Connecting Threads

Connecting Threads

Women's Lives in the Industrial North 1808-1909

Mavis Curtis

Copyright © 2021 Mavis Curtis
All rights reserved.

Maps contain OS data © Crown copyright and database right 2021
Original illustrations by E. Curtis

Cover image:
Blanket woven at Crowther and Nicholson's Ash Brow Mills

While Europe's eye is fix'd on mighty things,

The fate of empires and the fall of kings;

While quacks of State must each produce his plan,

And even children lisp the Rights of Man;

Amid this mighty fuss let me just mention,

The Rights of Woman merit some attention.

Robert Burns, 1792 (1759-1796)

For Barbara, Joan and Lucy

Table of Contents

PART I - Women in a Man's World

Preface	9
Chapter 1 - Pennine Country	17
The Woollen Industry	21
Turnpikes and Canals	27
Chapter 2 - Marsden Female Friendly Society	31
Chapter 3 - Smashed Frames, Murder and Retribution	44
The Murder of William Horsfall	53
Chapter 4 - Civil Unrest 1813-1820	67
The Radical Movement	67
The 1818 Election	74
Female Reform Societies	75
St Peter's Fields, August 16, 1819	79
Post Peterloo	90
The Cato Street Conspiracy	95
Chapter 5 - Two Unfortunate Marriages	97
Caroline of Brunswick and the Prince Regent.	97
Richard Carlile and his Wife	102
Chapter 6 - The 1830s	109
Parliamentary Reform	110
The Press	112
Working Conditions in Mills	115
The Royal Commission on Employment of Children in Factories (1833)	121
Chapter 7 - The Poor and the Workhouse	127
The 1834 Poor Law	127
Radical Attitudes to the New Poor Law	132
Conditions in the poor houses	138
The Swift Family of Newsome	142
Chapter 8 - Chartism	150
Chapter 9 - An Outsider's View of Britain: The German Diaspora	161
Prince Albert	162
The Great Exhibition	165

PART II - Women's Struggle for Independence

Chapter 10 - Education and Employment in the Second Half of the 19th Century	172
The Huddersfield Female Educational Establishment	176
Work available for women	182
Hospital-Nursing	184
Governessing	187
Higher education	188
Chapter 11 - The Women's Co-operative Guild	191
The National Organisation	193
The Huddersfield Branch	199
Chapter 12 - Florence Lockwood nee Murray. 1861-1937	203
Politics	213
Chapter 13 - The Suffragettes	224
The Huddersfield Suffragettes	228
Eliza Thewlis and her Daughter Dora	230
The Colne Valley By-election	235
Another Dora: Dora Marsden	237
The Pankhursts	241
Chapter 14 - Greenhead High School for Girls	243
The Municipal High School	244
What Was Taught	248
Chapter 15 - 1808 to 1909	261
Notes	268
Appendix 1 - Rules and Orders of the Marsden Female Friendly Society	282
Appendix 2 - Justice and Policing Before 1830	292
Bibliography	296
Index	302
Acknowledgements	311

Preface

Until fairly recently, the history we have been able to read has predominantly been about men, because women, generally speaking, lived within the domestic sphere and were thought to have had little influence on major events. War, kings, and heroes such as Wellington and Nelson are the ones that are recorded and form our ideas of the past. Fortunately, this situation has changed somewhat, and it is now recognised that women and the lives they lived are worthy of record, and that their experiences of life are very different from those of men.

An instance of this is a document recording the rules of a Female Friendly Society dated 1808 which I was given. These early Female Friendly Societies 'existed in significant numbers', according to a paper given at the Economic History Society Conference of 2004. This paper linked the existence of women-only friendly societies to the availability of work opportunities for women and because of variations in economic situations across the country, stressed the need to examine conditions in individual communities. The rules of the Society I had acquired had been formulated in Marsden, a township seven miles from Huddersfield, to the west of the town.

This focused my attention firmly on the Huddersfield area and the kind of work available to women: the textile trade. Indeed it was not just the women of the area who worked at making cloth. The whole family was engaged in the process, which in 1808 was mainly based, not in mills, but in the homes of the families involved, and because of that is called the domestic system.

In the eighteenth century Marsden was a relatively isolated community in the valley of the river Colne, separated from Lancashire to the west by forbidding moorland and to the east by a less than reliable road leading to Huddersfield, which in the census of

1801 is recorded as a town of some 7268 souls[1]. Not therefore in the midst of a bustling cosmopolitan business area, one would think. But by 1808 Marsden had recently become connected to the west by a turnpike road and to the east by a canal, which was at that time being extended under the Pennines to the Lancashire side of the hills. This may explain why the idea of a Friendly Society, for and run by women, had reached Marsden: Marsden was opening up to the outside world.

Were there, I wondered, stories to be discovered or re-discovered in the Huddersfield area about these women of the North as the century ran its course? What lay hidden in books and archives that would shine a light on their lives and show how those lives had changed for better or worse in the following years?

Much of the local history of the first half of the century covers the unrest that resulted from changes in work practices and the move from the domestic system of cloth production to an industrial model, with all the upheaval that involves. There are many stories of the exploits of the men in the area as they tried to improve working conditions, or establish some kind of control over their changing lives. By 1808, the very year of the formation of the Marsden Female Friendly Society, the men's patience was exhausted. They wrote, 'We petition no more, that won't do, fighting must'.[2]

So here we see the breakdown of what had been a relatively stable social situation but which now revealed two different ways of dealing with the changing circumstances. On the one hand the young men of the area formed what some of them hoped would be a revolutionary movement, this being less than twenty years since the French revolution, while the women struggled to maintain some kind of normality among the chaos by careful management of the family finances.

But in the Radical politics that swept the country in the first half of the nineteenth century, women were not just content to sit at home and struggle to make ends meet. They formed their own reform groups and were present in the crowds that flocked to hear Orator Hunt at Peterloo, in the crowds that followed Oastler as he agitated against the exploitation of child labour in the mills and the new poor law, in the Chartist movement and the Plug Riots.

As the century progressed and the country prospered, women woke up to the value of education and the need for political representation, which resulted in the suffrage movement. The two aspects of the suffrage movement, the suffragists, who worked within the law and tried to make their voices heard, and rather later the suffragettes, whose motto was 'Deeds, not Words', echoing the cry of the Luddites a century before, were all well represented in the Huddersfield area and took an active part in the politics of the region.

Mrs Josiah Lockwood, nee Florence Murray, a sophisticated woman from the London art scene married to a mill owner from Linthwaite, is a star in the suffrage firmament, not only for her account of how she became involved in the movement, but also for her depiction of life in the Colne Valley at the turn of the century, her involvement with the Peace movement and her descriptions of her encounters with Adela Pankhurst, the youngest daughter of the Pankhurst family. The Women's Social and Political Union, founded by Emmeline Pankhurst, had a thriving branch in the town with militant members who held rallies, demonstrated and were arrested.

Alongside this political awakening run other strands of awareness of a wider world: the first Female Education Establishment in the North of England for working class girls, the Women's Co-operative Guild and the Municipal High School for Girls, established in 1909.

As well as these initiatives, we should also recognize that the lives of many women and girls were restricted in the extreme, their life choices limited by their circumstances. Such was the case of the Swift family of Newsome, whose lives leap out at us from the diary of the head of the family, John Swift, a diary discovered by Jennifer Stead and sensitively and knowledgeably edited by her.

Women were not alone in their struggles to improve their lives and the lives of their children. They were supported along the way by enlightened men such as Samuel Bamford, a Radical involved with his wife in the organization of what turned into the massacre of Peterloo, Richard Carlile who wrote extensively about women's position in society and whose ideas were so far ahead of his time that he spent a substantial part of his life in prison, and even Josiah Lockwood, who attended the meetings his wife addressed and signalled to her when he thought she had spoken for long enough.

Occasionally, too, national events pushed their way into the consciousness of this corner of the world, among them the Queen Caroline affair, and the Great Exhibition, organized by Prince Albert, who contributed a great deal to improving the lives of the common people. The political and social life of the country as a whole was therefore reflected in and in turn reflected back the concerns of the day from this busy area of Britain.

As the founding of the Marsden Female Friendly Society in 1808 was the first event to feature in these stories of northern women, the final date, 1909 is that of the founding of a municipal grammar school for girls. Here we see the beginning of the kind of life that many Huddersfield girls would experience in the course of the twentieth century, a wider world with a multitude of possibilities unavailable to them in the previous century.

And finally, the appendices. I thought it would be useful for anyone interested in the detail of the running of a friendly society for the original rules to be included so that constitutes the first appendix. The policing of the civilian population was so different from today, and features so much in the early years of the nineteenth century, that I felt it would be useful to readers to have a summary of the situation which is contained in appendix 2. The rigid and punitive system of what can hardly be called justice helps to explain why there was so much unrest and makes one very sympathetic to the rebels who fought to change the system.

The Industrial North in the 19th Century

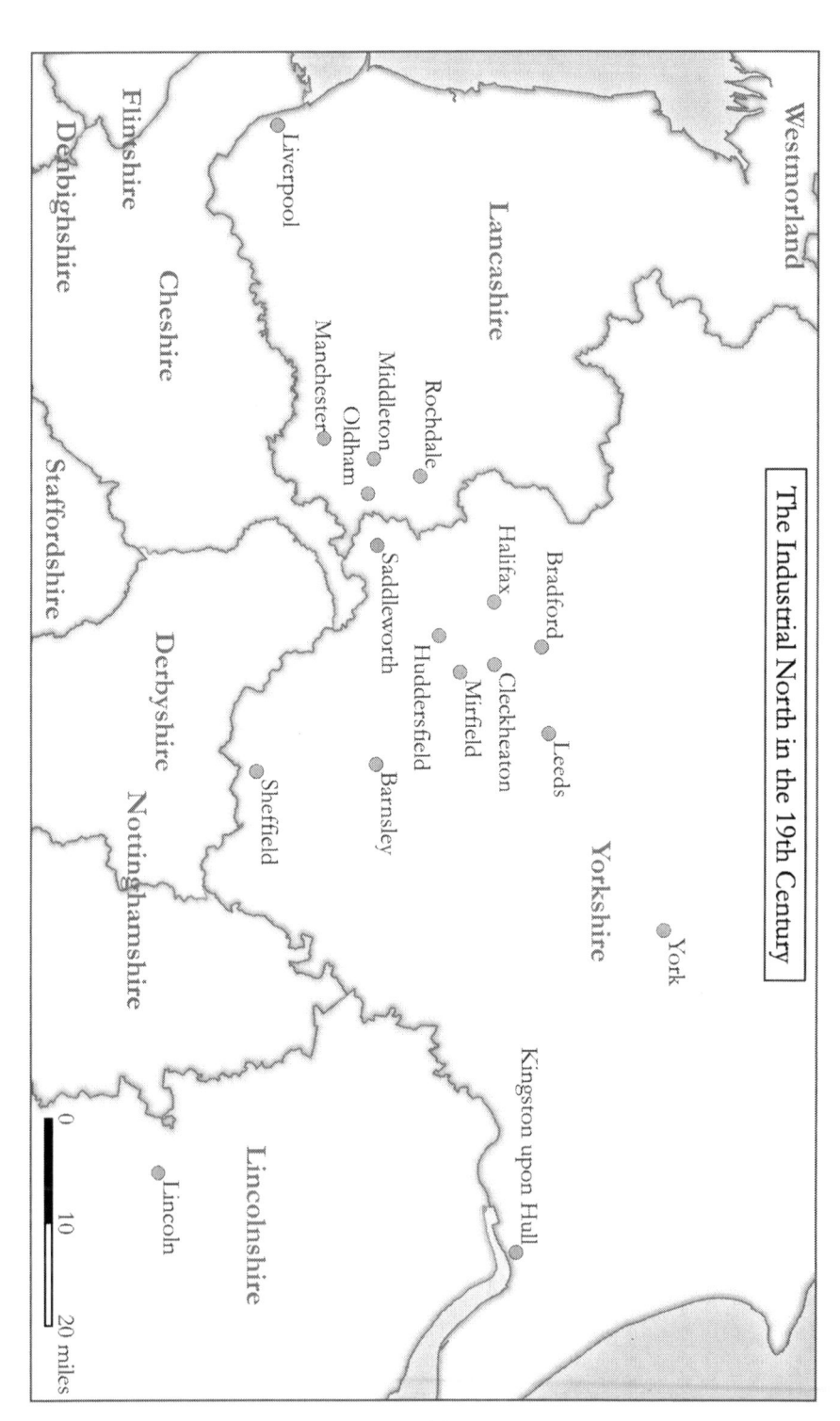

PART I

Women in a Man's World

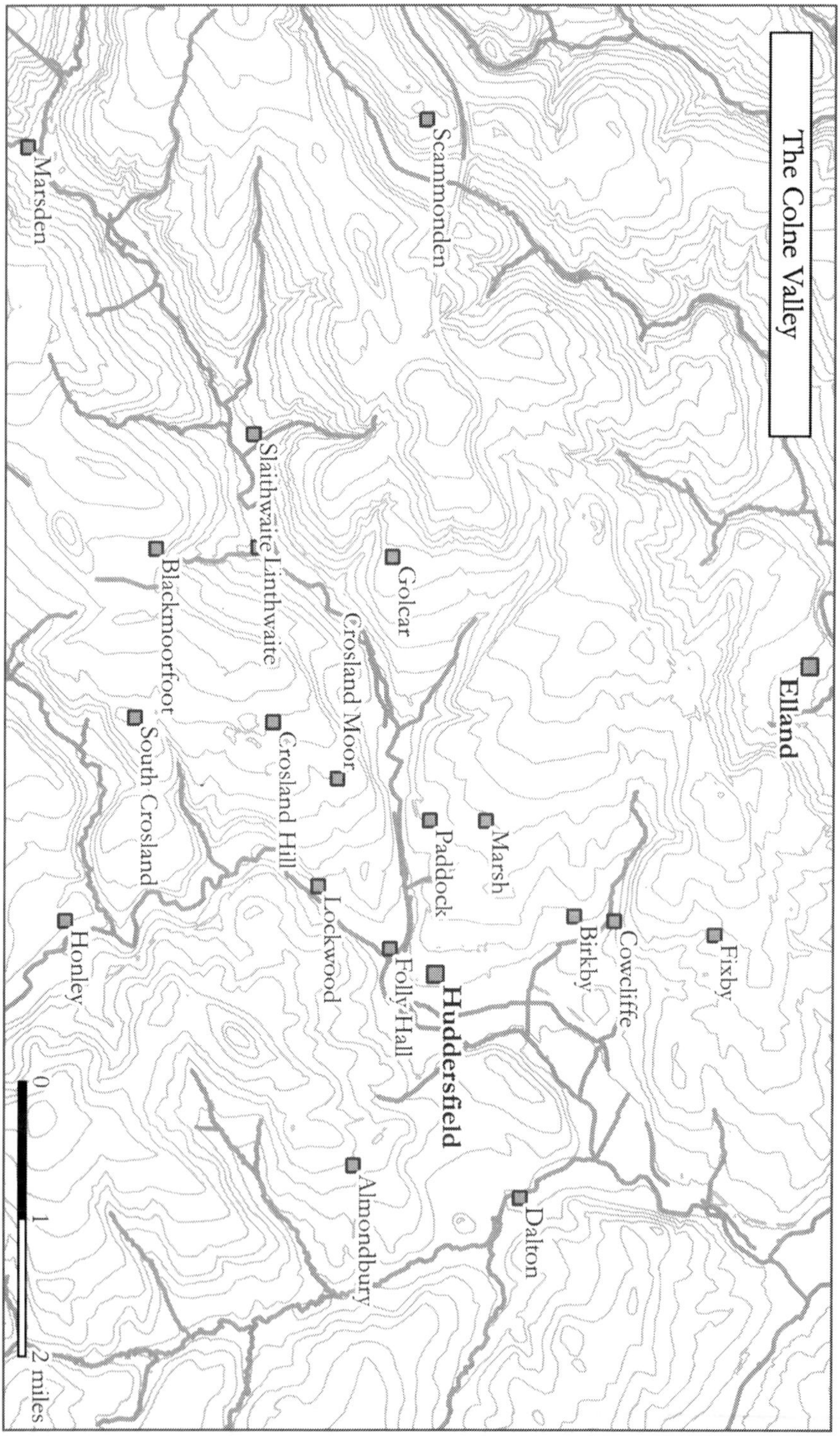
The Colne Valley
Scammonden
Marsden
Slaithwaite
Linthwaite
Blackmoorfoot
Golcar
Crosland Moor
Crosland Hill
South Crosland
Elland
Marsh
Paddock
Lockwood
Honley
Birkby
Cowcliffe
Fixby
Folly Hall
Huddersfield
Almondbury
Dalton
0
1
2 miles

Chapter 1 - Pennine Country

When Blake wrote about England's 'green and pleasant land' in 1804 it's unlikely he was thinking about the hills of the South Pennines in spite of the reference to 'dark satanic mills'. In the Colne Valley, the soil is thin and the underlying rock is millstone grit, a kind of sandstone[3]. The colour palate of the landscape, until recently, has been grey and purple, rather than green. Purple from the heather and grey from the stone, used to build the walls and roofs of the older houses and the dry-stone walling, which has criss-crossed the open countryside since the enclosure acts of the eighteenth century. In more recent times with the decline of heavy industry and aided by the actions of the Colne Valley Tree Society, the land has greened and now, when you approach Huddersfield from Lancashire by train, the purple of the moorland in the distance is hidden here and there by a curtain of trees.[4]

But the weather is often wet and, on the tops of the hills it can be very bleak, as Daniel Defoe witnessed in 1724 when he crossed from the west, from Lancashire into Yorkshire[5]. It was August but there was snow lying on the hill tops and as his little group, three gentlemen and two servants, made its way up towards the high moorland it began to snow in earnest. The wind blew the snow into their faces so they could barely open their eyes to see their way and the little spaniel who accompanied them whimpered, turned tail and would have run back to Rochdale if he could.

At that time the natives grew what they could, mainly oats, which will tolerate cold and wet conditions, and gave them porridge, gruel and oatcakes, the staple of the region. They needed to find other ways of eking out this meagre existence, however. They grew very little corn, Defoe noted, just enough to feed their poultry, but bought in grain from Lincolnshire and East Yorkshire. They bought black cattle from Scotland in autumn and salted it for eating during the winter months.

So if they had to buy in much of their provisions, where did the money come from for the purchases? Fortunately, the ground beneath their feet, though unconducive to growing wheat, had hidden riches. Immediately under their clogs, on the high hills, was peat, which they cut and burned. The millstone grit gave way here and there to an outcropping of coal and was an even better source of fuel. Defoe, observant as ever now the worst of the storm had abated, heard what he thought was a clap of thunder though some of the others thought it might be an explosion in one of the many coal mines which were, as he says, abundant in that part of the country.

In the eighteenth century and until about 1900, these small coal pits in the Calder, Colne and Aire valleys produced modest amounts of coal for local use. When the railways came to the Barnsley area in the mid nineteenth century, it was cheaper to use coal dug from the deep pits in that area transported by rail, rather than dig up coal locally, so the coal pits that had been scattered around the hills were abandoned.

Another resource was the sandstone, quarried not only for stone for house walls but flagstones for the roofs. The stone, unlike the pervious limestone of the Dales, resisted the constant pounding from rainstorms and channelled the water into rivulets, which tumbled down into the streams and rivers and, having no calcium dissolved in it, was as soft as the rain before it hit the ground.[6]

Defoe comments on the appearance of the countryside as he makes his way down from the heights towards Halifax. Everywhere he looked he could see houses, each surrounded with a small parcel of land surrounded in its turn by a wall where a horse or donkey and perhaps a cow and a pig might be kept.

Alongside each house was a tenter, and on every tenter a piece of cloth stretched on tenterhooks to dry, shining white in the sun. By each house there was a little stream piped by means of gutters and troughs into the 'manufacturies'. Then he reveals with a flourish that the source of the area's prosperity was making cloth, an occupation which involved every household and every individual in that household.

By the end of the century, even in the fastnesses of Marsden, at the end of the Colne Valley, the messiest processes of woollen cloth production – the dyeing and fulling – had moved into mills situated by the many streams in the valley, and the river Colne in the valley bottom, though the main processes of cloth production remained in the home. The rows of windows in the upper storeys of the houses in this area demonstrate the necessity of letting in as much light as possible, so the weaver could see and count the warp and weft he was weaving into cloth.

Defoe thought it was a splendid way to organize this difficult terrain where the soil was thin and the climate hostile but where there was an abundance of coal and clean, soft water. Every family was busily occupied with carding, spinning and weaving. Even four-year-olds, he notes with approval, were gainfully employed. There were no beggars in the streets here because everyone earned enough from cloth-making to supply their needs.

The terrain and the climate between them bred sturdy, independent men and women and, since there was no easy way to earn a living, and they were trained from an early age, they developed a strong work ethic. They fashioned a way of life which used the resources they had to the best of their ability, and traded their products for what they could not produce themselves.

A rather later visitor to the area than Defoe was John Wesley who in 1757 came to preach to the natives. He, like Defoe, made his way across the hills on horseback but unlike Defoe, travelled from the Oldham area via Saddleworth to the Colne Valley and thence to Huddersfield. Dropping down from the moors, he skirted the village of Marsden, at the head of the valley and came first of all to Scammonden, Bolster Moor, then Golcar.

He was less impressed with the area than Defoe had been. Of the people of Huddersfield he wrote, 'I rode over the mountains to Huddersfield. A wilder people I never saw.' He was rather more impressed with the inhabitants of Golcar, who, compared with the population of Scammonden and Bolster Moor, were as 'gentle as lilies'.[7]

The part of Marsden south of the River Colne was in the parish of Almondbury, a good seven miles away over the hills, while the northern part of the village was in the Huddersfield parish, equally remote from the parish church, so there was a Chapel of Ease in the village. Being so far distant from the mother churches, its parishioners had decided views on whom they wanted as their vicar. When the Reverend Marsden, the vicar of Marsden, died in 1779, the congregation did not take kindly to the appointment of the Reverend Murgatroyd of Slaithwaite as the new incumbent. In fact they barred the church door to him and demanded that Reverend Bellas, the vicar of Heights in Saddleworth, be installed.

The Reverend Bellas was an eloquent preacher but so fond of drink that he ran into financial difficulties and had to run a school to supplement his stipend. The inhabitants considered the flaws in his character were well worth putting up with when balanced against his entertainment value as a preacher.[8]

There was also a dissenting chapel alongside the river Colne, right in the centre of the village but on the northern bank of the river so in the parish of Huddersfield. In the turbulent years following the French Revolution, fear of a similar occurrence in England was rife. Some of this attached to dissenting chapels, perhaps because of the democratic way the chapels were run. Sylvanus Shaw was the first minister and in 1798 his house was visited by 'a drunken clergyman' – this was surely the Reverend Bellas – 'and a disorderly rabble' with a constable at their head who had 'a magistrate's warrant in his hand and shackles in his pocket.' Nothing of interest to the magistrate was found in Shaw's house. He had few books and those he had were religious tomes, so constable, clergyman and rabble left empty handed.

The Woollen Industry

The manufacture of textiles was the mainstay of the region, as we have already seen, and, if we are to understand how this impacted on the lives of the people living there, we really need to look closely at the process of producing cloth.

Spinning and winding in the home

The Colne Valley, and in fact the whole of the West Riding was noted for its production of cloth, a small amount being cotton or silk but the majority being wool, with each area specializing in a particular version of woollen cloth. In the Colne Valley at the end of the 18th century and beginning of the nineteenth, woollen cloth was made with undyed wool, so the finished product was white. The piece was then dyed resulting in a single colour for the cloth. Well into the nineteenth century the whole family, as Defoe noted, was engaged in its manufacture, and the survival of the family depended on the work of father, mother and children alike. Only the really messy parts of the process, the fulling and dying, had moved away from the domestic setting and this method of working is called the domestic system.

The processes in the making of woollen cloth by hand were often undertaken in the home. These were:

Picking the wool clean by hand, which was children's work; oiling the wool to protect it during carding and spinning; carding, which mixed the short fibres into a coarse mat. This was done either by teasel heads fixed to wooden batons, or later with iron nails fixed to leather, the making of which was done by women and children. Worsted cloth, on the other hand, not produced in the Huddersfield area but centred on Halifax, combed long–fibred wool and produced smoother cloth. Women, children and grandmothers did this.

The first part of the carding process was called scribbling. When scribbling and carding machines were invented by Richard Arkwright in 1775 they were not well received, as they were seen to be putting a great many people out of work. The early carding machines could be used in the home but very soon they were improved and began to be incorporated into the water-powered mills which had previously only been involved with the fulling process.[9]

Slubbing then turned the raw oiled wool into soft hanks, followed by spinning, which, until the invention of the spinning jenny, produced a single thread, using either the large wheel or later the Saxony wheel – the kind used to illustrate any number of fairy stories. It took the work of several spinners to produce enough yarn to keep a loom busy so the spinning jenny, invented in 1764, which could spin eight threads at once, was welcomed with open arms and was used both in the home and later in the mills. This was predominantly women's or children's work.

The yarn was then washed and spun in a 'wuzzer' just as salad can be swung round to get rid of the excess water. This was done with a stick fixed into a hole in the gatepost, and a basket. Again, this was women's or older children's work. At this point the spun wool was divided into warp thread and weft. The warp was fixed to a beam and sized i.e. coated with starch to strengthen it, and the weft was wound onto a bobbin. Sizing was sometimes done outside the home in a fulling mill, as it was messy.

With the warp fixed in place, the weaving could begin on the hand loom kept in the housebody. Broadcloth required two men to throw the shuttle from side to side, but after the invention of the flying shuttle in 1733, this could be done by one man. Woollen cloth was open-weave at this point and needed to be finished.

Finishing consisted of several elements: fulling, tentering, raising the nap and shearing it. The aim of the fulling process was to felt the fibres together to make the cloth thick, warm and windproof. It was first soaked in stale urine, called weeting in the Colne Valley or 'lant' in other parts of the country, for the ammonia content, which is a cleaner[10]. It was then trampled underfoot in a trough of water. Fullers earth was then added to remove the soap and oil.

Water-powered mills for fulling were in use in some places as early as the 13th century but in Marsden it was not till 1717 that one was established at Hey Green. By 1800 thirteen mills had been established in Marsden. Two of the mills, Fell or Woodhead's Mill and the New Mill were cotton mills while a third, in Warehouse Hill, was a silk mill. Being water- powered, the mills all clustered along the river Colne or its tributary, the Wessenden Brook, three along the Colne and ten along the banks of the Wessenden.

Tentering is a term that is unfamiliar to many people, except in the phrase 'being on tenterhooks.' Tenters were outdoor sets of wooden posts on which the wet cloth was fixed by means of tenter hooks to dry and stretch the cloth, to compensate for the shrinkage during the fulling process. To prevent the cloth being over-stretched and thereby weakened, a law was passed in 1737 to prevent this. The clothier had to incorporate his initials in the head of every piece of cloth and every piece had to be measured at the fulling mill while wet, by the millman and by a searcher. These were men of good repute who knew about the trade and who were appointed and their salaries fixed by a Justice of the Peace. It was allowed to stretch the piece by one inch per yard. The dry surface of the cloth was then brushed with teasels, the surface cropped with shears and the cloth was then ready to be sold.

The woollen industry boomed in the latter half of the eighteenth century and fortunes were made supplying the armies of several countries with great coats. The Yorkshire Woollen industry clothed most of the armies of Europe and North America, as well as supplying blankets to the Americas, to shelter the slaves who wore cotton by day but sheltered under woollen blankets by night.[11]

Atkinson writes of this period in Halifax saying that 'the industrial unit of the 16th, 17th and 18th centuries was the clothier. In the Halifax area the 'putting out' system was largely used, where the master clothier, besides using the skills of his own family, also employed outworkers, journeymen and women who worked with materials and perhaps even equipment provided by the clothier.[12]

The division of labour in a master clothier's household is admirably spelled out in a play in verse written in 1730. The words are spoken by the clothier to his family and apprentices telling them what to do while he is away buying wool. Having instructed his five lads – we are not told whether they are sons or apprentices - to collect spun wool from an outworker, collect the sized warp from the sizing mill, set up the loom with the warp thread ready for the next piece, he then instructs his wife to dye the wool. She has other ideas.

> So thou's setting me my wark.
> I think I'd more need to mend thy sark (shirt).
> Prithee, who mun sit at bobbin wheel
> And ne'er a cake atop o't creel.
> And me to bake and swing and blend
> And milk and barns to school to send,
> And dumplings for the lads to make
> And yeast to seek and syk as that
> And washing up, morn, noon and neet,
> And bowls to scald and milk to fleet
> And barns to fetch again at neet.

So his wife runs a large household with all the work that entails: mending, making oatcakes, which dry over the creel, milking the cow and, no doubt using a saucer made of sycamore wood, skimming the cream from the top of the milk[13], taking the youngest children to school, making the lads a filling meal, baking bread, washing up after every meal and fetching the children home at the end of the day. She no doubt had help with all this, but she also had to fit in swinging the wet wool and blending the carded wool, winding the spun wool onto bobbins and dyeing the wool, in this case before the piece was made.[14]

A task she didn't mention was scrubbing the stone-flagged floors of the house with weeting mixed with hot water and scouring stone[15], though this was probably a job performed by some poor maid rather than the mistress of the house.

However, Heaton has pointed out that there were few master clothiers in the Marsden area[16]. In the Colne Valley most cloth was manufactured on a much smaller scale, with a single piece produced by one family, much as Defoe describes. When the piece was finished the man of the family would take it to market either on horseback if the family was sufficiently prosperous, or over his shoulders if they were not. This type of production lasted well into the 19th century with carding still being done in the home in the 1840s.

Away from the Colne Valley however, by 1812 the clothier John Kay of Almondbury had made enough money for his wife to keep up with the latest fashions. Among her bills is listed five pieces of paper – wallpaper, at £2-6-3d, nineteen yards of border at 11s1d and payment for papering two rooms. She was also buying tea, coffee, lemons, hops and malt, so obviously making her own beer, and buying from her grocer, Mrs Scott, flour, currants, oats, cheese and butter. She also managed the land they farmed, paying for the fields to be ploughed, limed and dragged using four horses.[17]

As the nineteenth century progressed, the area around Halifax and northwards, where the putting out system was prevalent, went over from woollen cloth manufacture largely to worsted manufacture, a process borrowed, or perhaps more accurately, filched, from the cloth industry in Norfolk.

Woollen cloth manufacturers further down the Colne Valley from Marsden in the Huddersfield area began to specialise in fancy

A packhorse bridge in the Colne Valley

woollens, which used a variety of threads and patterns[18], and by the Great Exhibition of 1851 Huddersfield manufacturers were exhibiting and winning prizes for such exciting products as cashmerettes (cotton chain shot with woollen and silk shot with woollen for waistcoats), woollen beavers, valencias or toilinets, quiltings, plaids in challi wool for children's dresses. The list of incomprehensible specialities goes on, with prizes won for 'excellence of manufacture combined with economy', awarded to Armitage Brothers, for 'superiority of make and style of trouser goods' given to J. Tolson and Sons of Dalton and 'ingenuity in new application of materials to J. and T.C. Wrigley and Co.[19]

Turnpikes and Canals

One reason for the expansion of the trade was the improvements to the infrastructure of the valley. Defoe had travelled across the Pennines in the only ways possible at the start of the eighteenth century: by horse or on foot. He was heading for Halifax, seven miles north of the Colne Valley, but where the terrain and lifestyle were very similar.

The eighteenth century had seen an enormous increase in the cotton textile industry west of the Pennines, in Lancashire, 'Cotton Country' as it was known in Yorkshire. The only way across the hills was along packhorse tracks, which crisscrossed the countryside in a lattice of access routes between east and west. But the pressure for new markets for the Lancashire cotton industry meant that new roads had to be built. They ended at the Lancashire border. If the cotton industry were to expand further something had to be done to get manufactured goods across the border into the West Riding. In 1756, over twenty years after the Lancashire turnpike had been constructed, it was decided to build a turnpike road across the Pennines which would connect the Lancashire end of the road to the Colne Valley. Goods would then be able to travel freely between cities in the west of the country, notably Manchester and Liverpool, to Wakefield and thence to the east coast for transportation to Europe. This would also, of course, work in reverse, allowing woollen goods to travel to the west and to the New World.[20]

Because of the nature of the terrain, the road was extremely expensive to build and the first turnpike, built by Blind Jack of Knaresborough, was floated on rafts of heather, which cut the cost of the road and ensured good drainage. Unfortunately the route chosen, along the side of Pule Hill, proved too steep for horses to pull the carriages easily up the hill, so passengers were asked to step out of their vehicles and walk up the steepest parts. To cater for these people, a string of inns grew up along the roadside, which could make a decent living from the travellers.

The shortcomings of the first turnpike were such that a second

A farmhouse on the turnpike road on Pule Hill

was built in 1777, which was less steep and therefore not in need of wayside inns where passengers could rest. While better for the passengers, this arrangement bypassed the buildings on the first turnpike, making it necessary for those innkeepers to look for other methods of raising money.

One such couple was Samuel Lindley and his wife Martha. Like many people in Marsden they earned a living in a variety of ways: having a smallholding, making cloth and keeping an inn. When Sam died in 1805 he left the business to Martha, then aged 56. She ran it until handing it over to her son John shortly before she died in 1821[21]. It must have been something of a challenge to keep up the prosperity of the inn when their main means of support had suddenly been taken away.

They could however, and no doubt did, cater for the navvies who had come to the area to dig a canal connecting the two sides of the Pennines and who were housed, along with their families, in primitive shacks established near the tunnel construction site on Puleside, near the Lindleys' inn. It was a huge undertaking, very dangerous and thirst inducing for the men. They had no mechanical means at their disposal and every inch was hacked out by pick and shovel with the sometimes injudicious help of black powder, the forerunner of dynamite. To set fire to the powder, navvies would insert a quill into a crack in the rock and fill it with gunpowder, then beat a hasty retreat.

A second source of income, at least for the Lindleys, was the Marsden Female Friendly Society, which, in the event of ill health or accident, could help families over a bad patch.

Chapter 2 - Marsden Female Friendly Society

Friendly Societies worked in the same way then as insurance companies still do today. People paid a small amount in on a regular basis and could draw from the collective funds when the need arose. Nearly all societies at this time were strictly local and self-governing, and supported not just sick members but also provided a social life which included annual feasts and club nights.[22]

The manufacturing districts of Yorkshire were among the most active in establishing Friendly Societies. In 1800 there were 492 such organisations in the West Riding. They were especially popular in villages around Huddersfield. South Crosland, for example, just south of the turnpike road between Huddersfield and Marsden and with a population of 1500, had two registered societies in 1815 with 360 members, roughly a quarter of the population. Saddleworth, in the hills beyond Marsden had no fewer than fourteen societies totalling 3207 members, 24% of the population[23]. They included one female society with 499 members.

There had been a Friendly Society in Marsden since May 1776 entitled The United Society. Its rules were amended on June 6 1808, Whit Monday, the day before the Female Friendly Society, which was constituted on Whit Tuesday, one of the few days in the year when everyone was on holiday. The previous day, the men had held their annual get-together of every member well enough to attend. Now it was the turn of the women.

We don't know what time of day it was. The rules established that generally meetings would be in the afternoon, but on the anniversary of this momentous occasion, they would meet once a year in the morning and the celebrations would go on long into the afternoon.

We can imagine the first members of the society wending their way up the hill to Martha Lindley's inn, petticoats flapping, relishing the warmth of the June sunshine and glad to escape the confines of their cluttered houses and stretch their legs on the uphill climb. No doubt when they arrived there would be a glass of ale waiting for them in the cool of the inn. There must have been a solicitor's clerk who had perhaps ridden up from a legal firm either in Slaithwaite, further down the valley, or Huddersfield, to record the rules they had devised, and they would certainly have had a copy of the rules of the United Friendly Society which was now presumably exclusively a men's society. It seems obvious from the text of their rules that there was a clergyman of some kind present because the text of the women's society has a great deal of religious sentiment attached, though the United Friendly Society does not.

With the prospect of a free glass of ale, the clergyman in question was likely to have been the Reverend Bellas, who, being a vicar of the established church, and therefore unlikely to foment discord against the state, would be more acceptable than the leader of the dissenting chapel. While the introduction to the older organisation invokes 'antient custom' to justify their need to form a mutual support society, the women both begin and end the list of rules with an acknowledgement of the power of the Almighty. It begins 'when it shall please Almighty God to afflict any of us with Sickness, Lameness, or any other Infirmity, whereby we are incapacitated from following our usual Employments.' The document also ends with a promise of loyalty to the king and a prayer to the Lord:

'That every member shall to the utmost of her Power, by Precept and Example, promote the Interest and Happiness of the Society, by their mutual Affection and unfeigned Love and above all, earnestly and humbly praying that the Lord would make us thankful for all his Blessings we enjoy, under our present mild and happy Constitution and that He would shed his peculiar Blessings on all the Members of this Society, preserving them in Health, comforting them in Sickness, supporting them in Death, and crowning them with Glory to all Eternity.' Not exactly the language of a lawyer, but certainly showing the influence of either church or chapel. All it lacks is a heartfelt 'Amen' to complete the prayer grafted onto the legalese of the document.

The state, too, demonstrates its importance, with the reference to 'our present mild and happy constitution'. There was a reason for this. These friendly societies were something of a problem for the government of the day. Politically the last years of the eighteenth and the first part of the nineteenth century were turbulent times both locally and nationally. There were two major strands of unrest which the government tried to control with legislation. One was the struggle of working people to improve working conditions and wages, and influence the introduction of new working practices and the other was dissatisfaction with the Parliamentary system.

As meeting together to improve working conditions had been severely restricted by the Combination Acts of 1799 and 1800, workers had turned to legitimate associations to disguise their illegal activities. This was sometimes done under the guise of a friendly society. The Friendly Societies Act of 1793 acknowledged the usefulness of such societies and applauded the self-reliance engendered by these clubs which helped their members remain independent of poor relief. Under this legislation Friendly Societies obtained certain rights: for instance, they were exempted from stamp duty and were given powers to recover funds from defaulting officers. However, they had to be registered by a Justice of the Peace, who, in the person of George Armitage, duly signed this document in October of 1808.

The second challenge to the government was the political turmoil resulting from the ideas expressed by Tom Paine in his *Rights of Man*, published in 1791, in which he supported republicanism and proposed a social welfare system. Two acts were passed in Parliament in 1795: the Treasonable Practices Act which forbade, among other things, the fostering of hatred or contempt for the king, the government or the constitution. The Seditious Meetings Act decreed that all public meetings of over fifty people convened for discussion of public grievances or the circulation of any petition, remonstrance or address to king or parliament must be subject to the control of the local magistrates.[24]

Since the population of the West Riding and Lancashire had no representation in parliament, people's only means of expressing their discontent had been by petitions direct to the king, or rioting in the streets, a common occurrence at the time. Removing these possibilities would lead to more, rather than less, unrest and Friendly Societies were sometimes used as a cover for illicit political activity and were therefore of interest to the government.

So having assembled, with the Reverend Bellas supplied with adequate amounts of alcohol, and with the clerk sitting with pen poised, the women decided how they were going to organise their society. There are twenty-seven rules but rarely do they concern only one topic. It is as if they knew what happened in such meetings, as indeed several of them probably did, and they were remembering the order and having them written down as they thought of them. One can imagine the clerk struggling to keep up with the number of ideas presented in quick succession.

Rule I, for instance, covers the sort of person who will be allowed to join: of sound mind and body and not over the age of forty; how much she will pay at each meeting: one shilling and tenpence for ale every quarter; what time the meeting starts: two o'clock in the afternoon; what happens if a member does not turn up: she must send her money with someone who is attending.

They then go on to discuss who will look after the money and where it will be kept: there will be two wardens and three stewardesses, each chosen by the committee to act for a year and to be paid four shillings a year. One can hear someone saying,

'Yes, but what if somebody refuses to do it?'

'Fine her. That will encourage her to do her duty!'

'Yes, but how much?'

'Two shillings and sixpence.' A gasp at the price. 'Well, any less and it won't be a deterrent, will it?'

'And who will look after the lump sum and check the accounts?'

'The clerk, obviously.'

'And how much will he be paid?'

With the clerk in the room, any discussion could have been embarrassing, so it was left to another occasion.

The money was to be kept in a box with five locks and five keys. One key was to be kept with the box, and the other four given over to the officials. The stewardesses and wardens would meet with the clerk on each quarter day (i.e. four times a year) to see how the books were balancing, how much going out and coming in.

'Sometimes people might not turn up till half way through the afternoon', someone might have commented. 'Do we fine them for that?'

'Yes', comes the decisive answer. 'And anyone who wants to join the society must be interviewed by the Committee and must be honest about their age - no pretending to be younger than they are - and give her name, and address.'

They then go on to discuss the nitty gritty of what the financial arrangements will be. A member could claim benefits only after she had paid into the society funds for five quarters, i.e. five shillings and five lots of ten pence for the ale. She could then claim five shillings for twenty weeks and if she were still unable to work, could claim two shillings and sixpence for as long as she was incapacitated.

At this juncture someone may well have said, 'What about when you have a baby? What happens then?'

'There's no need to pay for the first four weeks after the birth but after that she should be able to claim.'

'Yes, but what about if the baby's not her husband's?'

'And what about if she's not married and has a baby by someone else's husband?'

No doubt there would be some discussion at this point about which women in the village might fall into this category. No mention, however, about children born to an unmarried woman who had a child, since this was quite a common occurrence. If a couple were courting and intended to marry, then they were considered to be married by the general population, if not by the church.

Stead confirms that up to 1750, a quarter of all brides were pregnant when they married and between 1800 and 1850 this rose to 38%[25]. She adds that there was no opprobrium attached to this, as an engagement was considered an unbreakable pledge.

It was the committee's responsibility only to admit those women who had a good reputation and would not exploit the resources of the society, so no one who was a malingerer, or who deliberately harmed themselves in order to draw their money would be admitted. Anyone who tried to claim benefits when they were not really ill would be thrown out of the society.

The stewardesses were expected to be diligent and take their responsibilities seriously. It was their duty to call on anyone claiming benefit the same day they applied, and if they couldn't manage it, to appoint someone who would. If not, they could be fined two shillings.

The way the money was lent out shows that a significant number of the women could read, write and add up[26]. Members of the society, whether literate or not, were expected to respect the written word, since they had to buy a copy of the rules when they joined. Of course, being in possession of a document does not necessarily signify an ability to read it. But as working women, whether in the home or the mill, they would be familiar with the weights of wool they had processed and the amount of money they might be paid for their labours. As managers of the family money, which many of them working alongside their husbands in the domestic system would be, and in a part of the country where they had to buy in provisions such as grain, cheese and meat, they must have been familiar with buying and selling. So the level of literacy and numeracy might have been quite high.

When the stewardess decided that someone was entitled to a benefit, she would draw the money from the box and write a ticket detailing the transaction and hand it over to the landlady. These would be inspected at the quarter day by the clerk. Quarter days were Whit Tuesday, followed by the fourth Tuesday of August, November and February.

Not only was the society involved on a day to day basis with people's lives and livelihoods, they were conscious of their duties to the dead and the bereaved.

'Now, ladies,' one can imagine the Reverend Bellas interposing, 'If a member dies, I hope to see some of you at the funeral.'

'Certainly, sir. The warden and stewardesses will attend, and the next in roll. With gloves and scarves. We know what is due to our dear departed.'

'I haven't got any gloves,' someone might whisper.

'We shall keep six pairs of gloves and six scarves here at Martha's next to the box, so we are all properly dressed for the occasion.'

'And may I expect you in church the Sunday following the interment?' Perhaps the Reverend has an eye on the increased amount of money in the collecting plate.

'Yes.'

Much emphasis was placed on the autonomy of the woman, casting the Society as protector of the woman's wishes and interests after her death. On the death of a member, four guineas were paid to the husband or relative, unless the member had specifically forbidden this. If a member's husband died, one guinea was paid towards the funeral expenses, providing she had not already claimed for a previous husband. A guinea would also be paid to the widower's family when he died, providing that he had not remarried.

Weinbren has pointed out that Friendly Societies had much in common with medieval religious and craft guilds. They stressed fellowship and conviviality, no more so than at the Whit Tuesday celebration. This was the highlight of the year. It cost every member attending the dinner two shillings and sixpence, of which sixpence was for ale. Officers assembled at eight o'clock in the morning and other members at eight-thirty. If late they would be fined twopence.

A possible further interposition from the Reverend Bellas:

'I hope a service to give thanks for the Good Lord's providence during the year will be in order,' he might say.

'Yes, straight after the roll-call. We will walk down to the chapel and you can preach a sermon, Reverend Bullas, on a suitable subject. We will decide later how much the fee will be.'

We don't know what they ate at the meal, but it is possible they ate broth, made from sheep's heads, and perhaps a leg of mutton, with vegetables. They may even have eaten wheaten bread. It was certainly coming into the diet of Leeds clothiers in 1800.[27]

After the celebratory meal came the annual settling of accounts, with each stewardess recounting who had received benefit during the year. There was then a ceremonial handing over of the keys and the re-appointment of officers.

Throughout the document there is one anxiety that the women keep returning to and that is time-keeping. They have a series of fines for anyone, including the officers, who are late arriving at a meeting. Anyone late for a meeting would be fined an increasing amount according to how late they were. This is something of a puzzle because while there were increasingly more clocks in private hands – Seidal has noted that of the 166 probate inventories since 1700, 106 listed a clock[28] – it is difficult to discover whether or not there were any external clocks on larger buildings. There was certainly no clock on the church tower at that point. Perhaps there were hooters at the various mills which had by then been established. But why the rigid insistence on time-keeping? Perhaps it was the need to emphasise the importance of the organisation as a modern Society.

A further cause for anxiety was the need for secrecy and keeping intruders out of their meetings. Every member had to be in her appointed place by the start of the meeting and 'if any member of this Society stand at the Door when the Roll is called over, or listen or inspect where the Business is carried on, or be any Hinderance to the Officers in the Execution of their Office, (she) shall for every Offence forfeit sixpence.' This seems to have been a precaution against informers, both men and women, who were paid by the local magistrate, in this case Joseph Radcliffe of Milnsbridge House. The Society needed to ensure that no unauthorised person could listen in and perhaps misconstrue what was being discussed. Knowing a person was no guarantee of their goodwill towards you. If there were money to be made by fabricating misdemeanors, then some people would not hesitate to stir up trouble.

The way a meeting was controlled gives an interesting insight into the kind of behaviour which might occur and gives the impression that the members could be unruly at times. Anyone who refused to be quiet after the third time of asking would be fined twopence for each offence; anyone who proposed gaming or fomented quarrels in the club room, or who was drunk, smoked or sang songs was fined fourpence or excluded; and any swearing was fined at the rate of twopence an oath. There were obviously some women in the village whose behaviour was not what respectable church- or chapel-going members would be expected to demonstrate!

While the rules of the society show us a great deal about the women's attitudes and priorities, it offers us no information about how the society acquired its funds or indeed who exactly was joining the society. There are some conclusions that can be reached, however.

If the amount of money in the stock reached £200, everyone receiving benefit was to be given an extra 6d a week, until the stock reduced to £150. If the level of stock fell to £100, everyone in the society was to contribute an extra 6d a quarter until it rose to £150. This was a lot of money. £200 in 1810 was worth over nine thousand pounds in today's money[29]. So where did the money come from?

The small amounts paid in by the members would hardly account for the £150 kept in the box. Perhaps employers paid into the funds to cover accidents or ill health in their workforce. The Canal Company, which was responsible for the construction of the narrow canal, was always short of money, but they were known to pay five shillings a week into a sick club. Perhaps the mill owners who employed most of the women and children did the same.

But in that case, how did the women manage to get to meetings arranged for two o'clock in the afternoon, when they should have been working in the mill? Minelotti has shown that by the age of forty many women were no longer working in the mills but in 1808 the Marsden Female Friendly Society certainly anticipated that there would be mature women as members, since provision was made for lying in at the birth of a child.

Minelotti's evidence also shows that there was no great dropping off of female workers when they were in their twenties, but the time when the mills were recruiting most females was between the ages of eight and fourteen. The women joining the society must have been under forty years of age, and could not have been working full time in the mill, because of the time the meeting was fixed. So perhaps we can assume that those people involved in the general running of the organisation were older women either working at home in the domestic system and/or bringing along the contributions earned by family members.

By 1833 when a government enquiry into the woollen industry was instigated, about a quarter of the employees in the woollen trade in Bradford and Huddersfield areas were women or girls[30]. Certainly by 1835, when the power loom was being introduced to Starkey's mill at Longroyd Bridge, fifty women and girls went on strike because of the reduction of their wages from 7s6d a week to 6 shillings.

There is also earlier evidence to support the predominance of women and girls in manufacturing. In 1819 there was a terrible fire at a cotton mill at Colne Bridge owned by Thomas Atkinson. The fire was started accidentally by a young boy, James Thornton, who had been sent downstairs to the carding room from the upper rooms used for twisting and spinning to fetch more cotton for the girls aged between nine and eighteen who were working on the night shift. He was carrying an unguarded candle – it should have had a glass chimney to shield the naked flame, but it didn't, and the cotton waste which filled the building was set alight. Seventeen of these young girls – many of them baptised at Kirkheaton church, therefore from local families, died in the flames. The building was completely destroyed. Eighty people had been employed at the mill, so by the standards of the day it was quite a large establishment and of course a terrible tragedy.

And how much were these women and girls working in Marsden in the earlier part of the century likely to be paid? There seem to be no details of wages in this area at this time, but we do have exact details of how much people were earning some twenty-five years later in 1833, when mill owners were obliged to complete forms sent out by the Royal Commission enquiring into the state of child labour in the mills. At Lockwood's mill in Huddersfield women were then earning nine shillings a week. If the rate of inflation over the intervening years is taken to be 1.6%, as the Bank of England suggests, then they were earning six shillings and a ha'penny. It's tempting to round the amount down, but a ha'penny was too important to be air-brushed out. Even farthings counted.

Turning to the structure of the society itself, it shows remarkable sophistication. Whoever designed these rules knew how organisations such as this worked, and how individuals within the group worked. They foresaw that some people might cheat if they could get away with it, that some officers might steal, that members might 'bad-mouth' others who were receiving benefits, that some might seek to undermine members' confidence in the Society. So they made rules against these possibilities and devised a set of checks and balances to guard against them. The officers were paid a small amount to ensure their commitment and access to the stock was only possible when all five of them were present.[31]

Any stewardess who took money from the stock had to write a receipt, which became part of the accounts, which was checked by the clerk. Furthermore, one of the wardens and the three stewardesses were chosen by the committee and appointed or reappointed every quarter, which meant that anyone thought to be less than trustworthy could be replaced before much damage could be done.

The committee played a central role in the smooth running of the Society and members were carefully chosen, one by each of the wardens, one by each of the stewardesses and the other six by the members, a total of sixteen. This meant a sharing of influence between the officers and the members.

These women, who took what must have been a really exciting step in the management of their own affairs, promised to not only look after one another but to abide by the Constitution. They were not to know that very soon, in this very village, the means of destroying the machines by which some of them earned a living, however meagre, would be forged. The Luddites would be on the march, armed with a hammer christened 'Enoch' after the blacksmith who made it, and who with his brother James plied his trade in the centre of Marsden; that there would be deaths and hangings and severe testing of the Constitution, to which they had just pledged allegiance.

Chapter 3 - Smashed Frames, Murder and Retribution

However much the members of the Female Friendly Society had expressed their loyalty to the king and constitution in 1808, some of them would soon be called upon to reject any idea of loyalty to the established government which had signally failed to get to grips with the changes in the textile industry.

As happened throughout its history, the fortunes of the woollen industry fluctuated with seasonal demand and the external forces of the market. According to official reports, the industry in the West Riding and the country as a whole was doing well in the early years of the nineteenth century, as we have seen in the previous chapter. The 1806 Parliamentary Report on the textile industry notes that the value of woollen exports in the three previous years had increased year on year from £5,285,719 in 1803 to £5,979,580 in 1805 and that it was by far the largest export earner of any trade.[32]

Life was nothing like as rosy as the picture painted by the gentlemen in London. The reality was very different. The report made no mention of the effect of the Combination Acts of 1799 and 1800 which forbad working people to club together to try to improve their working conditions, their chief weapon being the strike. The report had actually been ordered because of riots in the West Country – Somerset and Wiltshire, to be precise, and had been caused by the introduction of gig mills into the cloth manufacturing process. Gig mills and cropping frames were similar machines. Basically they sheared the raised nap of the cloth and were part of the finishing process which had traditionally been done by highly paid and skilled men wielding shears rather like present day garden shears but very much bigger. These skilled artisans thought the machines could not do as good a job as them, being difficult to control and sometimes cutting too close or not close enough. They were, in addition, fearful for their jobs.

Alongside this job insecurity there was the difficulty sometimes caused by bad weather and a poor harvest, as had been the case in 1802 when in November of that year the price of grain had rocketed, and the women of the Huddersfield area were angry. The shortages were being exploited, they felt, with badgers (travelling grain sellers) and merchants raising the price of a bushel of flour and oatmeal to a ridiculous level. A crowd of them had gathered on market day in Huddersfield, a Tuesday, and attacked the cart bringing in the grain.

They had no intention of stealing it. Hannah Bray, the wife of a waterman from Deighton organized a sale of the goods at six shillings a bushel. One of these was bought by another Deighton woman, Emma Holland, wife of a cloth dresser. Before she had time to do much else, the magistrate, Joseph Radcliffe, had turned up with a small posse of Volunteers, read the Riot Act and arrested Hannah and Emma, alongside a hot head by the name of Abraham Broadbent, who had kicked Radcliffe's horse. Emma and Broadbent spent two months in the House of Correction in Wakefield for their offence while Hannah was given a twelve month prison sentence.[33]

The gentlemen who wrote the 1806 report for Parliament were loud in their praise of the skill and hard work of the people in the textile trade, but said that because of all the various petitions from both master clothiers who wanted to introduce new practices, and workers who wanted to stick to what they knew, they intended to review all the old legislation and recommend what should be repealed and what modernized.

They recommended that the law preventing payment of the workforce in goods rather than money should be kept on the statute books; that modern laws preventing the export of certain materials and implements for the woollen industry should remain in force and also the refusal to allow workers in the woollen trade to emigrate. They suggested that laws concerning the quality of manufacture should be assessed. They found that gig mills and shearing frames, far from damaging the quality of the cloth, actually improved it and this was one reason the trade had flourished. The expansion of trade meant that any men thrown out of work by the new machinery could easily find other work, so the fears of these skilled artisans were groundless.

While appearing to give a reasoned summary of the situation, the Report was heavily skewed towards the manufacturers' point of view. Men who had served their apprenticeships in the cropping sheds, knowing that their work was highly skilled and that the value of the cloth depended on how well they worked, who were the most highly paid people in the industry and therefore at the top of the social hierarchy, could not simply step sideways and take up a similarly prestigious job. There were none. So any other work they could get would be less well paid and with a great deal less social standing.

They also knew that Ottiwells Mill in Marsden, run by William Horsfall, had been using gig mills for several years and that the number of men employed in cropping had been reduced from over a dozen to three. A similar circumstance prevailed at Bradley Mill where the owner, Thomas Atkinson, had also been using gig mills. In 1803 both mills had had fires which some people thought were caused by arson, though the owners did not.[34]

The 1806 Report gives a description of the woollen industry which differs little from Defoe's account other than that by this time the major towns in the area: Leeds, Halifax and Huddersfield had all acquired cloth halls – three in Leeds, each catering for a different kind of cloth. The report praised the factory system because they felt it was better equipped to produce fancy goods which sold well abroad. There was more room for experiment in the factory system which was less conservative than the domestic system. But they also recognised that the great advantage of the domestic system was that it required very little capital to set up independently, thus making it easier for young men to make their way in the world.

What really perturbed them, however, was not just isolated instances of rioting among the workforce - they were used to that - but the evidence of an organized network of workers from the West Country to Yorkshire and Lancashire and even up into Scotland. And this institution was beginning to take in people from other walks of life. They describe the structure:

In each town there is a society consisting of deputies from several workshops. One or more deputies are chosen to join the Central Committee. The powers of the Central Committee 'appear to pervade the whole Institution'. And they stress the ease of communication because of its hierarchical structure. Every member has a ticket and members pay so much a week depending on how much they can afford and they use this money to present petitions to Parliament. This, they say, is legal. But the Institution also funds strikes, which is illegal. (The Combination Acts were not repealed until 1824).

Locally in the Huddersfield area there was a thriving branch of this organization, called the Croppers' Institution. On being issued with a membership ticket, each member took an oath of loyalty to the organization. People who recruited new members were called twisters-in.

The gentlemen compiling the report were understandably disturbed about this ability of the working classes to organise on a national scale. It was, after all, only a little over ten years since the French Revolution, and they all knew what that had led to.

A letter had come into the possession of the gentlemen compiling the report which had been sent from clothworkers in Yorkshire to two of the principal Fire Insurance Companies in London advising them not to insure premises where machines were used instead of clothworkers, because they might lose their money if they did. The writers of the letter intended to petition Parliament about the use of machines and would go on strike if Parliament did not help. A postscript is attached: 'Only remember Bradley Mill in this County!' The letter had come following a meeting in Leeds but was posted in Huddersfield. Bradley Mill was owned by Thomas Atkinson who had resolutely refused to employ members of the Institution and whose fences and gates had been broken down in 1806 in the course of a riot.[35]

In 1807 following the defeat of the French at Trafalgar, Napoleon had abandoned any idea of invading Britain and had issued the Berlin Decrees, which prevented Britain from trading with Europe. This hit the woollen industry hard and led to a peace movement which was much in evidence in the Huddersfield area, with one meeting in March of that year being attended by 10,000 people.

The croppers were bitterly disappointed at the outcome of the report. They had, they thought, given trustworthy information to the Parliamentary committee but this had been ignored. A protest meeting was held at the Pack Horse Inn in Huddersfield by the Croppers Association which expressed their indignation at being represented as an unreasoning mob. They also asked that the law preventing the emigration of clothworkers be repealed, so allowing people without work to leave the country and seek employment elsewhere.

Dubbing the Croppers' Institution a subversive organization meant that there was no legitimate means for the work people in the woollen industry, whether in the West Country or the North, to put forward their complaints. In 1808 following the earlier report, a bill was put before Parliament repealing most of the old laws which had supported the croppers which meant that the Croppers' Institution was made illegal and the way was left clear for widespread introduction of gig mills and shearing frames. The only way forward was violence, which, as the letter suggests, was already happening.

Martha Lindley's Female Friendly Society was formed amidst this turmoil. Four years after the women of Marsden had organized their affairs independently, in 1812 the level of unrest in the country became difficult to control. It would culminate in the West Riding in the shooting of two so-called rioters, the murder of a mill owner and the hanging of seventeen men, leaving 57 children fatherless.

The troubles began in Nottinghamshire and were caused by the introduction of wide knitting frames for stockings. The men and women who made stockings were notoriously poor. One of the insults used in 19th century Britain was to call someone 'as poor as a stockinger'. People were not necessarily against mechanisation as such, but saw the dire effects these new machines had on employment and wages.[36]

The frameworks became targets for men put out of work by them, who called themselves Luddites, after a mythical leader, Ned Ludd. Such was the level of unrest in Nottinghamshire that Lord Liverpool's government felt it necessary to make frame breaking punishable by death. Lord Byron, who was familiar with Nottinghamshire and the poverty suffered there, made an eloquent and moving speech against the motion. He urged the government to plead the cause of negotiating with the rebels. Hansard reports him as saying,

> I did hope that any measure proposed by His

> Majesty's Government for your Lordships' decision,
> would have had conciliation for its basis;
> ...not that we should have been called at once,
> without examination and without cause, to pass
> sentences by wholesale, and sign death-warrants
> blindfold.

Then he draws their lordships attention to who these people are, whom they intend to hang:

> You call these men a mob, desperate, dangerous, and
> ignorant...; are we aware of our obligations to
> a *mob*! It is the mob that labour in your fields, and
> serve in your houses, that man your navy, and recruit
> your army - that have enabled you to defy all the
> world, - and can also defy you, when neglect and
> calamity have driven them to despair.

While Byron was defending the Nottinghamshire Luddites, what he had to say applied equally to the situation in the West Riding. The West Riding rebels were in general young men with wives and young families, and their anger and violent behaviour disrupted the communities they lived in. They had many supporters in the community, but also many who hated their unruly behaviour and feared their violence. In accounts of the troubles, we hear the angry voices of women who have to deal with the gig breaking, whose sleep is disrupted and whose homes are invaded by marauding bands of Luddites, but there must have been just as many who sympathized with the men's aims and who shared their anger, though we don't always hear about them.

The Luddites' first attack in early February 1812 was by a force drawn from Halifax, Huddersfield and many of the smaller towns of the West Riding. Chief among the rebels was George Mellor, a young unmarried man aged twenty-four who worked in a cropping shop at Longroyd Bridge, next to the newly opened Huddersfield Narrow Canal. They had identified a consignment of shearing frames which were being taken across Hartshead Moor to Rawfolds Mill in Cleckheaton and as the larger mills such as Ottiwells in Marsden or Rawfolds mill itself had been fortified to keep unwanted visitors out, this was an easier target than the mill itself.

The Huddersfield rebels then turned their attention to the small domestic establishments which were so prevalent at the time, wanting to frighten people into turning their backs on the frames, and collecting any guns they might have. This must have alienated some people intent on living a quiet life unconcerned with politics.

One night by the light of a full moon they marched to Joseph Hirst's shop at Marsh where he and a couple of his lads were still working. The armed men stood guard outside in the moonlight, while the others marched in and smashed the frames. One or two shots were fired, one bullet hitting the Hirsts' dog, and seven frames and twenty-four pairs of shears were destroyed.

Further attacks took place, often several in one night. In South Crosland, for instance, after smashing up the shearing frames of George Roberts, they warned his wife Sarah to pass on a message to her father, who owned Wood Bottom Mill in Marsden. 'Tell him to dismantle his frames', they said, 'or we and four hundred others will come and do it for him.'

They then marched to Honley to the workshop of John Garner, where they wreaked similar havoc, stealing his pistol. On their way home they broke into Clement Dyson's workshop in Lockwood. His wife, Hannah, was woken by the noise of the break-in, and had to watch as they broke up shears, tubs, frames and a brushing machine. They demanded something to drink, which she duly provided, but they left before they had drunk any of it.[37]

The violence escalated at Rawfolds with a joint venture of men from all over the West Riding who congregated outside the mill and attempted to storm their way in. It was too well defended however, and two men from Halifax were killed and many others injured. The Luddites had their first martyrs.

At this point the magistrate Joseph Radcliffe at Milnsbridge House received a letter informing him that if manufacturers persisted in using machines, it would be the signal for civil war, and that William Horsfall of Ottiwells mill in Marsden and Thomas Atkinson of Bradley Mill were on the list of targets. As one Luddite wrote, 'We petition no more. That won't do, fighting must.'[38] A remarkable precursor to the suffragettes' motto: 'Deeds not words.'

One couple who were definitely not supporters of the Luddites was William Milns, the Lockwood constable and his wife Fanny. In July Milns' house was shot into and the wadding from the gun set some bedding alight. Milns' main informant against the Luddites was his wife Fanny. They lived in the same fold as William Brook, a cloth dresser, who had three sons, Thomas, James and George. The boys disliked Milns, describing him as overbearing and purse-proud. He flaunted his money. Fanny, however, being a neighbour, was in the habit of dropping in and took a great deal of interest in what went on in their house. In March of that year, 1812, she had seen a pistol drying on the hob. Then, following a raid in Linthwaite in March, when it had rained very hard, Fanny had seen a coat drying. She had seen a pistol hidden from the view of nosy neighbours such as herself, which her husband, on investigation, found was the stock of a gun which he decided resembled one stolen from Linthwaite.

On the Sunday after the Rawfolds attack Fanny saw five or six men in the Brooks' house that she deemed to be suspicious. She loitered about and said she heard James Brook say that he wouldn't get involved in anything like that again because the sound of screaming from the injured and dying was too upsetting. All this information was laid before the magistrate, Joseph Radcliffe.[39]

The Murder of William Horsfall

William Horsfall, as we have already seen, was on the Luddite hit list, though nobody seems to have believed that threats would be carried through and even if Horsfall had known about it, his character was such that he would have probably thought it cowardly to take precautions.

He was the owner of 'a very large Woollen Manufactury', records a reporter from the *Leeds Mercury,* employing about 400 people at Ottiwells Mill, Marsden, and seven years previously had installed shearing machines which, at least according to the report, had achieved 'considerable perfection'.

On the day he was killed he had left Huddersfield after concluding his business there and made his way on horseback along the turnpike road, a very busy road on market days, which took him up Crosland Moor and out into open country. About a mile and a half from Huddersfield on land owned by the magistrate Joseph Radcliffe, he was attacked by four men, each armed with a horse pistol who stepped out of a small plantation, placed their guns in apertures in the wall (the wall would have been a drystone wall, so stones could easily have been dislodged), and all four fired.

The victim, injured on his left side four times, fell from his horse and 'the blood flowed from the wounds in torrents'. Several passers-by both on horse and foot rushed to him. Two boys who were gathering dung were immediately despatched to Warren House, a pub lower down the hill, and a cart was sent to collect Mr Horsfall. Dr Houghton arrived between eight and nine o-clock that evening but

*A contemporary etching of the murder of William Horsfall.
By kind permission of the Huddersfield Exposed web site.*

Horsfall's life could not be saved.

The four men walked then ran some yards away towards Dungeon Wood and escaped. A troop of the Queen's Bays stationed at the Red Lion in Marsden arrived three quarters of an hour after the event but had not caught up with the men.

The enterprising reporter had also managed to interview the doctor who attended Mr Horsfall. He told the reporter that of the four wounds, only one was serious, but that had been made by a musket ball which had penetrated the abdomen on the left side and had travelled down and lodged in the back part of the right thigh. The ball and a pistol ball had been removed the day after Mr Horsfall was shot but he had bled profusely, his leg had swollen up enormously and he died 'in full possession of his faculties'. A reward would be offered, the reporter understood, to the tune of £2000.[40]

In his lively account of working class rebellion in the first half of the 19th century Frank Peel gives a further account of Horsfall and his death, which although not written until the 1880s contains interesting details drawn from oral tradition. He tells us, for instance that William Horsfall was 'an excitable, impetuous man, violent in manner, but kind and forgiving to his own workpeople.' Marsden children enjoyed running past his house shouting 'I'm General Ludd!', which provoked him to chase them with a horse whip. Horsfall also refused to shake hands with Jonathan Brook of Longroyd Bridge, who had made cropping machines but stopped doing so when he was threatened with having his foundry smashed up. Horsfall said he would not shake hands with a coward.

The murderers, whom Peel identifies as George Mellor, Benjamin Walker, William Thorpe and Thomas Smith, ran away, with Walker and Smith hiding their weapons in Dungeon Wood. Mellor gave Walker two shillings because he had no money and told him and Smith to go towards Honley while Mellor and Thorpe took refuge at Mellor's cousin Joseph's house and hid their pistols among the piles of flocks (raw washed wool) in the workshop.[41]

After Horsfall's murder, Fanny Milns, the neighbour of the Brook family at Lockwood, gave evidence that she heard a cheer from the Brooks' house and rushed in to see what was going on. Fanny reported that James Brook said that whoever had done the deed deserved £100. When Fanny reported this to her husband, he must have decided he had enough evidence to detain James Brook, so accompanied by several soldiers he arrested James.

Unfortunately for Milns, he had failed to get an arrest warrant and was drunk, so James was only held overnight. On his release James took out a summons against Milns for assault and false imprisonment and won his case. One of the witnesses was George Mellor, who vouched that the gun stock was at the Brooks' house only for polishing and had not been stolen. James won the case and Milns had to pay £100 damages[42]. With the benefit of hindsight, it seems obvious that Mellor's evidence was unreliable, but this was before he had been arrested for the murder of William Horsfall.

The problem for the authorities was that the Luddites were in effect a guerrilla movement with a great deal of support within the community, whether generated by fear or fellow feeling. The day after Horsfall's shooting but before he had died, Betty Armitage, suspected of being an informer against the murderers, was beaten up outside an inn in Huddersfield and was rescued by a dragoon 'at the hazard of his life'. Undeterred, the following day she attempted to make her way to see the magistrate, Joseph Radcliffe, but was again set upon. This time her skull was broken and she was beaten so badly that she was close to death.[43]

Most people must have had an idea of who was involved with the movement, since in the little communities people lived in any unusual comings and goings would have been noticed by such as Fanny Milns, but it took several months before the murderers were arrested. Further evidence of community support for the Luddites is shown in the fact that croppers also contributed to a fund to support the men injured at Rawfolds.

The Huddersfield area was 'under virtual military occupation' and the view was expressed that if Bonaparte had decided to invade, the locals would have joined him against the British government, so disaffected were they[44]. By late 1812 there were 98 men of the second Dragoons and 300 of the Cumberland militia in Huddersfield, alongside the Devon Militia, the Kent and Stirlingshire militias with the Devon contingent often accompanied by wives and children.

The inns and lodging houses were bursting at the seams with the military and their families and inn keepers were becoming increasingly irate because of the trouble these 'foreigners' caused, with their almost unintelligible accents and strange ways. Curfews were imposed. In Marsden no lights were allowed after nine o'clock and the whole area had the appearance of a garrison town.

One of the jobs of the militias was to collect any arms they could find, which was another source of friction. In spite of the solidarity shown to the Luddites, various people, some under duress, laid evidence both for and against them. Among them were several women, who otherwise played little part in the dramatic events perpetrated by the young men of the area.

The landlady of the *Coach and Horses* at Honley, Mrs Robinson, where Smith and Walker supposedly went after the murder, gave evidence that the two men visited her inn, though she was never asked in court if she recognized them.

Benjamin Walker's mother herself gave evidence which was used against him. She had been taken into custody by J. Lloyd, a magistrate's clerk, who was known for his brutal cross-examining methods. He had, as he put it, 'run away with one of the witnesses to prevent her being tampered with and have placed her in my house where she will more fully and freely give her examination'. She held out against his questioning however, even resisting when told in the middle of the night that Benjamin had been arrested.[45]

Eventually after prolonged questioning Benjamin Walker accused the three others, George Mellor, William Thorpe and Thomas Smith, of being co-conspirators and eventually claimed the £2000 reward, which was not awarded to him, suggesting that he may not have been

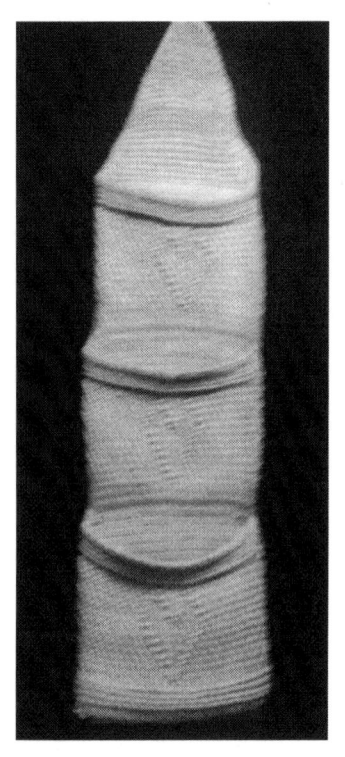

Hair tidy crocheted by Thorpe
By kind permission of the Tolson Memorial Museum

the first person to name them.

The trial lasted from 9am to 8pm before an excessively crowded court, *The Times* reported, and there was little attempt to find the men other than guilty. The government needed to make an example to the turbulent and riotous men of the county what the consequences of their acts would be. It was a show trial and could have been nothing less, held with a hanging judge who had recently sentenced 18 men to death in Lancaster, and a jury where the foreman was Henry Lascelles of Harewood and the rest of the jurymen consisted of an assortment of baronets and magistrates including Joseph Radcliffe.

Walker avoided the death penalty but the other three were found guilty, though Thomas Smith was recommended for mercy by the jury. This plea was ignored and on Friday 8th January 1813 Mellor,

Smith and Thorpe were hanged within 36 hours of their conviction, a shockingly short time, giving them no time to appeal, if they had decided so to do. Thorpe had spent the time in prison crocheting a hair tidy. As a young unmarried man of twenty-three, this must have been for one of the women in his life, a mother, sister or sweetheart. There is a heart included in the pattern, and is a touching reminder of the reality behind the bare account of the end of his life

The Times reported that the three men were well behaved on the scaffold, as were the spectators who stood solemnly by. Troops were stationed in front of 'the drop', and the avenues to the castle were guarded by infantry in case of any attempted rescue. After being hanged, their bodies were taken to the County Hospital in York for dissection, thus denying their families some kind of focus for their grief and at the same time avoiding the possibility of a further cause of unrest.[46]

After the three had been hanged fourteen others, all found guilty of the attack on Rawfolds mill, followed them to the scaffold. Seven of the men sang a hymn written by Samuel Wesley as they marched to their deaths.

> Behold the Saviour of Mankind
> Nail'd to the shameful tree.
> How vast the love that Him inclin'd
> To bleed and die for me.

When their bodies had been cut down, the second group was led out, still singing the same hymn:

> But soon he'll break death's envious chain
> And in full glory shine.
> O Lamb of God, was ever pain
> Was ever love like Thine?

These judicial murders left 57 children fatherless and condemned their families to penury.[47]

Those men who had been arrested for 'twisting in', i.e. recruiting for the Croppers' Union, were transported, missing the death penalty by days as the new legislation had not come into force. The magistrate Joseph Radcliffe received death threats and the hostility of the neighbourhood so affected his health that he considered retiring to some other part of the country. He had however asked for and received a baronetage for his pursuit of the Luddites.

The execution of those seventeen men at York Castle in January 1813 left their families bereft. The three hanged for the murder of William Horsfall were young unmarried men with no children, but the other fourteen had 57 children between them. How were their mothers going to cope?

It is unlikely, given the support for the Luddites within the general community, that they would be ostracized by everyone for being the widows of hanged men. There would nevertheless be some who would be prepared to castigate them. Not so the Quakers[48]. Joseph Wood of the High Flatts meeting wrote in his diary:

> After their execution, a concern came upon my mind to pay a religious visit to the families and near connections of the sufferers, but I think it so unusual a thing to engage in, endeavoured to reason it away, but the more I reasoned, the more my concern increased, so that in the second month, at our monthly meeting; having previously acquainted Thomas Shillitoe therewith whom I found under a similar concern, I spread our united concern before friends.

Thomas Shillitoe was a Quaker missionary and strong proselytizer for temperance. He had moved from London to Barnsley in 1812 to be near his widowed daughter, and was living there when the seventeen men were hanged at York. Hoping to bring solace to their families, he and Joseph Wood walked to Paddock, in Huddersfield, to visit some of the bereaved. They dined with elders of the meeting, John and Phoebe Fisher, and stayed the night with them. The following day, accompanied by John Fisher and Abraham Mallinson of the Paddock meeting, they began their mission of mercy.

They started with three visits to Longroyd Bridge, where Jonathan Dean, and John Walker had lived, both accused of riotous assembly at Rawfolds mill, then to the family of George Mellor, the organiser of Horsfalls' murder. Dean's widow had been left with five children, the eldest eight years old and the youngest a few months. She was, writes Thomas Shillitoe, 'under very great distress.' The visitors were much moved by her situation. 'All that was alive in us and capable of feeling for her, plunged as she was into such accumulated distress, we felt to be brought into action,' wrote Shillitoe.

They next visited John Walker's widow, who again had five children, the youngest still a baby. Again they were so distressed for her and the children that they could hardly bear to stay and take tea with her. However they sat and offered what sympathy and religious solace they could. They then moved on to the parents of George Mellor who, they noted, were in 'a respectable line of life'. The visitors were on their guard 'that nothing escaped our lips that should be the means of unnecessarily wounding their feelings.' The father acknowledged that they had considered moving to another part of the country, presumably because of the disgrace brought on by his son's death, but this visit, Shillitoe felt, had settled them down again and reassured them that they had friends in the community.

The following day they visited the Brook family. Thomas, the older brother of James and George, had been accused of riotous behaviour at Rawfolds, along with his two younger brothers. Fanny Mills had given evidence at the trial against them and pointed out that they were close neighbours whose house adjoined hers, with only 'a window between the two doors.' She was heard to say by Hannah Tweedle, a witness for the defence, that 'she was determined to have the Brooks distressed before they came from this place (i.e. York Assizes) and that some of them must be hanged before they left York.' Fanny obtained part of her ambition since Thomas was hanged, but the two younger men, James and George, were discharged on bail[49]. The Quaker visitors met Thomas Brook's widow and three children, his parents and two younger brothers and sat with the visitors for a while.

They made their way from there to Dalton Fold and talked with the widow of James Haigh at the place where she was employed where her employer made a room available for them and they had 'a comfortable time' with Mrs Haigh. The couple were childless, which meant that Mrs Haigh was perhaps less stressed than some of the poor women the Quakers visited. She had a job and the routine that brought with it, which must have helped her come to terms with the situation. They then visited the home of William Thorpe, one of those accused of the murder of William Horsfall.

In the afternoon they set off on another round of visits. They went to Cowcliffe to see the family of John Ogden, another man executed for rioting. His family seemed to have adjusted to the situation remarkably quickly. For a while they sat with his widow and their three children, his parents and two of his sisters. Then a third sister arrived, having married earlier that day. The men of the wedding party were off celebrating, leaving the women at Ogden's home for a post-wedding celebration. Joseph Wood's comment was that 'my companion had an extraordinary time with the bride and many other female guests'.

After visiting all these distressed (and not so distressed) families, the third day of their mission saw them going further afield towards the Halifax area, visiting the families of Joseph Crowther, William Hartley and Job Hey. Crowther's widow had moved to live with her mother and brought her three children with her. She was expecting a fourth child, Joseph Wood reports. William Hartley's wife had died only six months before, leaving eight children, who with their father's death were orphaned. The eldest girl, aged sixteen, had visited her father the day before his execution. He had at first refused to see her but finally gave in and they said their last goodbyes. Hartley had requested that 'the public should be informed of the number and unprovided situation of his orphan family'[50]. The whole family had been taken in by his parents. When the neighbours saw the strangers arrive, they filed into the Hartleys' house and sat down. Shillitoe suggests they were there to offer support to the family.

The last visit of the day was to the family of Job Hey, executed for burglary. A serjeant of the Suffolk Militia stationed in Elland had searched the house of the Hey family and found over eight pounds of gunpowder. With no visible means of support and left with seven children to support, his widow was in despair. Joseph Wood records that 'She appeared in a very tryed state both inwardly and outwardly & our labour with her was that she might endeavour to get into the state of stillness in which God is known & his power felt, and to stay comfort & console the mind, and bear it up in the depths of affliction.' How you do that with the worry of seven children to feed and clothe suddenly thrust upon you they do not explain.

At this point, on their return to Huddersfield, the members of the Paddock meeting were feeling distinctly uncomfortable about the activities of these men which might be interpreted as supporting the rioters. Consequently it was agreed that two of their number should inform the authorities of what they were doing. Two of the congregation therefore made their way to Milnsbridge House to explain to Joseph Radcliffe what they were about. They were well received by Radcliffe and his wife, who welcomed them and understood what they were doing. Of course, Radcliffe asked to be kept informed of what was happening among these families, which the Quakers were happy to do.

Wood and Shillitoe carried on their mission with a visit to North Dean, in Elland, the home of John Hill's family. They found the Hill family at home. Mrs Hill recounted how on the night of the Rawfolds attack, her husband had been forced out of bed by the gang. She ran after him for about half a mile 'without any of her upper garments on her', as Shillitoe delicately puts it, until the men forced her to return to the house, saying if she followed them any further they would blow her brains out. Shillitoe and Wood sat for some time with Mrs Hill and John's mother and aunt. His mother was at her wits' end because not only John but his younger brother had been involved with the Luddites. This younger boy helped his mother on the small farm she had, which was her only source of income. The boy was now on the run, though neighbours vouched for his good character and his god-fearing ways. The Quakers promised that if he were apprehended they would write a reference to put before the magistrate. His mother, Shillitoe adds, was close to despair as she contemplated the winter months ahead. How to keep her livestock alive must have been a major concern, and the loneliness of struggling out in the freezing winds which whistled down the valley and the snow that came with it in the following weeks must have made her very bitter.

The two final visits were to Briestfield and Thornhill Edge. Joseph Batley, who had been executed for robbery, had left three children. They had been sent to Mirfield workhouse but by this time had been returned to their mother. From there the Quakers went to see John Batley's widow, her husband having been executed for robbery and thence to see the family of John Lumb, who had been found guilty of 'twisting in' and escaped execution by the skin of his teeth but was sentenced to transportation. His family was without a settled home but they talked to his wife at her mother's home.

What a catalogue of destruction and despair which must have generated enormous anger among those bereaved families and bewilderment about how they were going to face the future. So where might these desperate and grieving widows have turned for support?

In the first instance, as we have seen, to where many people still turn in times of distress: to their immediate family. Steven King[51] notes that kinship ties were particularly strong in the West Riding compared with some other parts of Britain, and, as King says, 'kinship support was the mainstay of the relief strategies of a large body of the background poor'. E.P. Thompson points out that 'every kind of witness in the first half of the nineteenth century – clergymen, factory inspectors, Radical publicists – remarked upon the extent of mutual aid in the poorest districts. In times of emergency, unemployment, strikes, illness, childbirth, then it was the poor' who helped their neighbours.[52]

Kinship within the dissenting chapels was especially strong, the Quakers being an extreme example. They seem to have interpreted kinship as anyone belonging to their meeting. They addressed one another as 'brother' or 'sister', paid the travelling expenses of members wishing to travel to other parts of the country and were so aware of their separateness from mainstream religious life that anyone marrying outside the religion was referred to as being in 'a mixed marriage'.

If there was not enough support from the family, then the alternative was the poor rate, levied on the richest members of the parish. Before the 1834 Poor Law came into being, many of the poor of the parish would be supported by out-relief administered by the overseer of the poor. There was no general rule which governed the country on the levels of poor relief. In some areas it would be sufficient, in others a bare minimum. Mirfield, where the children of Joseph Batley were briefly confined in the workhouse, opened a public subscription in 1812 to provide for the poor of the parish and raised the substantial sum of £600.[53]

Overseers of the poor were overseen in turn by the church vestry which was made up of ratepayers, who had votes according to how much property they owned[54]. The kind of support provided can be seen in the 1809 overseer of South Crosland's account. He paid 6d a week to mothers of illegitimate children, though one of his duties was also to try and locate the father and make him pay for the upkeep of his child. Sometimes he paid for items of clothing such as clogs or cloth to make a shift. The rate for a lying-in was ten shillings and he would disburse small amounts of money to buy a cartload of coal or a couple of blankets. Medical expenses were also paid, often to the doctors used by the Friendly Societies since it was cheaper than paying the doctor direct[55]. This was a useful resource that could be tapped into when the industry was going through one of its many recessions and work was hard to come by.

Chapter 4 - Civil Unrest 1813-1820

The Radical Movement

As Lord Byron had predicted, lopping the heads off, or more accurately, hanging, a few leading dissidents in 1813 did nothing to solve the long term problems of a large swathe of the country, where the populace was far from happy. The cessation of hostilities with the French following the battle of Waterloo in 1815 meant that government money which had flowed freely in to clothing the army was suddenly withdrawn, leaving the weavers of the West Riding and the Cotton Country over the border in Lancashire worse off than before. Unrepresented in Parliament, their only means of changing the status quo was by petitioning the King, or in this case the much-despised Prince Regent. The radical movement set out to change the situation.

Walvin[56] has emphasized the importance to the radical movement in Yorkshire of the campaign against the slave trade. While this had begun over thirty years previously, the campaign, originating with the Quakers on either side of the Atlantic, had honed their lobbying skills and set out a pattern of behaviour which was adopted by various reforming movements and is still in practice today.

Their tactics were to research their subject meticulously and honestly, seeking out the testimony of reliable witnesses, to disseminate that information by means of cheap pamphlets and to ensure that the topic was discussed in their meeting houses. They also made good use of local newspapers and we shall see that in the coming decades newspapers would become increasingly important as an agent of change.

By 1830 Yorkshire had 1019 dissenting congregations and the largest number of Quakers in any county (though it was of course by far the largest county). In the first half of the nineteenth century Yorkshire also had the largest number of Methodists and Baptists. So there were lines of communication which spread radical ideas, not only about the necessity to abolish the slave trade but also the need for proper representation in Parliament, and the need for everyone, even women, to have a say in the laws which governed them. Women were used to running their own affairs within the women's groups, and while decisions made there might have taken second place to decisions made by the men, they did have organizational skills culled from this situation and the confidence to believe in their own opinions.

Following the disturbances of 1812 and the execution of the Luddite rebels, there was a short lull in overt rebellion. But the underlying problem of the mechanization of manufacturing processes continued and, as Marland has pointed out, 'high prices and poor wages, exacerbated by trade depression did …remain features of working-class life for much of the early nineteenth century'.[57]

It has to be admitted that there was a distinct difference in the level of political action between the militant Lancastrians and the less politically aware industrial West Riding but nevertheless the militancy west of the Pennines did cross the hills to awaken demands for revolution among at least some of the residents of the West Riding.

The two streams of discontent, the immediate problem of hardship caused by lack of work and the consequent lack of income, and the longer term problem of changing the political situation were both implicated in the unrest which dominated this period of life in the industrial North. This in turn resulted in three kinds of action: collecting arms to equip an uprising, as the Luddites had done, forming trade unions to improve working conditions in contravention of the Combination Acts of 1799 and 1800 and from a

A three-storey workshop and home

longer term political view, forming discussion groups to raise awareness of the need for political reform, epitomized by what became known as the Hampden Clubs.

By 1817 there was much talk about an armed rising but with leaders of the movement being regularly arrested and imprisoned, and their normal lives being disrupted, very little was achieved. One can't help thinking, too, that the enormous distances people had to walk after a hard day's work to meet fellow revolutionaries must have dampened their revolutionary ardour.

Among those arrested was a Huddersfield cropper Ben Whiteley, arrested following a meeting in Sheffield along with Joshua Midgely, a clothier from Almondbury and men from Leeds and Bradford. It is clear from the actions of the wives of some of these men that the radical ideas and great sense of injustice that drove the men to risk their freedom, and even their lives, was supported by their wives.

Ben Whiteley's wife was working at Whinney Bank when a letter arrived in Holmfirth from her husband, who had been incarcerated at

Wakefield House of Correction. The man bringing the letter waited at the Whiteleys' house while the children went to fetch her. The following morning she set off for Joseph Mellor's house at Burnlee, Upperthong, Joseph Mellor being the cousin of the Luddite George Mellor, to try to raise the money to bail out her husband. In a further incident, following the authorities' disruption of the Sheffield meeting, the wife of one of the men involved, Dawson, urged another of the rebels to go to Manchester to inform them of what had happened. He should go, she said, because 'something must be done or all these poor men will hang'.

With some of the working men of the Huddersfield area intent on collecting guns from their neighbours, women were involved whether they wanted it or not. When Sarah Jessop's husband was away from home, and her son and son-in-law were asleep upstairs, Sarah confronted a group of men who had come looking for guns. "I am a married woman. I hope you will behave yourselves,' she said to them. 'We will', they promised so she let them in and they searched the house. They didn't find any guns, though, because Sarah had hidden them too well. When they went to Clement Dyson's house again they had to contend with his wife Hannah, as her husband was away on business. She had dealt with the Luddites twice in 1812 and by this time she must have been heartily sick of being woken up by marauding bands of men. 'Your firelock!' they demanded. 'There's no gun in the house', she said, at which they promised to smash their way in. Knowing there was a pistol in the garret, she went up to get it but when she returned found they had done as they promised and broken their way in. She lost her temper. 'You're a damned set of Ludding rogues,' she shouted. 'You will never be quiet until you are hung by a string' Their reply was to say they would blow a ball through her, but instead, formed up in military fashion and marched off.[58]

These incidents occurred prior to what the men hoped would be an armed uprising. They were on their way to Huddersfield to join up with others, presumably to start the revolution. They marched to Folly Hall, at the foot of Chapel Hill, where they met with other like-minded rebels. There they came up against the newly formed Huddersfield Yeomanry, a volunteer force led by Captain Armitage. Shots were fired from both sides, Captain Armitage's horse was wounded in the head, though not fatally, and the Yeomanry turned and rode back to the town. The rebels likewise dispersed and returned home.

Several of the men went on the run but one of them, Richard Lee, was arrested after the magistrate's clerk accompanied by a posse of men had entered his house and forced him at pistol point to accompany them. He was given no time to wash or say goodbye to his wife, who was suffering from breast cancer. He was taken to York in irons to face trial for treason.

Ben Whiteley who had been out on bail for three weeks, was re-arrested. He was sent to Coldbath prison in London, then after a four day hearing before the Home Secretary, was sent to Worcester gaol where he languished for five months. By this time however, public opinion had changed somewhat. The *Leeds Mercury* had investigated the role of Oliver the Spy, who, they said, had falsely encouraged the men by telling them there was support for them in London and the men were seen as having been taken in by Oliver.[59]

The men who had been arrested and tried before a jury were found not guilty and released. They were welcomed home by a great crowd of well-wishers. Richard Lee and the man with whom he shared a cell, Riley, were not among that number. Riley cut his own throat in October 1817 and Lee was forced to clean up the cell. He was released at the end of the year, just before the Habeas Corpus Suspension Act expired.[60]

Political reform, that other strand of unrest, continued to concern people. At the national level there was a group of men known for their radical sympathies, among them Sir John Cartwright, William Cobbett, publisher and distributor of a *Weekly Register*, Sir Francis Burdett, and Henry Hunt so renowned for his fluency before an audience he was known as 'Orator' Hunt, and easily recognized by his white hat. Richard Carlile was also part of this group. He had set himself up as a publisher of political tracts. He split the works of Tom Paine, whose books were too expensive for working people to buy, into much smaller and therefore cheaper pamphlets and walked the streets of London selling them. They all wanted the abolition of rotten boroughs, universal male suffrage, annual Parliaments and secret ballots and had formed a Hampden Club. Richard Carlile was a firm believer in the equality of women with men, and was in addition an atheist.

A long way away from Westminster, in 1813, shortly after the hangings at York, Sir John Cartwright had been in touch with working people in the north and on a visit to Huddersfield saw the opportunity to channel the discontent into a force for Parliamentary reform. On his visit to the town he received a group of men who were interested in his ideas. He thought forming a Hampden Club would be a useful thing to do. The authorities thought otherwise. It was supposedly a private meeting, but the military commander of the area insisted on being present, took the whole group before magistrate Radcliffe and they were fined for tippling. In the opinion of the political establishment, Cartwright's ideas were nothing short of revolutionary. The idea of Hampden clubs spread throughout Lancashire and West Yorkshire, and the authorities' response was to harass the people involved, and to further develop the network of spies who infiltrated many of these clubs.[61]

From the political perspective the first overt indication of political unrest was in May 1814 when a local petition was organized and obtained 12,322 signatures against the Corn Laws, which kept the price of flour artificially high[62]. In 1816 the Huddersfield Union for Parliamentary Reform was established, while over in Lancashire three men, John Knight, John Saxton and James Wroe, put their heads together and published the first edition of the *Manchester Observer*, edited by Wroe, a Bradford man who had moved to Manchester. The paper was printed by Susannah and John Saxton at their shop on the outskirts of Manchester. This paper was sold all over the country and would certainly have been in circulation in the Huddersfield area, as was another radical paper, *The Black Dwarf*.

Joseph Johnston, another Lancashire Radical sent as a missionary from the Radical Union in Middleton near Manchester, was invited to speak at an open air meeting convened by the newly formed Huddersfield Union Club. Their agenda included a discussion of the dreadful economic situation with many looms now lying idle and brought about, they said, not by the transition from war to peace but 'as the result of a long and protracted War to subjugate the Liberties of this and other Nations.' They put the blame for this sad state of affairs squarely on the shoulders of the government, for, they argued with impeccable logic, 'if the general prosperity and happiness of a nation be indicative of a good government, poverty and wretchedness must indicate a bad one'.[63]

Reform Union Clubs were also springing up all over the West Riding, which in turn resulted in the formation of an anti-reform movement, the Loyal and Social League, whose members were made up of merchants, manufacturers and others not so affected by the economic situation. The government reacted strongly to this situation. They likened the Union Reform groups to the Spenceans, who sought to overthrow the rights and principles of property.[64]

The 1818 Election

The first Parliamentary election after the defeat of Napoleon occurred in 1818. After the new Parliament assembled you could have been forgiven for thinking there had been little change. Lord Liverpool was still Prime Minister, and the Tories were still forming the government. There had however been important changes, which showed that, whether they realized it or not, the movement for political reform put forward by the radicals was gaining ground.

In previous elections it had been the custom for candidates to be returned with no opposition. In the pre-election period candidates spent freely on food and drink, bribes, carriages to the polls, agents, bands, and general merrymaking for their supporters. Only the very rich could afford it. To complicate matters still further, the polls were not necessarily organized on the same day, so if a candidate did happen not to gain the seat, he could move on to another seat in the hopes of winning that. If, of course, he could afford it.

In 1818 there was a considerable number of MPs who could not face the upheaval and expense of a re-election, and retired. An additional complication arose from the fact that the franchise requirements had fallen into disrepair and in some areas no-one knew who qualified for a vote. The arguments went on for days in some cases. There were more seats contested in 1818 than at any time since 1734 so voters actually had a choice. Of the 380 constituencies, 120 were contested. The Radicals and Whigs had a set of coherent policies based on reducing taxation and state expenditure, parliamentary reform and greater emancipation, including for Catholics. They won 35 borough seats from the government, and now had a group of men in Parliament who were committed to reform and were prepared to speak up against the injustices of the system. 151 of the members elected had no previous parliamentary experience[65]. In spite of the political advances made in this general election, these were not recognized by the general population, and unrest continued unabated on both sides of the Pennines.

In Huddersfield the Union Society announced in the *Leeds Mercury* that there were would be a public meeting on 2nd August 1819. The meeting was meant as the first of a series of assemblies across the country to show Parliament that people were serious in their demands for Parliamentary reform[66]. The next meeting was scheduled for Manchester two weeks later on the 16th August when the speakers would be Henry Hunt and Richard Carlile. The meeting at St Peter's Fields was dubbed 'Peterloo' because of the number of people killed on that day.

Permission to hold the meeting in Huddersfield had been refused by the Constable so it was decided to hold an outdoor meeting in 'the Field betwixt the River and the Canal near the Dock Yard.' The meeting actually took place not by the river but on Almondbury Bank. Every contingent had brought a banner and a cap of liberty was hoisted on a flag pole carrying the banner demanding annual Parliaments.[67]

One speech proposed the formation of Female Reform Unions, a new idea, this, which had originated in Lancashire. At least one was formed in the Huddersfield area, in Paddock, the site of the only Quaker meeting house in Huddersfield. At the end of the Huddersfield meeting there were three cheers for Cartwright, Cobbett, Carlile and Hunt, among others.

Female Reform Societies

Women had been active in radical politics alongside men for many years though it was left to Samuel Bamford, the chronicler of Peterloo, to attribute to himself the novelty of encouraging them to vote alongside men at meetings of radicals. They played an important role in the formation of political opinion. The language and icons of the French and American revolutions still retained their power: the French Phrygian cap worn by Marianne, that epitome of the French spirit of resistance, and flags bearing dramatic messages, one of the more concise being 'No corn laws; Death or Liberty; arm yourself against Tyrants: Unite and be Free' still expressed what people were feeling, and these flags, or colours as Samuel Bamford called them, were made by women, as were the caps of liberty.

Female reform societies had their own characteristics. The very fact of their existence was a shock to society and they were painted in the loyalist press as harlots or drunkards, poor mothers and dreadful wives whose homes were a disgrace to themselves, their husbands and to the nation at large.

The first society saw the light of day in Blackburn in July 1819. According to the *Manchester Chronicle*, a loyalist paper, their aims were not only to support working men in their radical ideas but to 'instil into the minds of their children a deep and rooted hatred of the Government and the Houses of Parliament'[68]. One of the Blackburn society's first moves was to circularize women in other towns in the area and suggest they too form such societies. The idea was taken up with vigour in Manchester where a thousand women joined in the first week of its existence. Susanna Saxton, who had been helping to publish the *Manchester Observer* since 1816, was chosen as secretary and an activist called Mary Fildes as president.

Mary Fildes, nee Pritchard, was thirty years old in 1819, having been born in Cork. She had married a Lancashire reedmaker, William Fildes in 1808 and had eight children, three of the boys being called after famous radicals. So Thomas Paine Fildes, Henry Hunt Fildes, and John Cartwright Fildes all bore witness to the family's political opinions. She was prominent at Peterloo and was seriously injured then. This did not deter her from radical politics and some fourteen years after Peterloo she and a Mrs Broadhurst established a Female Political Union of the Working Classes in 1833 and she was active in the Chartist movement in the 1840s. She was also arrested for distributing information about contraception, which was considered pornographic. Eventually she retired to Chester to run an inn where she lived out her days in a more peaceful fashion.

Ruth Mather has some interesting insights into the speeches the Female Reform Society women delivered[69]. She makes the point that the women's rhetoric was couched in terms of their roles as wives and mothers. They were often apologetic for having the effrontery to stand up in meetings and express their thoughts. In fact the Stockport branch chairwoman asked for the men to withdraw before she had the courage to stand up in public and address the room. They stressed their need to take a stand because their children were hungry and their cottages, which had once vied for 'cleanliness and arrangement with the palace of the King' were now grubby and devoid of ornament and furniture. Everything which could be sold, had been. They blamed their poverty fairly and squarely on taxation which had been introduced to fund the wars with France, and the increase in land values which had enriched some while leaving the majority penniless. A good wife was seen as an asset to a man, and the way she showed that she was a good wife was to keep a clean and welcoming home and educate her children. All this had been taken away from them by the government.

The women were also aware of the drama of their situation. It was often the case that high-born women would present banners and write poems to celebrate the establishment of a volunteer corps, where the men were presented as heroes and chivalric defenders of their womenfolk not only against the enemy (i.e. the French) but also the regicides at home. These occasions, as Mather has pointed out[70], were highly visible and intended to be so, a celebration and also a warning to anyone who wanted to upset the status quo.

It is not surprising therefore to find women of a radical persuasion making banners and caps of liberty, that most iconic of symbols, and presenting them to their menfolk in ceremonies as public as the official ones. It was a way of showing publically their support for their husbands, fathers, brothers and lovers, urging them to keep the faith and be heroic in the face of adversity. These dramatic forms were a way of presenting information in situations where the spoken word was difficult to hear. After all, outdoor oratory necessitated large lung capacity and a loud voice. Even Samuel Bamford, that most dedicated of radicals, wanted to take himself off to the pub at St Peter's Fields, because he knew the arguments that were about to be presented and he could read what had been said the following day in the papers.

As part of the loyalist pressure on radical women, the loyalist press subjected women to vicious satire. In cartoons, as we have seen, they were presented as prostitutes and drunkards. It was not seemly, to many in the wider community, for women to have political views and to act on them, and this may be one reason the women were attacked at Peterloo. They were being punished for daring to have a point of view and daring to express it. After Peterloo, the image of women changed. The *volte face* of the loyalist press meant that women were now represented as tragic heroines trying to save their infants from the swords of the soldiery.

St Peter's Fields, August 16, 1819

There was at least one person from Huddersfield present on that fateful day: the twenty six year old magistrate Benjamin Haig Allen. Being a magistrate, he had ridden over the hills from Huddersfield to find out what was happening and to inform the Home Office about the meeting at St Peter's Fields. His terse account is the first to be written and does not describe the violence which is now its hallmark. The violence however was not unexpected in Whitehall. In March 1819 Henry Hobhouse, permanent undersecretary at the Home Office, had written to a Lancashire magistrate, 'Your country will not be tranquillised until Blood shall have been shed either by the Law or the Sword'.

Allen's terse message, written only an hour and a half after the demonstration began, said:

> The meeting took place at one o'clock. Hunt in the chair with 16 flags and seven caps of Liberty hoisted up among upwards of 60,000 people, the cavalry has just broken in upon them, the flags are taken, Hunt and his party secured, several lives are lost and a number are wounded. The cavalry are now securing the streets in all directions, half past 2 o'clock, yours H Allen.[71]

Graphic accounts of that day from a rather different perspective are given by Richard Carlile, the London-based radical, and Samuel Bamford, whose wife Jemima was there and whose experiences are included in his autobiography. Their accounts demonstrate what a happy event it was meant to be.

Samuel Bamford, a silk weaver from Middleton, was in and out of prison on a fairly regular basis, which must have been something of a difficulty for his wife. Their home, five miles north west of

Manchester, in Middleton, seems to have been a stopping off point for Radicals on their way to and from Yorkshire, including one old man by the name of John Knight. In 1817 Samuel had been consigned to prison in London, so his wife, in an attempt to find out from other Radicals what was happening to her husband, set off for Manchester. The weather was fine when she left home so she took neither cloak nor umbrella and had only a light cotton shawl around her shoulders. But there was a change in the weather before she arrived and by the time she stood on the doorstep of John Knight's house, whom she had welcomed into their home just a couple of weeks before, she was soaked to the skin. What did John Knight do in return for the Bamfords' hospitality? He kept Jemima on the step, and turned her away without inviting her in. No information, no umbrella lent, no invitation to step inside and dry out before the fire and certainly no cup of tea to warm her. John Knight was a Yorkshireman, said Samuel, but 'Few are the Yorkshiremen, I am convinced, who would have done as John Knight did'.

Knight directed Jemma to the Drummonds' house, an Irish family Jemima had never before met but whose son Samuel was also in prison alongside Sam Bamford. In spite of not knowing her, they took her in, dried her outer garments and gave her dry stockings and shoes and something to eat[72]. A proper way to treat people, to Samuel Bamford's way of thinking.

Sam Bamford had a high regard for women and considered them the equal of men. At a meeting on Saddleworth Moor where he was a speaker he insisted on the right and propriety of women voting alongside men. 'This was a new idea', he says, 'and the women who attended numerously on that bleak ridge were mightily pleased with it. …When the resolution was put, the women held up their hands, amid much laughter; and ever from that time women voted with men at the radical meetings.' He goes on to suggest that this practice spread to the dissenting chapels throughout the region and to the female political unions, with their chairwomen, committees and other officials.[73]

The radical movement had decided that they should present themselves well, so they could not be written off as a rabble. 'We had frequently been taunted by the press, with our ragged, dirty appearance and the confusion of our proceedings', says Bamford. It was time to clean up their act. So cleanliness, sobriety, and peaceful protest were the orders for the day.

The men had been drilling on the moors above Saddleworth so they could march in an orderly procession and were able, like soldiers, to fall into rank, march, face about and march in the other direction. This was no rabble. They had no guns, and their exercises were conducted after work during the week and on Sunday mornings, when they drew the interest of milkmaids from the surrounding farms who would sell them milk straight from the can[74]. An idyllic picture but easily misunderstood by officialdom, particularly as we are dealing here with several hundred men.

On the morning of August 16th the whole town of Middleton turned out either to take part in the procession or to watch them leave the town. The men were organised with twelve of the 'most comely and decent-looking youths' at the front each with a branch of laurel in his hand as a gesture of peace. Then came groups of men in fives followed by a band ready to play a suitable march. Behind the band came the flags called colours – embroidered with various slogans: Unity and Strength, Liberty and Fraternity, and a green silk one carrying the message 'Parliaments annual; Suffrage Universal'. In the middle of the banners was a pole with a red velvet cap of liberty atop embroidered with the word 'Libertas'. The rear of the procession was brought up by local men.[75]

They waited for the Rochdale contingent to arrive, and while they waited Samuel gave them a pep talk: when they got to Manchester they should not respond to provocation of any kind, they should leave sticks and staves by the wayside and if the peace officers should attempt to arrest anyone, they should not try to rescue them. They should abstain from alcohol and after the demonstration they should reassemble around the colours and march out of the city in good order, not loitering in any of the ale houses.

Then, 'with a hundred or two of women,' mostly the sweethearts of the young men and the young wives, among them his wife Jemima, their little daughter having been left with a neighbour, they set off. Some of the girls danced to the music or sang as they went along.

As they neared the city, a message came from Henry Hunt asking them to meet his contingent to the south of the city at Newtown, so he could make a grand entry into the city. Sam Bamford had a very low opinion of Hunt, who he thought too concerned with his own reputation as a charismatic speaker and not enough with the cause. He considered Hunt showed too much 'vanity of self-exhibition'.

However, the Middleton party duly changed course and proceeded to Newtown, where they were welcomed by the Irish immigrants, poorest of the poor, who worked for wages no self-respecting English man would accept. The Irish came out dressed in their best and 'uttered words of endearment', which the Lancashire people didn't understand though they appreciated the emotion behind them so much that the band struck up 'St Patrick's Day in the morning', which, as Sam says, electrified the Irish and left them 'capering and whooping like mad.'[76] They met up with the Saddleworth group marching before their black banner inscribed with the words 'Equal

Representation or Death' painted in white. They then marched into the centre of Manchester, arriving before Hunt's party, having lost them along the way.

Jemima was with a party of young married women when Sam caught sight of her, and he judged her to be protected from the general crush and safe from harm. Richard Carlile, from his viewpoint in Hunt's barouche, says,

> We had not proceeded far when we were met by a committee of women from the Women's Reform Committee, one of whom bore a standard with the figure of a woman holding a flag in her hand surmounted by a cap of liberty. She was requested to take a seat on the box of the carriage, which she did, and sat waving her flag and her handkerchief until we arrived at the hustings, when she took her stand at the corner of the hustings in front.' (This was probably Mary Fildes). 'Bodies of men were seen everywhere marching in military order with music, and colours flying, and carrying mottoes inscribed on them such as 'No corn laws' 'Liberty or Death. 'Taxation without representation is Tyranny'. Such cheering was never before heard! Women from the age of sixteen to eighty years were seen with their caps in their hands waving and cheering, and their hair consequently dishevelled.

In the carriage beside Hunt and Richard Carlile were Mr John Knight, presumably the Yorkshireman who had treated Jemima so abominably, and Mr Saxton, sub-editor of the *Manchester Observer*. Sam Bamford reckons there must by this time have been eighty thousand people present, who all cheered as they saw Hunt's carriage approach.

Hunt made his way onto the hustings, removed his white hat and began to speak. Richard Carlile reports that

> There were five women upon the hustings; four of them took a stand at the bottom of the wagons that formed the hustings, the other, Mary Fildes, I believe, was elevated on one corner of the front with her banner in her hand and resting on a large chain. A most singular and interesting situation for a woman at such a meeting; Joan of Arc could not have been more interesting.

He goes on to describe what happened when the cavalry appeared:

> I was standing by Mary Fildes, but I found her above everything like fear. I turned to cheer the other four women, and found them too in good spirits.' When the soldiers charged, many people 'were rushing on the hustings, and many others getting off, and an opening between the two wagons enabled them to pass down through. After many others had done so and just as Mr Hunt was arrested, I passed down through the aperture and had a narrow escape of my life in so doing, for the pressure of the crowd was so great that, just as I jumped down, the two wagons came together with a crash; and I lost my hat by its being jammed off my head, between the two wagons, in such a manner that I could not extricate it. I was no sooner under the hustings than I found the horses' feet up close to me; but the hustings being cleared, they moved around and followed the crowd who were driven from the hustings and then I walked out without a hat.[77]

Meanwhile Sam Bamford had suggested to a friend that they should adjourn to the pub, because they knew the arguments that would be put forward and they could read about them later in the papers. They made their way as best they could towards the edge of the crowd and as they did so heard a 'strange murmur' from the area near St Peter's church. Sam stood on tiptoe to see over the crowd and saw the blue and white uniforms of cavalry trotting forward, swords in hand.[78]

At first the cavalry was greeted with cheers from the crowd, but then they began to ride forward hewing their way through the defenceless crowd and, using the edges of their swords, inflicting head wounds and chopping at hands and arms. Not just men, but the boys and young women who had been at the front of the Middleton contingent and who had set off in such high spirits for a happy day out with the prospect of hearing one of the most charismatic speakers of the day, even these were hacked at and wounded. The crowd turned away from the hustings and fled, as best they could. The yeomanry cut down the flag staffs and demolished the colours and Hunt and his contingent disappeared. A dreadful silence descended on St Peter's Square. The ground was littered with caps, bonnets, shawls, shoes and the bodies of those killed. The only sound to be heard was the pawing of the horses. The Manchester Yeomanry wiped their sword blades.[79]

Richard Carlile decided the best he could do in the circumstances was to get back to London as fast as he could to report what had happened and to make sure that blame was allotted in the right quarters. His was the first account of the massacre to hit the streets and it was he who published the well known print of the Peterloo massacre.[80]

As the people fled the scene, the Cheshire Yeomanry arrived, to finish off the work of their Manchester colleagues. A number of the Middleton contingent found themselves at the foot of the Quaker Meeting House wall, and pulled themselves up out of reach of the soldiers. One of the young married women from Middleton, her face streaked with blood, her hair streaming down her back and her bonnet hanging by its string, filled her apron with stones and kept one of the assailants at bay, but then missed her footing and fell backwards. Badly bruised, she nevertheless managed to escape from both the Meeting House and the soldiery.[81]

One of the horses put its hooves through the Middleton big drum, which was kicked to extinction by the falling horse. Sam Bamford, not being in the middle of the melee had found shelter behind a corner of the Meeting House wall and had time now to worry about his wife. He was told however that she was well and was making her way home, so eased his anxiety.[82]

As he made his way towards home, he and a neighbour were passed by a troupe of the Manchester Yeomanry with one of them wearing wrapped around him the green silk banner now torn and bedraggled which had carried the proud words: 'Parliament Annual; Suffrage Universal.'

In her account, Jemima explains that she had been determined to go to St Peter's Fields. She felt that if she could keep an eye on Samuel she would be happier than staying at home. So she gave her little daughter 'something to please her' and left her with 'a careful neighbour woman' and joined the other young women at the demonstration. She had on her second best attire, dressed as the wife of a working man, as were her companions. She had seen Henry Hunt once before, but many of her companions had not, so they wanted to get good places in the crowd so they could see and hear what he had to say.

Her friend Mrs Yates linked arms with her but would insist on pushing forward, which Jemima did not want to do because she wanted to stay within reach of Samuel. However, Mrs Yates would not be dissuaded and they were swept close to the hustings. They were surrounded by men who were strangers to such a point that Jemime thought she might faint. Mrs Yates, being taller, managed rather better because she could see where they were. The crowd were pressing closer and Jemima thought she must get out of the press and asked the men to let her through, but they wouldn't shift. She then told them she might faint or be sick, which made them rather more responsive, and she was allowed to pass through, with the men saying 'Let her pass, she's sick'. She finally emerged from the crowds onto some higher ground in Windmill Street.

There was a row of houses, and she thought if she could stand in one of the doorways she would have a good view of the meeting and perhaps catch sight of Samuel again. She went along the row of houses till she found one with the door standing open. She stepped into the shelter of the doorway, since the occupants did not seem to object and it got her out of the crowd. Henry Hunt was by this time on the hustings addressing the people. A group of soldiers on horseback came riding up, which alarmed her, but the people in the house said they were only there to keep order, and there would be no trouble. But then a shout went up from the crowd. The soldiers started waving their swords and rode among the people and a moment later a man staggered past without his hat, wiping the blood from his head, which ran down his arm in a great stream. 'The meeting was all in tumult, she says, the soldiers kept riding amongst the people and striking with their swords.'

Jemima was terrified. She felt faint and turning away from the dreadful sight she went down a short flight of steps into a cellar and sat down on a pile of firewood. She could hear the people upstairs wailing at the sights they were witnessing through their window, and she put her fingers in her ears to try to keep out the noise. Then a young man was brought past her, wounded, followed by several men carrying the body of a respectable-looking middle aged woman, who had been killed. Jemima was terrified they were going to leave the body beside her, but they carried it forward into the house.

Jemima stayed there for who knows how long? Then a young girl came down from upstairs and bumped into her. The child in turn was terrified, probably thinking that here was another dead body, and fled upstairs to tell her mother of the intruder. The mother, Mrs Jones, came down and, having found that Jemima was well but very upset, took her up into the front room and offered her tea. Jemima refused the tea but accepted a cup of water but kept moaning, 'My lad! My poor lad!'. At this point Mrs Jones asked if she were married and where she came from. She told them but kept the name of her husband from them, being afraid that if she told them his name she might be put in prison, being the wife of one of the leaders of the event.

Jemima was determined to be on her way to Middleton, to find out what had happened to Sam, so Mrs Jones called a special constable to escort her into Market Street, from where she could find her way home. On her way she heard various accounts of what had happened to Sam: he had been killed, he was in the Infirmary, he was in prison and finally that he had gone home, which turned out to be the case. 'Soon after I had the pleasure of again rejoining him at Harperley, for which mercy I sincerely returned thanks to God'[83]. Of the Middleton contingent Samuel Bamford records eleven men and five women bruised or wounded by sabre cuts.

A week later at four in the morning he was arrested by Joseph

Nadin, the Deputy Constable of Manchester, along with a company of foot soldiers and a troop of hussars. Accused of treason, he was handcuffed and dragged out into the street where he bellowed, 'Hunt and liberty' at the top of his voice. 'Hunt and liberty' shouted Jemima, as the soldiers marched Sam away. One of the soldiers waved his pistol in her direction. 'I'll blow out your brains if you shout that again,' he threatened. "Blow away,' she responded. 'Hunt and liberty. Hunt for ever!'[84]. As might have been expected, Sam was sent to Lincoln prison to serve his sentence for his part in the events of that memorable day, and after a while Jemima joined him.

On his release they walked home from Lincoln to Middleton. At the first inn they stopped at, the landlady thought Jemima looked so young they must be eloping and seemed reluctant to give them a shared room. Sam said that they were more or less the same age and that Jemima was the mother of a fine nine year old girl They walked to Sheffield where they spent the night, but on leaving Sheffield took a wrong turn and ended in Derbyshire, so made their way towards Lancashire via Hathersage and Chapel-en-le Frith. They were by this time footsore and weary as they limped down from the hills into Stockport.

Here they stayed with friends who gave them a meal and prepared a bed upstairs. Jemima's feet were so blistered and sore she could not walk up the stairs. Sam offered to carry her but she refused and made her way up on her knees. One has to wonder if the wrong turning they took in Sheffield was Sam's miscalculation. If so, Jemima must have been furious with him. To try to make amends Sam got soap and warm water and bathed her feet, then wrapped them in her flannel petticoat. By morning they were both ready to embark on the last part of their journey.[85]

As we have seen, Jemima was not the only woman at St Peter's

Fields that day. Riding in Hunt's carriage was Mary Fildes. Riding on the box of Henry Hunt's carriage she was very visible in her white frock. She fell – or was pulled - from her seat on the box, but her dress snagged on a protruding nail and she hung suspended from the carriage. At this point an officer of the cavalry slashed her exposed body inflicting a serious wound.

Also arrested at Peterloo was Elizabeth Gaunt. Mrs Gaunt, who was pregnant, suffered eleven days of solitary confinement before being brought to court to be tried for treason. She had been helped into Henry Hunt's carriage to escape from the melee because of her injuries.

Mrs Gaunt, speaking from the chair they had had to provide for her because she was faint and weak from her injuries and prolonged incarceration, then gave her evidence. In the confusion in St Peter's Fields, she said, someone she did not know had pushed her into Mr Hunt's carriage for safety. She then fainted and when she came back to consciousness realized she had been wounded. She left the carriage and sheltered in a private house. The solicitor for the crown then said that as the evidence was very slight, he would not press for prosecution, at which Mrs Gaunt was immediately discharged.[86]

Fifteen people were killed at Peterloo. Four of them were women: Margaret Downs, who was sabred, Mary Hays trampled to death by the Manchester Yeomanry, Sarah Jones who was hit on the head by a truncheon and Martha Pilkington who was thrown into a cellar. There were 654 casualties, 168 of them women. Given that women comprised only 12% of the crowd, more than a quarter of them were injured in some way.[87]

Post Peterloo

Radicals in the Huddersfield area were as shocked as the people of Lancashire at the viciousness of the attack on the unarmed crowd.

Three days after the event, on the 19th August, a meeting was convened on Almondbury Bank, addressed by an unknown person, but possibly someone from over the county boundary, who called on those present to support their Lancashire brethren and to attend a meeting called for the following evening. The authorities reacted immediately and swore in special constables, and the yeomanry and 4th Dragoons were put on alert. The meeting did not happen but later in the month there were rumours of men drilling with pikes on Crosland Moor.

The unrest simmered for several weeks, and in October 1819 many people from Huddersfield attended a rally at Skircoat, on the outskirts of Halifax[88]. The *Manchester Observer* describes the size and the number of groups represented, the banners, seventy-four in all and sixteen caps of liberty held aloft in the driving rain. The paper recorded meticulously the messages displayed on the banners. The Lindley banner carried the message:

> With heartfelt grief we mourn for those
> Who fell as Martyrs to our cause.
> While we with execration view
> The bloody Fiends of Peterloo.

The Huddersfield banner must have been very large. It was surmounted by a cap of liberty and carried the messages: 'Universal, civil and religious Liberty.' 'Cursed be he that sheddeth innocent blood.' There was also a large bundle of sticks with the motto 'Unity' and a large bough of the willow trimmed with black crepe with the motto 'Sleep no more. Manchester hath Murdered sleep', a parody of the phrase from 'Macbeth' after his murder of Duncan.

The Brighouse flag was rather more concise. 'Truth is fallen into the streets, equity cannot enter.' And the bitter comment 'Buy the truth and sell it on. Unite and be free'. There was no doubting their

The Skelmanthorpe Banner
By kind permission of the Tolson Memorial Museum

beliefs and their anger.

This was followed by another rally rather nearer to home in Huddersfield town centre on November 8th. The organisers were refused permission by the Constable, but went ahead with their arrangements anyway. The aim of the meeting was 'to take into consideration the late events at Manchester and the propriety of reform in the Commons House of Parliament'.

Crowds of people marched into the town from the outlying villages some of them led by a band playing 'Rule Britannia' and the Dead March from 'Saul'. They marched through the town carrying sixteen banners and caps of liberty, bunches of laurel and cypress mounted on poles. The Halifax contingent brought two bands, 28 flags and caterpillar-ridden cabbages depicting corruption. The banners had slogans such as 'No corn laws; Death or Liberty; Arm yourselves against Tyrants: unite and be free.'

While descriptions in the Press describe these banners, only one seems to have physically survived intact in the Huddersfield area. That is the Skelmanthorpe flag, which, lovingly crafted and carefully buried after each rally, has survived to this day and is displayed at the Tolson Memorial Museum in Huddersfield.[89]

At the 1819 rally in Huddersfield following Peterloo there were over 8000 people massed before the hustings. The chairman, John Dickinson of Dewsbury, a weaver, concluded the meeting with an exhortation to the crowd not to buy taxed goods. His family was saving six shillings a week, he said, by this means and denying the government the taxes.

An unusual part of the proceedings was the presentation of a silk cap of liberty by Alice Tittinsor to John Dickinson, who read out an address written by Alice to her fellow female reformers of Huddersfield[90]. We have no record of what Alice wanted to say at that meeting, but it is likely to have been along similar lines to the addresses prepared by Lancashire women earlier in the year.

This was the last meeting in the area they were able to hold, because the following month, December 1819, the 'Six Acts' came into force. These were:

- The Training and Prevention Act (unlawful drilling) Punishable by transportation. This remained in force until repealed in 2008!
- The Seizure of Arms Act This gave magistrates the right to search private property and seize arms. The owners could be arrested. This was set to expire in 27 months.
- The Misdemeanors Act. This reduced the opportunities for

bail and speeded up the court process.
- The Seditious Meetings Act. Meetings of more than 50 could only be convened by a magistrate for a particular parish. Repealed in 1824.
- The Blasphemous and Seditious Libels Act. This gave more punitive punishments with up to 14 years transportation being a possibility.
- The Newspapers and Stamp Duties Act extended to cover publications which published opinion and increased the amount paid to 4d. Publishers had now to post a bond. The amount was reduced in 1836 and phased out soon afterwards.[91]

Peterloo stood out to the general population as an example of state brutality, made worse by the political response to it. Not only the government with its six acts to stifle debate and neutralize political unrest, but the Regent himself, that spoiled, spendthrift degenerate, expressed the opinion that the magistrates had been right to send in the cavalry. As Chase says, 'In the popular view, Peterloo was rapidly fixed as an unprecedented example of official violence and the moral bankruptcy of aristocratic government.'[92] Revulsion against it was expressed by Shelley in *The Mask of Anarchy,* a poem of over ninety stanzas which ends with an exhortation to the multitude to stand firm Stanza 85 reads:

> With folded arms and steady eyes
> And little fear, and less surprise
> Look upon them as they slay
> Till their rage has died away.

And the final stanza:

> Rise like lions after slumber
> In unvanquishable number

Shake your chains to earth like dew.
Which in sleep had fallen on you.
Ye are many. They are few.[93]

The Cato Street Conspiracy

The six acts may have pushed radical discontent undercover but it had not eliminated it. 1820 was to manifest the unrest in two ways, the Cato Street Conspiracy and the Queen Caroline affair. The country was also troubled by the death of George III and the succession of the wildly unpopular George IV.

Radical discontent in the south of England centred round a group of men led by Arthur Thistlewood. Their aim was to assassinate the entire Cabinet by blowing them up, just as the Gunpowder Plot in 1605 had aimed to kill King James I. This group had extensive connections in the north of England, Scotland and Ireland.[94]

Radicals in the Huddersfield area sent a man called John Crowther to London in mid-February to discover what was happening there. Unfortunately for the conspirators and fortunately for the politicians, the conspirators had been betrayed by spies and the group had been arrested on February 23 in a barn in Marylebone. John Crowther was late arriving home because of being delayed in Nottingham where a secret meeting was held to discuss the Cato Street conspiracy. When the leaders were brought to trial on May Day of that year, five of them including Arthur Thistlewood were hanged and beheaded (!) and a further five transported to Australia.

In the West Riding unrest continued, with various attempts to revive the radical fervour of the previous few years, but what is striking when one reads about these sporadic attempts at revolution was how difficult it must have been to rally people to the cause. The people were spread over a wide geographical area, their only means of transport being on foot and the only time they could march being after dark, when they would not be seen and set upon by the militia. In addition they had the difficulty of sending and receiving messages to rally other groups.

The six acts, with their ban on large public meetings had stamped very successfully on the drama of revolution and the threat of hanging and transportation, which had not deterred men in the past, were now perceived as a very real threat. There was one spark however, which survived the government clamp-down: the Queen Caroline affair.

The year of 1820 had begun with the death of George III at the end of January, and the accession of his son George IV. This led directly into what became known as the Queen Caroline Affair, a matter which both enthralled and appalled the country, who, without the delights of television soap operas, had to content themselves with real life marital discord and the drama of court proceedings in the highest court of the land, the House of Lords.

Chapter 5 - Two Unfortunate Marriages

The two marriages in question both took place a long way south of the Pennines, but nevertheless made an impact on the Radicals of the North.

The first of these was the marriage between Caroline of Brunswick and the Prince Regent, a very reluctant bridegroom. The second is rather a long way down the social scale from this inauspicious coupling, the radical writer Richard Carlile and his wife, a woman seven years older than her husband, and of an uncertain temper, at least according to her husband, though she would no doubt have had a different tale to tell.

Caroline of Brunswick and the Prince Regent.

> Queen Queen Caroline
> Washed her hair in turpentine.
> Turpentine made it shine
> Queen Queen Caroline[95]

Whatever did Queen Caroline do to project her personality into the public domain to such an extent that she is remembered over two hundred years later in a children's skipping rhyme? It makes a riveting, though complicated, story!

Queen Caroline of Brunswick, was the wife of the Prince Regent, who, on the death of his father, became George IV. He had led a dissolute life and was a hate figure for the Radicals. In 1785 George had married his mistress Maria Fitzherbert who was a Catholic. The priest who married them had had to be bailed out of the Fleet debtors' prison by the Prince who provided £500 to clear the debts.

If this marriage had been recognized, he could not have succeeded to the throne, since it was illegal for a monarch to be married to a Roman Catholic, even or perhaps especially, one whose marriage had been acknowledged by the Pope. However, in 1795 his debts were of such an order that he had to approach his father George III for help. His father promised to pay off what he owed providing he made a legitimate marriage. This he very reluctantly did, marrying Caroline in 1795.

The Prince of Wales was drunk throughout the ceremony and, according to Caroline, spent his wedding night insensible on the floor of the apartment. His mistress at the time of the marriage, one of a succession of women, was Lady Jersey, whom he insisted should be part of Caroline's household and the only woman to accompany her on the honeymoon. Not unreasonably, Caroline kicked up a fuss, the first of many.

The year following their marriage a daughter, Princess Charlotte, was born and was immediately taken to the heart of the nation because here at last was a legitimate heir. This did not improve the relationship between the royal couple. Three days after the baby was born, the prince, who thought he might be dying, made a will in which he stated that Mrs Fitzherbert was his true wife and he left one shilling to Caroline with the rest of his estate going to Mrs Fitzherbert. He recovered from his illness however, and Caroline moved out to live in Blackheath where she had a lively time entertaining politicians of a variety of opinions.

King George III liked Caroline, but when he became mad in 1810, without his protection Caroline became more exposed to her husband's whims. She was excluded from Court and found it more difficult to keep in touch with her daughter. In 1814 she left England and made her way down to the Mediterranean. Here she incorporated into her household what were painted by the innumerable spies who surrounded her as unsavoury characters and became more and more eccentric, eccentricity being equated with short Tyrolean skirts and no corsets and an affair with a man of lesser status than herself.

While Caroline abroad, out of sight and mind, posed little threat to George, the death of their very popular daughter Charlotte in childbirth in 1817 roused the emotions of the whole country. The doctor attending the birth, Sir Richard Croft, was censured so publicly and vehemently that he committed suicide in November of that year.

George was determined to obtain a divorce before his father died, but his father defeated him and died in January 1820 while there was a three-man commission investigating Caroline's behaviour. On becoming king, George immediately ordered that Caroline be excluded from prayers for the royal family. Incensed by this decision, Caroline set off for England but her progress was intercepted at St Omer by messengers from the king, who offered a bribe of £50,000 per annum if she would stay abroad. She refused. The King then had a Parliamentary bill drawn up, called the Bill of Pains and Penalties which would deprive Caroline of the title of 'queen' and grant him a divorce.

Expressions of support for Caroline poured in with Greenwich alone sending them in seven carriages, headed by the officers of the vestry and escorted by the beadles bearing the ceremonial maces[96]. People who had met her had a low opinion of her taste, manners and cleanliness but she had the great advantage of being at odds with the King. And what's more the soldiery were firmly in her court. It was even suggested that prostitutes were refusing to offer their services to guardsmen who did not support the Queen[97]. Caroline seems to have made the most of this public sympathy. 'A deserted Queen be only a deserted woman' she confessed to the women of Bristol.

Radicals seized on the Queen's cause as a way to circumvent the six acts, since, as Henry Hunt pointed out, 'no seditious meeting act can apply to her, no multitude, however numberous, can be deemed sedition for its number', seeing as it was in support of the monarchy. There was a profusion of homewares all printed with messages of support for the Queen: plates, wall-plaques, jugs, cups in cheap earthenware meant for sale on market stalls. Loughborough lacemakers made her a dress. Coventry weavers made monogrammed ribbons. Five old ladies from Kent gave her a 'very fine fat pig.'

Women's support for the Queen and their public participation in both loyal addresses and on the streets was a surprise to the general population. Many of the loyal addresses contained as many women's signatures as men's. In Exeter, for instance, with a population of 23,000, 9,000 women and 10,000 men signed a loyal address.[98]

In the wake of Peterloo and the six acts, the Radicals, deprived of any means of expressing their political ideas or furthering their aims, could at least carry on their agitating under the guise of support for the queen. The movement in her support, and more importantly to some, against the king, spread not only among the working classes but among the middling classes as well, both men and women, and this was seen as a frightening development by the Cabinet.

The government was so concerned that to keep the peace in London the Tower of London garrison was increased to full strength, the guard on the British Museum was doubled, three hundred cavalry were on stand-by within two miles of Parliament and sixty of them guarded the Regent's residence at Carlton House. A fifth of the troops stationed in the North were moved to London to maintain order and the Russian ambassador's wife noted that any available wall was scrawled with the message 'The Queen forever, the King in the river.' George meanwhile took himself off to his yacht anchored in the Solent, only venturing ashore at Cowes.

The whole country was caught up in the drama in the House of

Lords as the petition for divorce was argued. Every day Caroline drove to Westminster to hear the discussion, every word of the proceedings was reported in the Press, the crowd cheered her on her way. Caricaturists were in their element and £2,500 had to be spent on buying up the most scurrilous of their cartoons. The bill passed its third reading but Lord Liverpool refused to allow it to go further because he was afraid of the reactions of the radical elements in society, whereupon the whole country took this as a sign that Caroline had been exonerated and prepared to celebrate.

Among the celebrants were many of the Friendly Societies who in some places took an active role in the demonstrations. Large numbers of people, including women, took to the streets to celebrate. This mostly took the form of illumination in one way or another. In some places it was torchlit processions and the burning of effigies, often of the King. In Huddersfield an announcement came from the Friends of the Queen requesting

> On Thursday Evening Next, in Honour of Queen Caroline's TRIUMPH!
>
> All LADIES who join with them in thinking her conduct deserving of Imitations
>
> And are desirous of being thought like her, will make a point of Appearing at their Windows,
>
> During the Illumination, in order that Gentlemen may know their Female Friends.
>
> Huddersfield, November 15th 1820.[99]

Caroline was refused entry to Westminster Abbey for the coronation ceremony in spite of banging on the door insisting she should be let in. Eventually however, the crowd became tired of the antics of the royal couple, and Caroline lost popularity to such an extent that one wit wrote:

> Most Gracious Queen, we thee implore
> To go away and sin no more.
> But if that effort be too great,
> To go away at any rate.[100]

Which she obligingly did, dying the following year. Her death was marked in the radical newspaper *The Black Dwarf* by a satirical verse:

> Ah me! What news is this? Alas. They say the Queen is dead.
> Bless me! The onions will be dear, for tears of fashion must be shed![101]

Chase sums up the extravagant celebrations in support of the queen as a kind of social bonding where the local divisions between factions would be subsumed into the Queenite demonstrations. Charlotte, in spite of her eccentric and uncouth behaviour, stood as a representative against aristocratic misrule. Addressing a meeting in Hull, one speaker said, 'I rise to defend the cause of an injured, persecuted, desolate and most innocent women. Our interests and hers are united; we must sink or swim together.'[102]

Richard Carlile and his Wife

Once the furore over the Queen had lost its fervour, radicals turned their attention to spreading the word and thereby influencing the thinking of their fellow men and women about Parliamentary reform. In this women shared alongside men. A prime example of this is Richard Carlile and his wife and sister. They did not live in the West Riding but they certainly received a great deal of support, both political and economic, from the Huddersfield area.

As we have seen, Richard Carlile determined to spread the word of Tom Paine's revolutionary ideals by issuing his work in short tracts at

1d a copy, thereby making Paine's ideas well within the means of working men and their families.

Carlile, who had been intending to speak at Peterloo, made an early escape from St Peter's Field and on returning to London wrote an eye witness account of the event. Being an atheist, he was arrested shortly afterwards on a charge of blasphemy and sedition, which earned him three years in prison. While he was behind bars, his wife took on the publishing of his tracts and when she was arrested on a similar charge, Richard's sister Mary took over.

Carlile not only printed the works of Tom Paine, he wrote copiously himself, published a weekly 32 page newspaper, *The Republican,* and carried on writing in prison. Here is what he had to say about women and their position in society:

> Philosophers in general have not paid that deference which is due to the female in society; in speaking or writing for the improvement of society they have passed by woman as a secondary or insignificant object, whereas she forms the most important channel through which virtue can be propagated and the social state be rendered peaceable, prosperous and happy. Every impression that is attempted to be made on the female mind that she is an inferior being, every step that is taken to degrade her, is a bar to virtue, an inlet to vice. It interesteth the welfare of society to raise the female character to the highest possible pitch in the scale of intellect, even to a competition with the male in all the fine arts, science, and general literature.'[103]

Carlile was here expressing a common assumption at the time that the care of children, not only their physical welfare, but their spiritual and moral development, was the responsibility of the mother of the family, and therefore how well she was educated and treated mattered because on her shoulders rested the future welfare of the country.

The irony was that during his trial for blasphemy and sedition, the day's events were written up and printed every day, and he and his wife made more money from issuing accounts of the cut and thrust of the courtroom drama than they had ever made in the past. There were queues outside their shop every evening to read the latest instalment.

When he was finally committed to Dorchester prison for three years, it was a rather different matter. As his daughter later recounts,

> Mrs Carlile was persecuted by the authorities in the form of threats of prosecution. She was frequently arrested but her trials were as frequently postponed from time to time, only making matters more aggravating by their uncertainty. They were finally brought to an issue and were laconically announced in the *Republican* thus: - 'Trial of Mrs Carlile. Verdict, as usual. Guilty!'

Mrs Carlile was eventually sent to prison, and Richard Carlile's writings were then published by his sister.[104]

Richard Carlile's marriage was not a happy one. His wife was seven years his senior and, in his own words, 'Her temper could not be relied on'. Any little kindness he bestowed on his mother or sisters was resented. She made his life so difficult that 'I never considered my life safe, and lived for years in almost daily apprehension of some terrible domestic tragedy... To me imprisonment was a great relief'. While they were imprisoned together in Dorchester gaol, they worked out a separation settlement. She agreed to the separation if he would provide her with an annuity, which he was able to do within two years of leaving prison. She wanted the wherewithal to set up in the business she had learned from him and he notes with some bitterness that she took every article of furniture, £100 worth of books and set up in the nearest empty shop she could find so she could be in direct competition and ruin him. Of their five children only three boys survived to adulthood. He wrote about them 'Such a family as I have neither God not the Devil could manage'.

On Mrs Carlile's release from prison she was again harassed, their premises were set on fire and Mrs Carlile and the children escaped through a bedroom window. Theophila, Carlile's daughter by his common law wife Eliza Sharples, expressed the opinion that there was a concerted effort by the authorities to ruin the business by destroying books.

He was released in 1823 but immediately rearrested for non-payment of fines. He was eventually released in 1825, and in 1826 published *Every Woman's Book*. Being about contraception and explaining how women could enjoy sex, it was immediately condemned as pornography. This may have been the book Mary Fildes was keen to promote in the years following Peterloo.

It is a surprising book. Its first sentence is 'Love is the source from whence flows the stream of human happiness'. You have to wonder how he arrived at this conclusion, considering his strained relationship with his wife! This stream of happiness however is diminished by the fear of pregnancy so he will explain how this can be avoided. He reassures any possible female reader: 'The modest and chaste woman may be assured that there is nothing here which is meant to offend her'. He then acknowledges that women have sexual urges and should be able to express them and approach a man in a straightforward way without the coyness that they usually employ. Long courtships lead to sexual frustration, which in turn leads to young men frequenting brothels and young women pining, often suffering from chlorosis, the green sickness.[105]

He outlines the dangers of abortion, detailing methods of bringing them about which have a strangely modern ring – knitting needles, gin, herbal concoctions – and concludes that 'It is better to prevent than cure'.

Knowledge of contraception is common in the North of England, he avers, where handbills circulate telling people how to avoid unwanted children and states that 'no married couple should have more children than they wish to have and can maintain.' The methods he describes are a sponge inserted in the vagina, condoms available from brothels, waiters in taverns and by some women and girls in the 'neighbourhood of places of public resort such as Westminster Hall'.

He stresses the need for cleanliness. A hundred years later women such as Marie Stopes were running into the same shock and horror that Carlile's book provoked.

While in prison, Carlile's supporters in Marsden collected £12.0s.3d which a tinplate worker, Abel Hellawell, sent to him, with an assurance that he had friends 'most hearty in your cause'. A list of 103 names from Huddersfield, Almondbury and Marsden was sent to show support for Carlile and his fight for a free press[106]. One of his many supporters was a man named James Penny, of Heckmondwyke, who sent money collected in Dewsbury, Hightown and Millbridge with a contribution from 'your Huddersfield friends'[107]. Penny was on the brink of marriage with Hester Brooke, a Huddersfield woman, so moved to the area, setting up as Carlile's agent and selling his publications.

Lawrence Pitkethley, a well known Scottish radical, had also moved to Huddersfield by 1824, and gave Mrs Carlile a piece of black waistcoat material which Hester Penny made up for Richard Carlile. He wore it through the winter of 1824-5 to try to keep warm in the cold of Dorchester prison.

Happier times were in store for Carlile after he left his wife. The daughter of a Bolton family, Eliza Sharples, had once seen him at a friend's house, though the girls had been banished to their bedrooms when he was there as his presence was considered a moral danger, but they sneaked down and listened at the keyhole to what was being said.

They also applied their eyes to the keyhole so they could see what this dangerous man looked like. They were rather impressed. Eliza was intrigued and decided to read what he had written. Coming from a strictly religious background she was immediately enthralled by his ideas on religion. She read back-copies of the *Republican* and eventually via a local book seller wrote to him and offered her services to help him in his work.

Following the death of her father, she was very lonely. 'I have no-one to whom I may impart my thoughts,' she wrote to him, so in 1829 she travelled down to London and began helping him with his publishing business. Her family was extremely upset that she had rejected her Evangelist Christianity and their way of life to align herself with what they must have thought of as troublemakers, which indeed they were.

At first she helped with the production of Carlile's radical literature but in 1832 he was engaged in another project. He hired and repaired a run-down building called the Rotunda just across the Blackfriars bridge in Southwark. Eliza organized radical speakers of the day both in the political and the secularist tradition. She also edited a journal, *Isis,* then began to speak herself twice or three times a week under the name of Isis. She became his common law wife, at which point they moved to Enfield, and she bore him four children, the third of whom, Theophila, wrote a biography of her parents.

Richard died suddenly in 1842, leaving no will, so his estate went in its entirety to his eldest son by his first wife. Eliza struggled to provide for her children, receiving no help from her mother, who, when Eliza asked for help, replied that she had made her bed and must lie in it. Eliza died in poverty in 1852.

Chapter 6 - The 1830s

The last few years of the 1820s were a time of great financial insecurity and hardship among the fancy weavers of Huddersfield. Weavers, especially the journeymen, who were liable to exploitation by manufacturers, their only recourse being to join a union, now that the Combination Acts had been repealed.

Radical thinking at the time associated their poverty with the employment of machinery and the reduction in wages which had led to a great deal of pauperism and crime.[108]

Even the parliamentarians in London were aware that all was not well. The changes in the country over the previous thirty years: movements of population from country to town; the unrest caused by a lack of representation at Parliamentary level; the growth of the factory system with sometimes appalling conditions of work: these had been known about for many years but few satisfactory solutions had been sought or found, an honourable exception being Robert Owen, who many years before in 1799 had set up his model factory in New Lanark.

As we have seen there had been a great deal of agitation about these matters but following the six acts passed in 1819 any discussion had been swept under the carpet, or rather into prison, by the suppression of radical newspapers and the imprisoning of journalists. The 1830s was a time when an attempt was made to remedy at least some of these difficulties. There were rallies to complain about the various problems that society needed to fix, and the banners of the period show just how mixed up were the various strands of discontent.

The Reform Act of 1832 dealt with parliamentary reform, the 1834 New Poor Law attempted to get to grips with the increasing expenditure on the destitute, and the Ten Hour Act, which was met by opposition from most mill owners, went some way to improving working conditions in the mills, in particular the employment of children, which found an ardent supporter in Richard Oastler.

Parliamentary Reform

In 1830 the Tories were ousted from government and the Whigs came in, led by Earl Grey (of tea fame). He was a wealthy landowner but realized that the country was in such turmoil that something had to be done 'to avoid the necessity of revolution'.

The Great Reform Act of 1832, though improving matters somewhat, left a lot to be desired. The vote was given only to men who owned property to an annual value of £10, which excluded six out of seven men, and a secret ballot had to wait until 1872 to be introduced. It did have a subtle effect on society, however. It separated out what might be called the intelligentsia of the Radical movement, supporters of the Hampden clubs, for instance, from the rest. In effect it widened the gap between the haves and the have-nots, thus accentuating the social divisions in society.

On the plus side it disenfranchised 56 boroughs which had very few inhabitants, and re-allocated them to the North. Newly enfranchised boroughs in the West Riding were Huddersfield and Wakefield, who both got one MP. Bradford, Halifax, Leeds and Sheffield all got two MPs, while the whole of Yorkshire, which previously had had four MPs for the whole county now got two for each Riding.[109]

Huddersfield's first MP was Captain John Fenton, a Whig, who had commanded the Volunteer Corps in Huddersfield in the two previous years. His tenure in Parliament only lasted two years, he spoke only twice, once about a Beer Bill[110]. In his speech in Parliament, he bore witness to the demoralizing tendency of the Beer Bill. Scarcely a murder, fire or robbery but had its origins at a beer shop, he said[111]. He was right. By 1833 one in eight heads of households in Huddersfield was a drunkard[112] and the situation led to the rise of the Temperance movement.

His second contribution was about the Volunteer Corps. Huddersfield needed one, he said, 'because the conduct of some of the operatives was calculated to excite the most unpleasant feelings'. He opposed the Ten Hour Bill which sought to limit the hours women and children could work in the mill[113]. His Parliamentary career was cut short in November 1833 when he fell out of a bedroom window at his Huddersfield home and was killed. The following by-election resulted in another Whig, barrister John Blackburne, being elected.

Naturally Richard Carlile criticised the Reform Bill and raised the question of votes for women.

He wrote:

> Will the new reform bill allow women who are householders to vote for members of the House of Commons? …. If no express exception be made, female householders will be allowed to vote. And what existing law is there to reject a woman if she were returned to Parliament? I have no such high opinion of men as to think them intellectually superior to women. We shall not make this leap at once but I am sure we shall come to this: women will claim and exercise the franchise and sit in Parliament…. The ladies may be assured that whenever they stir to assert the rights of women, I will assist them.[114]

What a splendid sentiment, but not one that would be needed until the next century.

The Reform Act enfranchised small shopkeepers and businessmen, but carefully excluded the working class, so it was hardly surprising that unrest continued long after the improvements to the voting system had been brought in. By enfranchising men running small businesses, however, it did provide a means of bringing pressure to bear on the owners of these establishments. Women, who were the ones who bought in provisions, could and did boycott those who did not support their own political views. This was known as 'exclusive dealing' and had been used in the 1820s when working people boycotted taxed goods to demonstrate their opposition to the government.[115]

The Press[116]

The Newspaper and Stamp Duties Act of 1819, one of the Six Acts which came into force following Peterloo, had attempted to stifle political discourse by imprisoning writers and publishers for sedition as we have seen with Richard Carlile.

Newspapers had begun their life at the beginning of the eighteenth century as advertising sheets[117]. By 1712, when stamp duty was introduced, there were about twelve papers established in the provinces but in the following decade the number had doubled, and now included the *Leeds Mercury,* established in 1718.

The Six Acts, passed after the Peterloo massacre in 1819, tightened up the definition of a newspaper. Radical papers had to choose between being a pamphlet, unstamped and appearing monthly, or being a paper which carried news, which meant it had to be stamped, which raised the price, the tax being four pence on top of the expense of distribution. Newspapers were then bought by inns and drinking houses, where they were read by the literate and read to the illiterate and the ideas discussed.

The London papers and pamphlets were sent out by stagecoach, and eagerly awaited not only by the agents who sold them – people such as, in Huddersfield, Lawrence Pitkethley, - but wives who wanted to buy them to prevent their husbands having an excuse to go to the public house to read[118]. Writing about the distribution of the papers, Robert Lowery, a Newcastle Chartist, recalls how in 1819 women with children in their arms would often be waiting to collect a paper, and were disappointed if they failed to arrive. Assured of the arrival of the bundle of newspapers later in the week, they would say,' Yes, yes but I like to get it on Saturday, and then he doesn't go to the public house when he's done his work, but stops at home and reads it.'[119]

Provincial newspapers had a lower circulation than the London papers but were more numerous. Generally they represented local factions. In 1801, for instance, the editorship of the *Leeds Mercury* was taken over, with the backing of a group of wealthy Dissenting manufacturers and merchants, by Edward Baines, who made it the premier Whig Dissenting newspaper in the West Riding. It generally took an anti-government stance, and by 1817 was the leading provincial newspaper. The *Manchester Guardian,* set up in the wake of Peterloo, was another such. Papers such as these not only reported the news, they facilitated discussion among their readers, and even undertook what would now be called investigative journalism, with the *Mercury* for instance revealing the role of Oliver the Spy as an *agent provocateur*. The newspapers formed a focus for agitation for Parliamentary reform.[120]

A local paper in the Huddersfield area was *The Voice of the West Riding,* printed by weaver Joshua Hobson for the Huddersfield Political Union. Joshua was familiar with the workings of the unstamped press since his mother, Mary Hobson, was a landlady who sold them. Established in Huddersfield, Joshua started to print his paper in June of 1833 in Swan Yard in Kirkgate.

Its first edition covered the working conditions of children in the mills. One of the first items was the coverage of an incident at Norris and Sykes' New Town Mill. A case came before the magistrates concerning a Cowcliffe boy, Joseph Firth, who had been beaten by an overlooker, Robert Clay. Joseph had been one of a group of boys who had 'baa'd' at one of the workmen, who they deemed to be a black sheep, the equivalent, I suppose, of today's 'black leg'. Clay was found guilty of the offence and told to pay two shillings to the surgeon who had attended the boy, a week's wages to the boy and £1 to the Infirmary where Joseph had been taken after his beating. The account of the event in the paper drew attention to the fact that the boy had not been given anything for his injuries, which the magistrates had refused to inspect, and that pain and bodily injury deserved more recompense than loss of labour.

The *Voice of the West Riding* only survived till June 1834, Hobson being imprisoned for selling an unstamped paper. He put up a spirited defence during his trial, maintaining that the prosecution had been instigated not because the paper was unstamped but because of its content. He nevertheless ended up in the House of Correction at Wakefield with common felons, rather than being held as a political prisoner, so could have no food supplements from his friends in the radical movement, and had to wear prison uniform and have his hair cut.

An even more short-lived publication was *The Demagogue*, edited by William Rider and printed by Alice Mann. There were only two of these published, aimed at the editor of the *Leeds Mercury*, Edward Baines Senior, for his lack of support for factory reform.

Earlier radical unstamped papers were the *Black Dwarf*, a very popular satirical paper which ran from 1817 to 1824, and William

Cobbett's *Political Register* first published in 1802. This had a circulation of 6,000, a highly successful achievement at the time. To reach a wider audience he then took out any news and published only comment, in a cheap pamphlet called the *Register*, which sold at 2d, thereby avoiding the necessity to pay stamp duty, and reaching an audience of 40,000. It remained in print until 1836, the year following Cobbett's death. It was known as the 'Tupenny Trash'.

The papers were distributed through a series of agents in the provinces recruited by London agents. Most agencies began as part-time businesses, such as James and Alice Mann's in Leeds but such was the profit to be made that there was no shortage of people wanting to sell the papers. As with much printed material, the number of people reading the papers very much exceeded the number buying them, since they were stocked in coffee houses, inns, and ale houses. Although there was considerable rivalry between publishers, if one of them was committed to prison, their families could usually rely on these rivals and their supporters within the community for financial help.

Working Conditions in Mills

The Yorkshire MP William Wilberforce had been a leader of the fight against the slave trade, and the Lascelles family of Harewood had acquired much of their fortune from it. The repugnance felt by many had finally had its effect by 1807 when the Act against the Slave Trade had come into force. When people considered the working conditions in the mills, it seemed a small step from the slavery of the West Indies to that of the West Riding. Having moved mountains to get the abolition of the slave trade, if not actual slavery, perhaps something could be done about the 'wage slaves' in the West Riding.

Following the dreadful fire in 1819 at Thomas Atkinson's cotton mill, when seventeen girls between the ages of nine and twenty had

Fixby Hall

lost their lives, legislature had been brought in to regulate working conditions in cotton mills. These laws did not apply however to woollen mills and in any case there was no mechanism for ensuring that mill owners abided by the laws. So rather an ineffective piece of legislature.

Foremost among the agitators for a change in the way mills were managed was Richard Oastler. He had been brought up in Leeds and worked as a commission agent. As such he was very successful and in 1816 he married Mary Tatham, the daughter of a wealthy Nottinghamshire lace manufacturer. They had two children but by 1819 both children had died. Oastler lost interest in his business, and who can blame him, with a weeping wife at home and an empty cot? The business went downhill and in 1820 he was declared bankrupt.

However, that same year, his father died. What might have been considered a sadness was also an opportunity. His father had been steward at Fixby Hall, in Huddersfield, for the Thornhill family, who had moved to Norfolk in 1809. Richard was taken on in his place and moved from Leeds to Huddersfield, where he began to live the life of a squire, travelling round the estate and re-invigorating old customs. He was by this time a keen supporter of the movement for the abolition of the slave trade, and a friend of the Leeds MP, Michael Sadler, also a keen abolitionist.

Having heard a pompous and self-satisfied speech in Leeds Cloth Hall on September 22 1830 by the Reverend Hamilton, in which he congratulated the country on having no slave existing on her soil and concluded that 'the air which Britons breath is free - the ground on which they tread is sacred to liberty', Richard Oastler, in a rage, was driven to reply to the clerical gentleman in the pages of the *Leeds Mercury*.

> Thousands of our fellow creatures and fellow subjects, both male and female, the miserable inhabitants of a Yorkshire town (Bradford) are at this very moment existing in a state of slavery more horrid than are victims of that hellish system – 'Colonial Slavery'.

- he wrote.

He goes on to highlight the hypocrisy of a town renowned for its religious zeal and whose inhabitants 'are striving to outrun their neighbours in Missionary exertions, and would fain send the Bible to the farthest corner of the globe.' Look nearer to home, he urges them. Look at the boys and girls as young as seven who work in the mill from six in the morning till seven in the evening with thirty minutes allowed for eating and recreation. 'Ye live in the boasted land of freedom,' he says to the children,' and feel and mourn that ye are slaves, and slaves without the only comfort which a Negro has. He knows it is his sordid master's interest that he should live, be strong and healthy. Not so with you. …When your joints are in action no longer, your emaciated frames are cast aside, the boards on which you lately toiled and wasted life away, are instantly supplied with other victims who in this boasted land of liberty are HIRED - not sold - as slaves and daily forced to hear that they are free.'

Although written on the 29th September 1830, it was not published until October 16, delayed while the editor compiled a suitable editorial to accompany it.

The Reverend Hamilton was a powerful force in the religious life of Leeds, being the dissenting minister of the Albion and Belgrave Independent chapels and Henry Lascelles was the Lord Lieutenant of the County. Not people to be unnecessarily provoked.

The letter catapulted the cause of factory reform into one of the foremost social issues of the day, alongside Parliamentary reform, and Oastler into the leadership of it. It led immediately into the formation of Short Time committees, one of the first being that brought together in Huddersfield.

As well as working for restrictions on the employment of child labour, the Short Time committees were hoping that by so doing they would limit the working hours of adults. This is because much of the work done by children was 'piecing' or 'piecening': connecting up the broken threads in the slubbings and spun thread as the slubbers and spinners produced the hanks of wool and the actual threads used for weaving. The children were often family members paid by one of their parents, a remnant of the domestic system.

The Huddersfield Short Time committee (HSTC) consisted of seventeen men mainly employed in the woollen industry, the most important on a national level being Joshua Hobson, the weaver and publisher of the *Voice of the West Riding*, and Lawrence Pitkethley, the general dealer from Scotland, who had married a Huddersfield woman. By 1833 there were people touring the country to drum up support for the cause. One such was George Crabtree, a mill worker from Huddersfield who talked directly to the mothers of Halifax[121], saying 'Mothers of Halifax and its neighbourhood, rouse yourselves in your children's cause; if the RICH ladies won't use their influence to emancipate your infants, you as mothers ought to be alive to the amelioration of their condition.'

Alongside the Short Time Committees there were also Political Unions, concerned with the reform of parliament and there was, as one might expect, a considerable overlap in membership of the two.[122]

The role of the HSTC was to gather reliable evidence about the treatment of children in mills in the area, to support Michael Sadler MP, who was involved in the presentation of a bill to Parliament, and to organize meetings to spread the word. These were all tactics which had been found to be effective in the campaign against the slave trade.

Oastler decided that a pilgrimage to York would bring the topic of factory reform to the forefront of people's attention. As a renowned public speaker – a tall man with a very loud voice, which was needed if you were to be heard outdoors by a large crowd – he realised that it would be an excellent way to promote the cause.

On Easter Monday 1832, the Huddersfield contingent led by Oastler having walked forty-five miles, joined crowds of people from all over the West Riding converging on the Castle Yard at York to make their feelings known. The poster advertising the event had promised 'all will be Peace and Joy'. Well, not quite. Having walked for two days, footsore and weary, they arrived in York to find their lunch of bread and cheese had not materialized. It was only the arrival of Oastler that saved the day. The meeting went on for five hours and resulted in the drafting of three petitions, two to members of the House of Commons and one to the Lords. The presenters of the petitions then went on to give evidence to the Factories Inquiry Commission.

Michael Sadler, who was promoting a Ten Hour Bill in the House of Lords, lost his seat in the 1832 election, so the following year Lord Ashley (the Earl of Shaftesbury) took responsibility for it. The Bill achieved some of the changes the Short Time Committees had hoped for but by no means all. It was agreed that no children under the age of nine should be employed and that under eighteens should work no more than ten hours. This failed to be incorporated into the act, and the age was changed to thirteen. Young people under twenty-five should not work nights.

In 1835 the physicians and surgeons of Bradford issued a memorial to the effect that they supported a ten hour working day, but not an eight hour day. This was because if the hours of work were cut to eight hours a day, it would mean mill owners might well run two shifts, with the possibility that children would be able to do two shifts a day and earn two wages. By fixing the working day to ten hours, this would be an impossibility.

Importantly, the Ten Hour Act created a factory inspectorate which would police the Act, though there were only four inspectors to cover the whole country. It was, however, a start, though it depended on the enthusiasm of magistrates to enforce the legislation. Richard Oastler's outspoken and emotional rhetoric against the lack of enthusiasm for enforcing the new law by the magistrates was considered revolutionary. Addressing an audience in Blackburn which contained several of the said magistrates, Oastler said,

> If the law of the land, intended to protect the lives of the factory children, is to be disregarded, and there is

> no power to enforce it, it becomes my duty, as the guardian of the factory children, to enquire whether in the eye of the law of England, their lives or your spindles are most entitled to the law's protection.

He went on to suggest that the children could obtain their grandmothers' old knitting needles which he said he would show them how to apply to the spindles.[123]

Alongside the legislation, a Royal Commission explored what mill owners thought about bringing in new legislation. Thanks to the *Huddersfield Exposed* web site, it is possible to read the forms which were sent back to the government enquiry about the make up of the work force in each mill, and the working conditions therein.

The Royal Commission on Employment of Children in Factories (1833)

Questionnaires were sent out to mill owners asking for details about what kind of mill it was, how many people were employed, how much they earned and how much holiday the work force was allowed. Answers came back which give a vivid picture not only of

Weavers' Cottages

working life at that time, but also of the employers' attitudes to their workforce.

Of all the mill owners who completed the forms sent out by the government, only one was a woman. This was Mary Horsfall who ran a slubbing and scribbling mill in Golcar. Her mill was very small. It had been built in 1807 on the banks of the Hawm Brook in Golcar, was water–powered with the wheel producing only eight horse power, and dealing with only scribbling and slubbing. She employed only thirty people, excluding office and warehouse staff and the workforce when broken into its component parts consisted of

	M	Paid	F	Paid
Under ten	2	3 shillings	2	3 shillings
10-12	8	3 shillings	8	3 shillings
14-16	2			
21 +	8			

She fails to give the average pay of the workforce, but the children acting as piecers for the slubbers and scribblers are paid their three shillings by the adult they are working with, so the domestic system is still a reality in this mill. There are 17 children paid by the slubbers in this way. There is very little overtime but people are not paid extra for working overtime.

The mill starts work at 6 am and ends at 8pm five days a week with Saturdays being two hours shorter, and ending at 6pm. Sunday, of course, is a rest day, or at least a day when the mill is not running. If there is a lack of water during a drought the mill begins work when there is water and stops when the supply runs out.

There is only one official break in the day, for an hour from 1pm to 2pm for dinner and at this time the machinery stops running. All other meals and drinks are taken while the machinery runs, and the work is covered by another person. If time is lost due to an accident or other obstructions, for instance to the flow of water, then if trade is brisk, the time has to be made up, but if not, time and the attendant money is lost to both mill owner and employees. No time is allowed for sickness. Wages cease with the work, though if anyone is off work sick, their job is kept open for them.

There are several days' holiday a year: New Year's Day, two half days at Easter, two half days at Whitsuntide, two days for the village feast and two days at Christmas. No-one is paid for the holidays. There are no fines for non-attendance or late arrival, however.

There is no shift work, so only one set of people is employed, and the same applies to the children. When the question of corporal punishment is raised, Mary Horsfall's answer is enigmatic. 'We do not allow children to be ill-used,' she says firmly, 'but we allow them to be punished for willful neglect or mischievous conduct.' One suspects her interpretation of 'ill-used' may differ from a modern interpretation. She considers that she is doing families a favour by employing children under the age of twelve, as the work can be done by older children, but these young ones come with their family, are employed at piecing and are there 'out of charity for their needs'. In other words, the family needs them to work.

Her comments on the legislation supports this, 'I am decidedly of opinion that a ten hours bill will be injurious to the labouring classes; for, if the legislature restrict the hours of children's labour to ten hours a day, or five days a week, the adults, whose labour depends upon the labour of the children, will not be able to work more than five days a week; consequently they can expect to receive only five days' wages per week.'

Mary Horsfall is obviously running the mill in the way it has been run since its inception, and cannot envisage anything else. In this she is no doubt in accord with her employees, whose work patterns would be likewise set in a rigid pattern with no way of imagining a different way of life. Her mill is run as a sort of halfway house between the domestic system and the factory system.

If we move further up the Colne Valley to Marsden, to Schofield, Kenworthy and Co., we find a very similar picture in an even smaller establishment. Isaac Bottomley, who signed the form, and was asked for comments, basically told the government to mind their own business. 'We are of the opinion,' he wrote, 'that in the woollen business there is no occasion for the interference of the legislature to regulate the hours of labour'. As with Mary Horsfall, we see a similar refusal to accept the need for change.

A third example from the Colne Valley is that of Scholes, Varley and Co. whose mill at Waterside, Slaithwaite cards and spins cotton. Working conditions were more or less the same as the previous two examples and Richard Varley, who completed the form, had a lot to say to the men in Westminster. He thought 'twelve hours per day, exclusive of meal times for five days a week and nine hours on Saturday is not injurious to the health of children employed in factories; and that ten hours per day would be very detrimental to the manufacturer himself, as it would decrease the produce of his machinery at least one sixth, and would therefore reduce the wages of the workpeople in proportion.

Josiah Lockwood of Upperhead Row, Huddersfield is a fourth example, and possibly an ancestor of the Josiah Lockwood who lived rather later in the century and whose mill was established at Black Rock in Linthwaite. His mill is much the largest of these described here and obviously using modern methods. It is steam- rather than water- powered, with the steam engine providing 40 HP, with 3HP let to another company. The mill was built in 1825 and finished in 1827 and 1828, so what might be called state of the art at that time. Josiah employs 211 people to make fancy goods from cotton and wool. His workforce and their pay is as follows:

Age	M	Paid	F	Paid
Under 10	13	2/3d	4	2/3d
10-12	34	2/9d	34	2/9d
12-14	16	4/3d	14	4/3d
14-16	4	6/3d	5	6/3d
16-18	28	7/6d	12	7/6d
18-21			10	8/-d
21+	56	20/6d	3	9/-d

They work a 70 hour week and 192 of them are on piecework. 94 children are paid as pieceners for slubber-spinners and twisters, and any overtime is paid in proportion to weekly wages. They work, as all the other mills do, from 6am to 7.30pm during the week though a shorter time on Saturdays, from 6am to 5pm.

They have a half hour break at 8.30am, half an hour at 12.30pm and another half-hour at 4.30pm.

If there is an accident they gain the time lost then by one hour a day, paid accordingly. If the mill is not busy, they don't make the time up and people lose pay correspondingly. If someone is sick or off work because of an accident, they are paid in full for a while then half wages if they are good workmen. If they are poor at the job, they get nothing. Holidays are very much in line with other mills in the area: half a day at Shrove tide, two and a half days at Easter, two half days at Whitsuntide and two full days at Christmas. No wages are paid for holidays but people are not fined if they are late for work. The mill is not particular to half an hour.

There is no shift work either for adults or children and punishing children is not allowed. If they don't do their work satisfactorily, they are dismissed. The mill has no need of children under twelve to get the work done, but they are taken on when their parents bring them with older siblings so 'they don't stay at home to be idle, and they

An early textile mill

take half work with the rest.'

Josiah Lockwood sounds very impatient with the members of Parliament who have commissioned this enquiry. 'For my own part I think twelve hours per day neither too much not too little. The sooner the factory question is decided the better; it was never intended to do the working class good,' he says.

It is obvious from these examples that mill owners resented the intrusion of government in what they considered their particular area of expertise. They were dismissive of Parliamentary concerns about the welfare of their employees, and, in the case of Mary Horsfall, puzzlement about how the new law could possibly work successfully for her workforce, given that children's employment was intimately linked to family structure and the child's wage was part of the family's means of survival. Oastler and his followers would have their work cut out to change this entrenched system of exploitation.

Chapter 7 - The Poor and the Workhouse

The 1834 Poor Law

Before the 1834 Poor Law was brought in, poor relief, as we have seen in a previous chapter, was administered at local township level (large ecclesiastical parishes such as Almondbury or Huddersfield, were broken up into smaller administrative areas called townships), and funded by the better-off in that township. Overseers were members of the townships delegated to do the job, unpaid, for a year. It was not a popular position[124]. In Huddersfield it was mainly old people, the long term sick and the infirm who were supported, though people suffering from temporary crises could be helped with payments such as doctors' bills and funeral expenses, clothing such as stays, shoes and petticoats, or even food and drink, gin and rum being paid for in at least one instance[125]. So the payments were, if not generous, at least cognizant of the actual circumstances of people's lives.

Single women who were pregnant were where possible sent back to the township they were born in though it was the responsibility of the overseer to track down the putative fathers and make them pay maintenance. This would consist of expenses for the lying-in and maintenance of the child until the age of seven. It was such a common occurrence that there was a standard form to fill in. The mother had to swear before a Justice of the Peace when giving the name of the man who was the father. A feature of the South Crosland overseer's book was 'money received of lads' and 'Payment to lasses'. Fathers who would not pay could be arrested and sent to a House of Correction. This was not always as straightforward an arrangement as one might expect. In 1830, for instance, a bastardy order was made against Thomas Murgatroyd of Berry Brow to make him pay for the lying-in costs of £2-8-6d for Sarah Horsfall, who was an inmate of Almondbury workhouse, plus a shilling a week for maintenance of the child. Murgatroyd, a married man, was an ex-soldier, who denied having a relationship with Sarah. It then turned out that Sarah already had two illegitimate children. Sarah said Murgatroyd called himself Matthew Jessop and he had ginger whiskers. She purported to have seen him more recently when she visited Berry Brow, but he had shaved off his whiskers, though she recognized him by his voice.

Even before the 1834 Act there were some fairly substantial poorhouses such as the Huddersfield one in Birkby, built in the 1700s to house 60 inhabitants, or Almondbury, also catering for 60 people. Smaller ones for up to 20 people provided accommodation in Lockwood, and Kirkheaton, while there were also houses at Honley and Lepton. Small poorhouses existed in the Colne Valley at Golcar, Linthwaite, and Marsden. So there was quite a considerable amount of provision for the poor. The Poor Law Commissioners in 1834 reported that most townships were without a workhouse, but about a third of the townships in the Huddersfield area did have some provision[126]. Much of the relief given to the poor was out-relief, administered by the overseer in each township and so varied in its provision. Some areas were generous in their provision, others much less so.

As has already been pointed out, the end of the Napoleonic wars had brought yet another slump in trade for the cloth industry, the population was increasing and many people found it impossible to find enough work to keep the wolf from the door. The introduction of the Corn Laws made the price of corn artificially high and the eruption of Mount Tambura in Indonesia in 1815 brought on disastrous farming conditions, with 1816 being known as the year without sun. Bad harvests in the 1820s made the position even more stark.

Voluntary subscriptions for relief of the poor were organized with a meeting at the George Inn in 1820 raising large amounts of money with generous donations from the Ramsden family and the Earl of Dartmouth. The money was used to subsidise the cost of oatmeal. Meanwhile the ladies' committee organized the collection and distribution of clothes. By 1826 there was a full-blown banking crisis which added to the woes.

We have a picture of the difficulties weavers faced at this time from the diary of John Swift, who eventually left the textile trade and went on to become a self-styled aurist. He was a witness to an enquiry about working conditions at the time. John Swift was himself then a journeyman weaver affected by the wage cutting. The only recourse men had against the people who employed them was to join a Union, a movement which was in its infancy, but if they did so manufacturers were promising to sack them.

Some manufacturers had reduced their payments from 8d to 3d a yard, and a long yard at that: not 36 inches (roughly 90 cm) but 36 inches plus a thumb's width, so 37 inches (92cm). All the manufacturers employed the same measure so there was no point in looking for another employer and if taken before a magistrate to argue their case, a weaver would gain a reputation as a troublemaker and be unemployable.

In addition manufacturers refused to employ journeymen who had joined a union. Enter John Swift, vice-president of the West Riding Fancy Union, who we shall meet later in a rather different context. In 1825, since trade was in the doldrums, manufacturers had reduced the wages they paid to journeymen by more than half and many of them were close to starvation. John Swift tried to mediate between manufacturers and their employees to little effect[127]. The meeting ended with one manufacturer finding he was paying considerably more than some of the worst payers, and a promise that they would work to ensure manufacturers all paid the same amount for their cloth.

The fact that poor relief topped up earnings had led to employers paying low wages, and with a surplus of men looking for weaving work, there was no way the men could take action to combat this. If anyone was unaware of the conditions the poor were living in, a piece written in 1829 which appeared in the *Leeds Intelligencer* would have enlightened them.

Two reporters visited 1100 families at dinner time to see what living conditions were really like. They were shocked and horrified by what they saw and heard and almost in tears. The people they visited were eating gruel, or salted potatoes. Their houses were 'stripped of every article they possessed' in an attempt to feed themselves and pay the rent. The men were often too weak to work, sometimes going twenty-four or thirty-six hours without food. They had the clothes they stood up in and nothing else. On Saturday night the husband and children would go to bed so the wife could wash and dry their clothes overnight, so they could have them clean on on the Sunday. These conditions, the reporters said, 'do not apply to the aged and infirm, nor to the thoughtless and gay, but to the sober, honest and good workman, whose character will bear the strictest scrutiny.'

The subsequent strains on the poor relief were blamed on lack of initiatives to encourage men to work, the fact that poor relief was used to subsidize the low wages paid by employers, and the idea that the poor were encouraged to have large families because relief was geared to the size of the family.

In 1832 a Royal Commission was set up to look at the whole

matter and to see how money could be saved. They came up with a scheme which would abolish the small local poor houses spread around the townships and erect large purpose buildings which became known as 'bastiles'. Townships would be grouped together in a Poor Law Union, which would be administered by elected Poor Law Guardians. These elected members would be supplemented by the local JPs and they would be responsible for hiring staff and keeping a check on conditions in the workhouse. Conditions and rules governing the running of the workhouses were set out and would apply to every workhouse in the country. They would be aimed at discouraging anyone who was capable of work from applying for poor relief. Out relief would be abolished and overseers of the poor would be paid.

In these new workhouses incumbents would be divided into separate units depending on sex and age and would be housed in different wings of the building. Men would be separated from women, and children from their mothers unless under three, though mothers would have access to their children at any reasonable time of day. Inmates would be dressed in workhouse clothes, get up in the morning at five or six o'clock and go to bed at eight. Their hair would be cropped on entry to the workhouse. (Presumably this was to rid them of headlice). And the food would be as cheap as possible: gruel, potatoes, cabbage and cheap meat were a feature.

The position of mothers of illegitimate children changed. They were given the responsibility of supporting their children up to the age of sixteen. If the mother needed poor relief the overseer could pursue the father for reimbursement of parish money until the child was seven, but there was no punishment for the father if he evaded payment. The Chairman of the Huddersfield Union wrote to the Poor Law Commissioners in 1840 to complain that enforcement of the filiation orders was difficult as they could not punish the evaders, so in 1844 the Poor Law Amendment Act allowed the mother to apply for an affiliation order for maintenance for her and her child.

Radical Attitudes to the New Poor Law

Radicals were very much against the new law, as they saw it as yet another example by central government of the whittling away of local responsibilities and the imposition of a 'one size fits all' approach to local problems. The working class networks - the short time committees, the political unions and the public houses - were bitterly disappointed at the failure of the 1832 Reform Act to facilitate any access to power by the working classes, and took exception to this latest exercise of government power.[128]

They resented not only amalgamation of township poor houses, but the provisions of the law. Separating men from women meant that married couples would be separated, which went against their marriage vows. Richard Oastler had something to say about it. 'I tell you deliberately, if I have the misfortune to be reduced to poverty, that the man who dares to tear from me the wife whom God has joined to me, shall, if I have it in my power, receive his death at my hands!'[129], he declared melodramatically.

The Huddersfield Poor Law Union was set up in 1837, amalgamating all 32 townships of the area and thus becoming the largest poor law union in the country, caring for the welfare of a population of 89,000[130]. It was run by an elected Board of Guardians which was immediately filled by radicals and anti-poor law activists, who prevented the proper functioning of the act. They resisted government pressure to build large, centralized workhouses and the first in the area, Deanhouse, at Netherthong, and Crosland Moor were not built until 1862 and 1872, respectively.[131]

In Richard Oastler's township of Fixby in 1837 the townspeople refused to elect a Poor Law Guardian, for which understandably Oastler was blamed. This, combined with his rhetoric urging children to industrial sabotage meant that mill owners felt something should be done to curb the man. Pressure was brought to bear on his employer, Mr Thornhill, and Oastler lost his job at Fixby Hall. He was also seriously in debt to the tune of £2000 and, the following year, unable to settle his debts, he was committed to the Fleet debtors' prison, thus removing him physically from the scene. As with Carlile, however, he continued to write and publish his writings.

In support of the Ten Hour Bill, for instance, he wrote about the detriment to family life when the wife had to work to support her husband and children. In 1842 he published extracts from the report of a West Riding radical by the name of Mark Crabtree who described how the women's friendly societies had developed in the West Riding.

> Female clubs are composed of a certain number of females (married and single) generally about fifty or sixty in number, who hold their meetings weekly at public houses. The ostensible purpose of these clubs is to protect each other from want in case of sickness, a provision also being made in case of death. ...It may easily be imagined what will be the consequence of fifty women meeting together in a public house and enjoying themselves in drinking, singing and smoking for two or three hours and then being brought in contact with a number of men assembled in some other part of the house, the husbands should bethink themselves of the family at home, and urge the wife to depart, she will generally show signs of vexation and insist on having her own way in these matters. He, poor man, *well knowing that*

HIS livelihood depends on HER labour, is obliged to submit and quietly wait her pleasure to go to his neglected children alone.[132]

From a 21st century perspective it is heart-warming to think of these women whose days were spent in drudgery meeting together and having fun after work, even if the power balance within the family was seriously upset. It's possible, as Thompson has pointed out[133], that the situation was exaggerated to underline the need for reform of working hours and conditions, but nevertheless it is reassuring to know that the friendly societies were still providing both financial, social and psychological support which must have made these women's lives less dreary than they otherwise would have been.

Back in 1837, however, much of the unrest was focused on the New Poor Law. A 4,000 signature petition had been presented to Lord Harewood and had been rejected, so to give vent to people's discontent a rally was organized which took place at Peep Green, on Hartshead Moor on Whit Tuesday.

The *Leeds Times* gives a vivid description of the event. There were processions from Huddersfield, Dewsbury, Halifax, Bradford and Heckmondwyke. There were bands, banners and flags. The hustings were set at the foot of the slope down from the moor while people congregated on the slope above and wagons from various pubs in the area set their stalls up on the periphery with the name of each pub blazoned on the side of the cart from where they dispensed refreshments. People who couldn't get near enough to hear the speakers paraded with the bands who played national airs. There were roughly 250,000 people present on that day.

The flags and banners carried slogans, all relayed to the reading public by the indefatigable *Leeds Times*. Paddock brought a banner declaring. 'England home, liberty, local rights, wholesome food and no bastiles'. From Dewsbury: 'Dewsbury can manage the affairs of their poor without the interference of commissioners; Men of Dewsbury arise and be emancipated or forever be slaves'. Linthwaite: 'Comfort for the poor is protection for the rich'. Fixby: 'Fixby and defiance: we will be free or we will die.'[134] And of course the Skelmanthorpe flag made another appearance. Both the rhetoric of the speakers and the slogans on the banners combined messages against the Poor Law and for reform of the voting system.

The speakers at the rally were some of the foremost in the land. Oastler, of course, and Robert Owen, but also two Irishmen, Fergus O'Connor and Bronterre O'Brien. Bronterre O'Brien had moved to England from Ireland in 1829, turned his hand to journalism and joined the London Working Men's Association, formed by Willian Lovett, founder of the Chartist movement. (See Chapter 8.) He had also been imprisoned for publishing an unstamped newspaper and led the struggle against stamp duty.[135]

Forty-one year old Fergus O'Connor, an Irish Protestant from a Radical family, had studied law but been disinherited by his father when he had to swear an oath of allegiance to the King of England. His father thought it inappropriate for a descendant of the Kings of Ireland to do so. A passionate household, therefore, and suitable training for a radical orator. Fortunately his uncle left him an estate, so he was not held back for lack of money.

O'Connor was involved with a Land Plan which would share out parcels of land to working class people. Opinions differ about his motivation, but one reason could have been that it would give working men the land qualification needed to enfranchise them. Up to this time he had been active in the London area, was excited by the strength of feeling and potential for action among these northern radicals. At some time in the day, he fell into conversation with Joshua Hobson, who printed and distributed the *Voice of the West Riding*. Together they realized that, given the huge crowds gathered there, it should be possible to harness the political energy of the crowd and give it direction. What was needed was a newspaper which would carry O'Connor's message and help him spearhead another drive for political reform. So it was that Hobson set up his printing works in Leeds and began to print the *Northern Star*, which became the most successful radical paper yet seen in England. By 1838 it was selling 10,000 copies a week and its circulation extended across most of Britain. Chase sums up its achievements: 'The *Northern Star* gathered up news of local and regional activities, and steadily promoted the idea that all were part of a coherent and vital whole.'[136]

So strong were the emotions aroused by the new poor law that following the Peep Green rally in June of the same year the Huddersfield workhouse was stormed by a crowd mainly of women and effigies of the Act's supporters were burned[137]. Emotions were kept on the boil by broadsheets such as that published by Christopher Tinker a radical bookseller, who in 1834 published a poem entitled, 'The Cottager and his Wife, and the New Poor Law'. After establishing his characters, John and Sarah Loy, who had led blame-free and happy lives, he describes their position now in their old age:

> When John no longer could maintain the board
> And not one child to help them could afford
> They for relief must to the parish go;
> With heavy sighs and hearts o-erwhelmed with woe.
> No kindness there, but harshest words were said, ...
> No more for them the cottage fire-side glows
> No more they in each others' arms repose...

> You that are called the Guardians of the poor
> Oh think on this if you ne'er thought before;
> Pay due respect to God's most holy laws,
> Protect the poor and lessen human woes.
> Such ways I ne'er approved in all my life
> To separate the husband from the wife.[138]

Peep Green was one of the last outings that Richard Oastler was able to make before being committed to prison in 1840. As soon as Oastler went to prison, a Central Liberation Committee was set up to work towards freeing him but it was not until all his debts had been paid off in 1843 that he was released.[139]

He immediately planned a return to Huddersfield, which he saw as his spiritual home. He wanted his first speech on his release from the Fleet to be in the town which had supported him in his confinement. His incarceration however had modified his oratory and he was less of a firebrand than before. Nevertheless his arrival in Huddersfield, on Shrove Tuesday, having travelled to the newly opened Brighouse station by train, was in the tradition of heroic homecomings. The ballad sellers were out in force, small children waving white flags, three bands, banners bearing messages such as 'Oastler our defender' and 'Oastler and no bastile' turned out to accompany him on his triumphal return and form the procession which accompanied Oastler in his open carriage.

It wound its way out of Brighouse up the hill towards Fixby being careful to skirt the Thornhill estate. It took over two hours for the cavalcade to arrive at the Druid's Arms at the bottom of Halifax Road where the hustings had been erected. Oastler spoke movingly to an attentive audience and thanked them for their support. 'I thank you with a true Yorkshire heart for this right Yorkshire welcome', reported *The Times*. Songs were sung to welcome him home, one such being *Oastler is welcome!* Eight verses and a chorus, one of which is

> They come, they come from every mountain
> Hill and valley, moor and plain.
> In numbers far beyond the counting
> To welcome Oastler back again.

It was estimated that between 12,000 and 15,000 people crowded round the hustings that day and listened attentively to what the great man had to say.

'You know, my friends, that our object has been simply this – that labour should have its due reward'. As can be imagined this was met by a rousing cheer.

But Oastler had been weakened by his long incarceration and the fire and drive that had made him such a leader was sadly diminished. He died in 1861. John Hargreaves sums up the achievements of this largely forgotten man:

'All three major agitations in which Richard Oastler engaged brought significant results during his lifetime: the slave trade was abolished in 1807; slaves in the British Empire were emancipated in 1833 after serving a seven year apprenticeship; factory regulation and machinery for its enforcement were introduced into the textile industries between 1833 and 1853 and the operation of the New Poor law was modified in the north of England through the continuation of outdoor relief after 1837.[140]

Conditions in the poor houses

Opposition to the Poor Law continued for many years. Meanwhile the township poor houses continued to a large extent to cater as best they could for the poor of their own township. Huddersfield poor house, situated in Birkby, was squalid and the medical officer for the Northern Region, T.R.Tatham, had been complaining for years about the inadequacy of provision for the elderly and sick supposedly catered for in the workhouse. This came to a head in 1848 when the vestry committee asked the overseers of the poor to investigate certain allegations about the inadequacy of the care of the sick.

Mr Tatham reported that the workhouse was filthy, with 'unclean linen and neglect in every corner'; the water closet had been stopped by filth for several months and the cesspit was too close to the house and caused 'foul exhalations'. Lack of ventilation was spreading illness and death among the inmates, in his opinion.

Joshua Hobson, one of the Guardians of the Poor, reported on conditions in the Poorhouse and this was printed in the *Leeds Mercury* of May 1848. It was a blistering attack on the terrible conditions people were living and dying in. There was not enough clothing and bedding so if sheets were washed they had to be dried and put back the same day. Consequently, given the impossibility of drying anything outside for much of the year, this was not a high priority. Patients were put into beds where patients had died of typhus without changing the bed linen. 'Beds' was rather a misnomer. The 'beds' consisted of bags of straw on the floor and the straw was heaving with lice. Living patients were left in bed with corpses for considerable periods and there were no proper nurses to care for the sick, with male paupers looking after female paupers. Patients were left unwashed in their own excrement, medication, if there was any, was not administered and there was no wine, which was used to treat fevers.

Inmates had no change of clothes. They were often clad in their own, some of which were mere rags, and because there was nothing to change into, they wore them for up to nine weeks. The food was often unfit to eat, consisting as it did of soup containing such a lot of cabbage that it smelled foul and had to be thrown away. Dinner often consisted of soup and a quarter of an oatcake, with the soup made from four shillings worth of shin beef and forty-two pounds of potatoes, for 150 inmates. To say the house was overcrowded is an understatement. There were forty children in one room eight yards by five who often slept ten in a bed and thirty women lived in a room of similar size.

The overseers blamed the men on the Board of Guardians for this lamentable state of affairs, saying they were 'beyond the reach of public opinion and whose main concern was keeping down the rates.' The Board of Guardians reacted immediately to this report. They recommended that 484 yards of cotton and hessian, 79 pairs of blankets, 38 yards of ticking for pillows, 226 yards of cotton and hessian for pillow cases, 57 coverlets, 14 mattresses, and two iron bedsteads be bought (Why only two?); that the privy in the hospital be removed and a 'patent torrent water closet' be substituted; that the hospital be thoroughly lime washed by a plasterer (to keep down the lice); that the copper in number three ward be removed; that a proper brick oven be provided in the baking room, a washing machine in the washhouse and a cask of lime be procured for disinfecting.

By August the workhouse committee reported that the windows had been fitted with ventilators; the duck pond had been removed and replaced with the dung heap (was this an improvement?!); gutters and spouting had been repaired; rooms had been set aside for lying-in; stud and lathe partitions had been taken down and the privy in the hospital had been removed and replaced with a water closet. The copper in ward three had been removed, a washing machine had been provided and cotton and hessian sheeting had been purchased.

The committee then recommended among other things that a new oven be obtained for the kitchen, a room be set aside for the laundry, a specified room be used as a deadhouse and that more privy accommodation be provided for women and children. As something of an afterthought, they also suggested that the children be sent to school.[141]

The Birkby Poorhouse came under scrutiny again in 1866 by the *Huddersfield Chronicle*.[142] It reported that it now had accommodation for 121 people with a separate building used as an infirmary. It was, they said, wholly unfit for purpose and devoid of comfort and convenience. There was however a paid nurse who did the best she could under the circumstances. The beds were too close together and some of the old men slept two to a bed. The day rooms (at least there were some!) were too small and overcrowded and there were two violent insane or idiotic inmates who were very disruptive.

Kirkheaton poorhouse also had its problems. Although they had managed to keep men and boys separate from the women and girls, their sleeping arrangements left something to be desired. There were three boys who wet the bed. The urine had soaked not only into the bedding but had seeped through the floor to the room below! There were twenty-nine women, girls and infants. Two of the older girls wet the bed, so they slept together. Foul linen was boiled in the same copper as the food was cooked in.

Similar cooking facilities existed in the Golcar poorhouse. Fourteen men slept in seven beds, seven women and five children slept in four beds in one small room. This was also the lying-in room. In spite of this, the women and children were reported to be clean and healthy.

Honley poorhouse was newly built but unfortunately the waterclosets had been built so that the foul air was drawn into the main body of the house, instead of escaping to the outside. There were no dayrooms, poor ventilation and the twenty-four children were supervised by the paupers themselves. Whether they went to school or not is not recorded.[143]

The Swift Family of Newsome

It was amid the muddle that followed the introduction of the new Poor Law and the attempts to establish it that we have a glimpse of family life and how the workhouse impinged on the lives of ordinary people. The Swift family was not the usual kind to come into close contact with the overseer of the poor. The family was relatively prosperous, but their story, as described in John Swift's diary, shows not only how the workhouse impinged on life but also how little room for manoevre many women must have had in the control of their lives.[144]

In the 1830s and 40s John Swift followed various career paths during his eventful life. Born in 1784, as might be expected at such a time, he began his working life as a weaver and seller of fancy waistcoating and, as we have already seen, tried to negotiate a settlement between weavers and merchants, to no avail.

His business prospered for a while, during which time he married his first wife Nancy, whom he probably met at the Methodist New Connexion Old Bank Chapel. Nancy died in 1806 at the age of twenty-six, having given him two sons. Jennifer Stead, who recounts the story of his life, thinks he truly loved Nancy, which was more than can be said for his second wife, Hannah North, nee Lumb, a widow, with four children: Betty, aged fifteen, Charlotte, thirteen, John aged eleven and George aged nine.

Swift married Hannah in 1815 and moved from Honley, where he was born, into Hannah's house in Towngate, Newsome. He may have married her for her property, and again he probably met her at chapel. By 1815 the marriage was over and he records in the family bible that Hannah Lumb, his second wife, was 'filth above common'. Hannah disappeared, leaving her four children in the care of their stepfather.

By this time Betty, aged eighteen, was pregnant with Swift's child, Anne, who was born in January 1815. Stead avers that there could not have been a formal marriage, so Betty became Swift's common law wife, though 'living 'ovver t'brush' must have been fairly common given the impossibility of getting a divorce. It was also commonplace, says Stead[145] for the eldest girl to step into her mother's shoes if her mother died, including 'marrying' her stepfather.

After the birth of their second child, Mary, the family seems to have transferred their religious allegiance to the Church of England, which may have been less disapproving than the Methodists, and all their subsequent children were baptized at Almondbury parish church.

In the first five years of her relationship with Swift, Betty produced one child a year: Anne when she was eighteen, then Mary, William, Tom (died in infancy), Tom North Swift, Dean (died aged one), William (died aged eight), Jane. By this time Betty was twenty-nine. In her thirties, the pace of reproduction slackened and she had only three more children: another William who was born when Betty was thirty-one, and who died in infancy, three years later another Dean who again died in infancy, Dean number three, who died when he was six, born when Betty was thirty-seven, and finally when she was forty, John Henry made his appearance. She had therefore between the ages of seventeen and forty produced twelve children of whom six had died.

By this time John Swift had changed his career. He had become an aurist, a specialist in ear complaints and trying to improve people's hearing. This was quite a fashionable trade at the time and Swift seems to have made a good living at it, though he worked very hard and travelled widely across the North of England. Completely without formal qualifications, he studied what qualified doctors had to say on the subject, though he seems to have steered clear of the blood-letting which was so popular with the qualified of the medical profession. Swift also made up medicines in both liquid and pill form which he sold throughout the North of England and the Midlands. He travelled across the north from Liverpool in the west, to Sheffield in the east, charging his patients five shillings a consultation, though it varied according to how much he thought they could afford to pay. He was prosperous enough to set up three of his sons as druggists: James in Rochdale, Joseph in Westgate, Huddersfield, and Tom North Swift, who became a druggist and medical botanist in East Parade, Huddersfield.[146]

By this time he was travelling away from home, and complaining in his diary that his wife was jealous and unhappy. She may well have had cause as he seems to have been pursued by several women in various farflung cities, Mary in Manchester and Mrs Grundy in Preston being two of them.

On 21st April 1850 he records that his wife 'was very poorly, she was lost in a cold, but the primary cause is, and has been, cursed jealousy and without cause. She has reduced herself to a scelliton(sic) her cloths hang on her like a consumptive person'. Perhaps his wife's unhappiness was one reason he spent so much time in his garden. He was a dedicated gardener.

He does however seem to have made an effort occasionally to take her out and to please her. He bought her a silk umbrella and took her to the fair, where they saw a jiantess(sic) and a dwarf[147] and he took her on several of his selling trips: Ashton, Sheffield, Preston. Occasionally he commented that her health was better, and noted that when he returned at 11pm from one of his evenings out with the

Druids his wife was 'getting over her wims and emty visions'(sic).

She also helped him with these pills and potions, one which was much in demand being 'Infantus quietus', which kept babies quiet and peacefully sleeping, hardly surprising when two of the main ingredients were spirits (brandy or gin) and opium, sweetened liberally with treacle and flavoured with liqueris(sic) juniper berries and saffron. Up to this point the Swifts had kept well away from the poor law Guardians, being one of the more prosperous families in the neighbourhood. Their eldest daughter Anne, however, was about to bring disgrace upon the family.

The Swift children had grown up alongside several other families in Towngate, among them the Bottomley twins, Luke and John, James Lodge and Charles Kaye. In 1837 in Almondbury parish church Anne married Charles Kaye. James Lodge gave them a wedding present of two ducks for the wedding celebrations. The following year produced a son, Joseph.

Then Kaye enlisted in the army and was drafted to some farflung post in India, which left Anne on her own. Not for long, however. In 1839 she married again, at Elland parish church. This time it was James Lodge, who had given them the ducks as a wedding present. The little boy, Joseph, was passed on to his grandparents at some time in this period, perhaps when Anne took up with Lodge. Twins were born while she was living with James Lodge, two little girls whom she called Keziah and Jemimah. Jemimah died aged 17 months and was buried in January 1842. Anne lived with Lodge for two years and four months, at which point Charles Kaye returned from India.

Within two weeks, Anne had decamped and moved in with her lawful husband, leaving Keziah with James Lodge. Lodge, however, refused to look after the child and put her in the workhouse. Neither Charles Kaye nor James Lodge would support the child because they said one of the Bottomley twins was the father and the upshot was Anne's bigamy became known to the authorities.

Anne was arrested and would have been taken into custody had not her father stood bail for her, an expense he resented. The child Keziah was sent along with a letter to John Swift from the Constable demanding that he take the child so she was not an expense on the poor rate. He got a short message back, conveyed by the child, saying, 'I will not take the child at your bidding nor shall I do, who are you, strutting in a little brief authority, you cannot, nor your master, you cannot intimidate me'.[148]

In spite of his bravado, Swift was very upset at his daughter's fall from grace. She was terrified of being arrested and going to prison, so her father arranged for two of his sons to go to discuss with the Prison Governor in Huddersfield what could be done. Because of the men's standing in the community, the Governor agreed that she should live in the Governor's house and sleep with their servant. She was then bailed to appear at York Assizes in the following March. Her father was very angry at the cost of going to York for the two weeks it would probably take.

The social disgrace, too! He thought Anne's behaviour reflected on her upbringing, so he and Betty would be blamed for their daughter's misdemeanours. He notes however that Betty is in good health. 'This rumpus does not seem to take any hold on her', he comments. Anne was imprisoned at York Castle for four calendar months.

This raises the question of why Anne went to such lengths to marry, when she could perfectly well have lived with James Lodge without attracting any undue criticism. Perhaps she thought that the marriage vows she had made in Newsome only applied to the immediate neighbourhood, and that marrying in Elland, some six miles away would absolve her from her commitment in Huddersfield.

Perhaps James had family in Elland who weren't aware that she was already married and that, having been presented to the family as unmarried, she found herself carried along by the lie.

Whatever her thinking, from the point of view of maintenance for her and the children, there would be none forthcoming from her husband. In theory, married men were not recruited as soldiers, so Charles Kaye had enlisted illegally and as a soldier had no obligation to support her. He had in fact abandoned her. Between 1837 and 1873 soldiers were exempted from supporting any family they might have by the 1837 Mutiny Act. This would be in force when Anne married both her husbands, since she was in court for bigamy in 1844, having married Charles Kaye in 1837 and James Lodge in 1839.[149]

Having been left alone, what could she do? She could try to find work, but mill work was in short supply, with starvation a real threat to many people in the textile trade. She could apply to the Poor Rate for support, she could approach her parents, though they were already looking after Anne and Charles Kaye's son Joe or she could 'marry' James Lodge. Perhaps that seemed the best option. If she were lucky she might also find him attractive and fun to live with. When all the options are considered, her decision does not seem quite so crazy as it first appears. She certainly paid for her mistake, as did her father! The Bigamy Act of 1861 fixed the terms of imprisonment for an offence as between three and seven years.

Though Anne was such a trouble to the family, their son Tom was a source of great delight, to his father if not his mother, having found favour with Emily Learoyd, daughter of a prosperous manufacturer. Emily Learoyd was at the other end of the social scale from poor Anne. Favourite daughter of a wealthy mill owning family, nothing but the best would do for her. Tom had to ditch a previous young lady to marry her. In a letter to his daughter Jane, who was living in Rochdale with her half-brother James, Swift writes that when he was in Bolton, a young woman called Miss Hall presented him with a small package, weeping bitterly as she did so. Miss Hall read the contents of the letter she had received from Tom, to the effect that they were both at liberty to chuse for themselves a companion to associate with them through this Vale of Tears. Even wrapped up in Victorian sentimentality, the result was devastating for the poor girl.[150]

In 1843 following the announcement of the engagement between Tom and Emily, Swift gleefully makes a note of all the wedding arrangements, though he is quick to point out that Tom was not marrying for money, having a thriving business of his own. The preparations for the coming nuptials were well on their way: bed hangings, carpets fitted, superb mahogany bedsteads, feather beds 'are all in a forward state of preparation'. Mary is to be a bridesmaid and has a brown satin dress and a white drawn, i.e. gathered, bonnet.

On the wedding day two carriages arrived at the Swifts' house in Newsome by 7.30 in the morning to convey the bridegroom's family to Mr Learoyd's. Here breakfast was laid on before the church service at 10 am. After the church service they all repaired again to the Learoyds' establishment where they took a glass of wine.

The Swifts then returned home, while the wedding party went to Leeds for the day, as was the custom at that time. Much to Swift's delight, Mr Learoyd handed a cheque for £200 to Tom. By Swift's reckoning - and he spent much of his energy adding up his own income -Emily would have an income of £44 per annum from the lump sum invested in the 4 percents.

The happy couple appeared at the Queen Street Chapel the following Sunday, still probably dressed in their wedding finery, as again was the custom, and Betty Swift, who had not attended the wedding, as was customary at the time, since someone had to stay at home and organize the refreshments, sent Jane 'a good thick slice of spice cake' and a pair of gloves to mark the occasion.[151]

A footnote to this story is that in 1860 Keziah Lodge married and her marriage certificate records that her father was James Lodge, the man she married was John Lodge, who signed his own name in the register, while Keziah made her mark. Both of them are listed as living in Lepton and the fathers of both were weavers. They were married at Kirkheaton church.

Chapter 8 - Chartism

The Great Reform Act of 1832, though disappointing in its limitations, did, as Dorothy Thompson has pointed out[152], bring in a system of representation which was uniform throughout the country. Its great drawback, from a working class point of view, was that it gave the vote only to those men who held land worth £10, thus excluding six out of seven men, and drew a firm line between what might be called the lower middle classes, publicans and small businessmen, and women and working class men. In this way it underlined class distinctions which had been less securely drawn before.

Radicals noted the centralization of power, shown in the imposition of the new Poor Law designed to regulate provision for the poor, and, as Chase has pointed out[153] they were of the opinion that workhouses were 'an insensitive and inappropriate mechanism through which to deal with cyclical unemployment and short-time working'. Even the Parliamentary 'interference' to limit the hours of children and women, was seen as another example of paternalistic meddling and they were afraid this tendency would lead to more of the same.

Peterloo was remembered and toasts were drunk every year on the anniversary of the massacre, and the name of Henry Hunt, who died in 1835, was still revered in the North[154] so although unrest might not be showing itself overtly, it was simmering in the background. Radicals also noted that political action backed by demonstrations had frightened Parliament into re-configuring the franchise, thus demonstrating the power of this approach. They were therefore hopeful that a new pressure group focusing on widening the franchise had a fair chance of succeeding.

The Charter was set out by William Lovett, a member of the

London Working Men's Association in 1836 and had six demands:
- A vote for all men over twenty-one.
- A secret ballot.
- No property qualification to become an MP.
- Payment for MPs.
- Electoral districts of equal size.
- Annual elections.

They also originally included votes for women, but this was quickly deemed too extreme to stand any chance of success, so was dropped. There was some discussion about it, however. Writing in 1842, Elizabeth Pease, founder of the Women's Anti-slavery society of Darlington, and a Quaker, wrote, 'I believe that the Chartists generally hold the doctrine of the equality of woman's rights – but I am not sure whether they do not consider that when she marries, she merges her political rights in those of her husband'.

Writing from jail, (where else?!) in 1840, R.J. Richardson in his *Rights of Women* pamphlet certainly thought that she would lose her rights as an individual when she married, since to posit any other position would mean greater changes in the law. He thought that unmarried and widowed women were entitled to full political and social rights, including the vote. As Dorothy Thompson comments, however, 'his case was argued from the standpoint of a north country workman, who saw the women as educators in the family and as workers in the industry in the locality[155]. Of the six demands of the Charter only one appears exceptional today: the idea of an annual election.

Fergus O'Connor was already building up a following in the North because of his articles in the *Northern Star* edited by William Hill, with leaders written by Bronterre O'Brian and printed and distributed by Joshua Hobson. In 1838 he drew together in a very loose affiliation most of the radical organisations of the industrial north in a Great Northern Union, launched in Barnsley in the wake of a meeting on Hunslet Moor, near Leeds.[156]

The movement in support of the Charter was up and running somewhat earlier than that, by 1836, and lobbied Parliament three times: in 1839, 1842 and 1848, this last obtaining six million signatures[157]. In 1839 some centres collecting signatures listed men's and women's signatures separately, though not in Huddersfield. In those areas women's signatures constituted between 13% and 20% of the signatories. Chase considers that there were likely to be a substantial number of women in Huddersfield signing the petition, since there was a significant number of women taking part in the movement. They participated in the 'exclusive dealing', where shopkeepers unsympathetic to radical causes were boycotted by radical families, a scheme pioneered in Huddersfield from 1837. Joshua Hobson had been a leading advocate of this, writing, 'The *way* to their brains is through their pockets – FIND IT!'.[158]

Women Chartists were lampooned in *Punch,* so they must have had a sizeable presence in the movement. One cartoon shows women Chartists, carrying banners with slogans such as 'Vive Georges Sand" being driven off not by soldiers shooting at them or even threatening them with their swords, but by unleashing rats and mice which chased the women away.

Following the imprisonment of Oastler in 1840, Fergus O'Connor stepped into the lead of the movement. Like Oastler before him, he was a powerful man with 'lungs of brass and a voice like a trumpet'[159].

Although, as Chase has pointed out, we see through a glass darkly where women's involvement is concerned, there were some women who managed to break through the fog. In the Huddersfield area one such was the wife of John Leech, a draper at Shorehead who was a close associate of Oastler. In 1840 she collected money from Chartist women to support men imprisoned for their involvement in the movement, and Amelia Gledhill and Mary Collins were such ardent followers of Fergus O'Connor that they named their baby sons after him. They were not alone. According to the 1851 census there were 316 boys called Fergus and 46 of them had O'Connor as a middle name[160]. One child in the Helliwell family, living in Sowerby was christened Fergus O'Connor Vincent Bronterre leaving little doubt about his parents' political leanings.[161]

There were also radical associations specifically for women. Elisabeth Hanson and her husband Abram were important people in the Chartist movement. They lived in Elland and Abram had been a speaker at the Hunslet meeting when the Great Northern Union was formed. Abram was a shoemaker, though by this time the actual making of shoes and boots was being taken over by commercial manufacturers so shoemaking had become more centred round cobbling and making clogs.

Abram was a republican and caused an outcry at a parish meeting when he tried to stop plans to celebrate Victoria's coronation. The couple also had strong views on the New Poor Law. Elizabeth was not averse to physical action. In March 1838 she founded the Elland Radical Association and in the following months she with a group of other women met the assistant Poor Law Commissioners, who had come to inspect the local workhouse and ensure the new law was being put into practice. The commissioners were rolled in the snow.

Women were afraid of the new Poor Law because it made them dependent on their husbands' wages rather than as contributors to the family income. Chase puts this most eloquently. People resented the Poor Law because it was 'a major assault on the integrity of the family, the dignity of old age and the powerful popular ideology that held relief from poverty to be a legal and moral right.' Having to dress in shoddy, their hair cropped and with the threat to have one's children taken way was seen as an assault on what it was to be a woman.[162]

Another instance of direct action from the Elland women was when two hundred of them prevented a donkey and cart train from leaving the village. It was loaded with wool owned by a local cloth merchant who had reduced the wages he was prepared to pay to Elland weavers and was taking the wool out of the village to be woven elsewhere.

Elizabeth was also well informed about politics and economics and had a fine turn of phrase. When discussing the idea of introducing paper money, she is quoted in the *London Dispatch* as saying 'You say, extend our commerce. We have ransacked the whole habitable globe. If you can find a way to the moon, we may, with the aid of paper, carry on our competition a little longer, but if you want to better the condition of the working classes, let our government legislate so as to make machinery go hand in hand with labour, and act as an auxiliary or helpmate, not a competitor.'

The Elland Radical Association was not interested in votes for women but felt it was their duty to increase their knowledge of politics and to co-operate and support husbands and sons, so they held evening classes to educate themselves. To this end they read the radical press and wrote to the *Northern Star*. Abram shared in his wife's interests and ambitions. 'Should the men fail in their allegiance,' he said, speaking at the inaugural meeting of the Great Northern Union, 'the women of Elland, who had sworn not to breed slaves, had registered a vow to do the work of men and women'. Of course their son born in 1839 was called Fergus O'Connor Hanson.

The original charter had made the point that those working for the Charter were not a threat to the realm and that they abjured violence.

> We desire by peaceable and legal means, and by them alone, to alter and amend the institutions of the country: by establishing its legislative system upon the only true basis—the ascertained will of the majority, at once the guarantee of present order, and the promise of peaceful growth and happiness for the future.

They did not manage this. An uprising in Newport in November 1839 frightened both the establishment and the locals, many of whom feared for their lives. The showground Sanger family, who were on their way to Newport to entertain the town with its collection of comic and topical peepshows, turned their caravan round and headed away from the town. They parked by the side of the road and Mr Sanger guarded the door armed with his blunderbuss while his wife collected the children around her. They held their breath while the unruly crowd rushed past, swearing, shouting, waving their cudgels. A truly terrifying sight. The knowledge of the rising had been conveyed to the authorities who sent in the militia. The mayor was holed up in the Westgate hotel with 31 Infantrymen who shot into the crowd, killing twenty-two of the demonstrators.

A hundred and twenty-five people were brought to court and the ringleaders were sentenced to be hanged, decapitated and their bodies quartered. Many Chartists expected that they would be pardoned before the queen's wedding to Prince Albert took place. This did not happen but the sentence for the three ringleaders was subsequently commuted to transportation for life.

The next manifestation of discontent was in 1842. There was

massive unemployment and wage-cutting. That year workers went on strike and resorted to the time-honoured practice of rioting, but this time with a purpose. The trouble started in Lancashire but in August spread across into the Colne Valley. Men and women poured over the moors and descended on Bankbottom Mill in Marsden. They were told to get out by the owner, John Fisher, but instead went into the boiler house and knocked out the boiler plug, doused the fires and released the steam, while another group raised the sluice at the mill dam and drained it. The mill then had no steam power and it would take some considerable time to restore order.

The following Saturday five thousand men, women and children came over Standedge and proceeded down the Colne Valley, doing to mills further down what they had done at Bankbottom. On the Sunday troops arrived from Leeds to deal with the breakdown in law and order, but on the Monday the strikers moved on to the Holme Valley where pits were closed down. The workers were demanding 'A fair day's pay for a fair day's work' but their demand fell on deaf ears and in spite of many people feeling sympathetic to their reasonable requests, they returned home with no improvement in their working conditions.[163]

These events were called the Plug Riots, for obvious reasons. There was no doubting the presence of women. Looking back on his experiences at the time, F.H Grundy wrote 'all were hungry, evening was coming on, and although a few stones were thrown, chiefly, of course, by women... the mob dispersed for that time peaceably.'[164]

Similarly Frank Peel from the distance of 1880, recalls about the Plug riots reaching Brighouse. 'No inconsiderable number of the insurgents were women 'and, strange as it seemed to him by that time, they were more violent than the men.' The thousands of women were looked on with some commiseration by the well-disposed inhabitants, as many were poorly clad and not a few were barefoot. When the Riot Act was read and the insurgents were urged to return to their homes, a large crowd of these women, who stood in front of the magistrate and the military loudly declared they had no homes, and dared them to kill them if they liked. They then sang the Union hymn:

> Our little ones shall learn to bless
> Their fathers of the Union
> And every mother shall caress
> Her hero of the Union.
> Our plains with plenty shall be crowned
> The sword shall till the fruitful ground
> The spear shall prune our trees around
> To bless a nation's Union.[165]

The Chartists tried to get men from the Chartist movement into Parliament and collected money to that end. They were hampered by the fact that most of their supporters did not qualify to vote, so though their candidates had a vociferous reception at the hustings, most of them failed to gain seats. A notable exception was Fergus O'Connor himself who in 1847 gained the seat of Nottingham. This was so unexpected that the *Northern Star* had not bothered to send a reporter and had to complete their account from those printed in other newspapers.

1842 marks the high point of Chartism. A National Petition was organized which was signed by 3,317,752 people. It contained 6 miles of paper and weighed over six hundredweight (305 kg) and was presented to Parliament on a Monday so it would have a large procession accompanying it, Monday being the traditional day of rest, St Monday, for weavers. There were seven bands, including the Grenadier Guards, marshals on horseback and of course flags and banners galore. The petition itself was carried on a box built specifically to carry it by a succession of tradesmen. Unfortunately, brought directly to the House of Commons, it proved too big to go through the door. It jammed in the Members' doorway with attempts to dismantle the box and even parts of the doorway failing to give it enough space. Eventually the roll of paper had to be dismantled and deposited in bundles on the floor of the House[166]. It failed to move the Honourable Members and the Charter was no nearer to being adopted.

There was a brief revival in 1848, though not so much in the North as in London. The Address of the People's Charter Union of 1848 argues their case succinctly. They deal with the objections that have been put forward against the charter with admirable clarity.

> We are told that 'The mass of the people are not fit for the franchise'. We answer 'The exercise of the franchise will be their have it? Reading and writing, what is called education, will not be sufficiently clear. They are not knowledge, but only the tools of knowledge.' 'The difficulty of election'. ' A sufficient number of polling stations will obviate that'. 'The swamping of the intelligent by the unintelligent'. 'Then, as now, we believe, intelligence will now how to win its way. It will hardly be intelligence else....'[167]

Dorothy Thompson comments that radical expressions of discontent largely disappeared, especially among women in the late 1840s. She tentatively attributes women's retreat from overt politics as being due perhaps in part to the influence of the Temperance movement. She suggests that by the late 1840s higher paid workers were able to participate in local government in newly established boroughs, thus separating them from lower paid workers and

Weavers' cottages rented from a landowner

women, so the social bonds that tied many disparate groups during the first thirty years of the century had been whittled away to some extent. Victorian sentimentalisation of the home seems to have affected even working class women, who turned away from open political participation.[168]

Chartism up to this point had been sustained by its commitment to a political end, but that was not the whole of the movement. Chartism was often mingled with a radical social gospel but had many facets to it, some of them contradictory. On the one hand there were the chapels with their rousing Chartist hymns and the belief that the Chartists were a chosen people working towards a legitimate end, and on the other there was the support of the Friendly societies which met in pubs. So some Chartists were teetotal but they all had a strong drive towards self-improvement. Abram Hanson, for instance, was an autodidact able to quote from the classics and familiar with the philosophy of the ancient world. There was a lively creative side to their meetings, with acting and poetry playing its part alongside the music[169] and thus enriching the social life of the movement.

As Chase has pointed out, Chartism left an abiding affection and a feeling of pride in the movement because it was 'inspired by great ideals, because it called forth a spirit of devotion and self-sacrifice' and Chase concludes that it was in essence Britain's civil rights movement.[170]

Chapter 9 - An Outsider's View of Britain: The German Diaspora

There is little in this chapter about women, unless we count Queen Victoria, hovering in the background. It is all about her husband. That is because he achieved so much and was so aware of the needs of the working classes, the need to rejuvenate university education and to stimulate trade that he was a revolutionary force in his own right.

During the 1840s there had been a shift in the power imbalance between the landed elite and the manufacturers of the North. The 1832 Reform Act had helped a little. The repeal of the Corn Laws in 1846, which had imposed tariffs on imported foodstuffs since the end of the Napoleonic wars, meant that, though many small farmers on marginal land found it difficult to cope with the lower prices for corn, the majority of mill workers were less hungry than they had been and the landowning elite was less able to wield the power they had once had.

On the domestic front the 1850s ushered in what Brears, has called 'the golden age of baking'. Compressed yeast, cheaper sugar, jam and dried fruits were much more in evidence and reliable baking powder was available from 1850. The invention of mass produced cast-iron domestic ovens meant that women could bake their own bread, which had not commonly been the case.[171]

The year 1848 - the year of revolutions on the Continent – left Britain relatively unscathed. Since 1837 Victoria had been firmly on the throne with Albert, - her 'Angel' – equally firmly by her side since their marriage in 1840.

Albert was one of many German immigrants and he brought hope to the working classes. Though Albert's motivation in moving to

Britain was to marry the woman he loved, and in doing so improve his social standing, other immigrants had less romantic reasons.

The first wave of immigrants were merchants, many of whom settled in the north. Among them was Friedrich Engels, whose father owned a cotton mill and who sent him to England so he could rid himself of what his father considered a lot of silly ideas about politics. It must have been quite an embarrassment for Engels Senior, a manufacturer, to have a son so enamoured of communist ideas.

Young Engels was very pleased to go. His parents were strict Calvinists who disapproved of dancing and reading novels. His mother missed him enormously when he came to England. She sent him money with instructions to buy a good winter coat and drawers and a bed jacket and would have liked to send him warm socks, but his father said it would cost too much. Poor Mrs Engels. She would have been horrified to know that he was living with his common law wife Mary Burns, an Irish mill girl, and far from rejecting his political ideas, he was supporting the newly arrived Karl Marx who could not earn enough to support his wife and growing family from his journalism, so relied on his friend Engels to do so.[172]

German bankers such as the Rothschilds and the Huths had settled in England early in the century though Little Germany, the centre of the German merchants' trading in Bradford, was not established until 1855.

Prince Albert

In some ways, Albert held the same values as his compatriots. Younger son of Ernest I, ruler of the Bavarian dukedom of Saxe-Coburg Gotha, he was a highly educated, highly intelligent and cultured young man, with a wide knowledge of Continental countries and a delight in modern thinking and inventions, who reacted against his father's dissolute ways by being hard-working, principled, a devout Christian and a faithful husband. When he arrived in Britain he was amazed to find a country held back in many ways by antiquated thinking and traditions.

His very first task which showed his interest in humanitarianism and reform was an Anti-Slavery speech he gave at the World Antislavery Convention in 1840. He referred to slavery as 'a stain upon civilized Europe' and 'repugnant to the state of Christianity'. The five thousand strong audience gave a him a great ovation. Given that many of the aristocracy had made their fortunes and built their mansions on the proceeds of the slave trade, though, it did not make him any friends among the upper classes. But his sympathy and knowledge of the living conditions of many of the poorer of Victoria's subjects made him friends among the liberals.

He then moved on to a review of the royal household. By collaborating with the Prime Minister, Sir Robert Peel, he managed to break the stranglehold the aristocracy had on the running of Buckingham Palace, with its multiplicity of opportunities for corruption, thereby saving enough money for Victoria to be able to buy Osborne House.

His organisational skills were applied equally successfully on the restoration of the Palace of Westminster, and the university syllabus of first Cambridge, then Oxford, making them more suitable for the modern, technically advanced country that Britain was becoming.[173]

In May 1848, when almost the whole of the Continent was beginning to erupt into revolution, Albert gave a speech to the Society for Improving the Condition of the Labouring Classes. It had been established in 1844 with Albert as President. It concerned itself with providing good housing for the working classes, funded from philanthropic investments. The first project had been completed in 1846 in Pentonville, guided by Albert's insistence on the importance of sanitation and ventilation. His speech at the meeting in May pointed out that, in his opinion, 'the interests of classes too often contrasted are identical, and it is only ignorance which prevents their uniting for each other's advantage'. He appealed for more people to join the organization. 'To dispel this ignorance, to show how man can help man...ought to be the aim of every philanthropic person but it is more particularly the duty of those who enjoy station, wealth and education'.

Having highlighted the importance of social housing, Albert then turned his attention to pensions for servants. Albert had discovered that in London 70% of domestic servants ended up in the workhouse or dependent on charity to eke out a living in old age. Albert led a drive to allow people employed as servants to pay into an annuity scheme which would cover not only the servant but their spouses and family members. This scheme proved an immediate success.[174]

Albert saw the dangers and destructiveness of revolution, and realized that the causes of people's dissatisfaction should be addressed before their anger boiled over into direct action. 'The unequal division of property and the dangers of poverty and envy rising therefrom, is the principal evil,' he wrote to his brother.[175]

Following a visit to Birmingham, the centre of Chartist agitation in 1843, he worked out a list of improvements which would ameliorate the lives of working people. These were:

- the education of children particularly in industrial training
- improvements in the housing stock
- allotments alongside the housing for growing food
- savings banks and benevolent societies, if possible managed by the workers themselves.

Albert's ideas on how to improve British society were shared by German immigrants to the North who adopted his ideas and were in positions of influence where they could put his ideas into action.

Savings banks, friendly societies and from 1846, building societies were within reach of most of the population in the North. Leeds Building and Investment Society opened in 1846, the Halifax Permanent Benefit Building and Investments Society (how the Victorians loved explicit titles!) later renamed the Halifax Building Society, in 1853. The Huddersfield Equitable Building Society which became the Huddersfield Building Society, was something of a late starter, having to wait until 1864 to be established by five men: a manufacturer, a dentist, a currier, a woollen draper and a bookseller. The Yorkshire Penny Bank founded in Leeds by Edward Akroyd of Halifax was aimed directly at people with limited means. The annual amount deposited could not exceed £30 while the cumulative total was limited to £150. In its first year it established twenty-four branches and in the second year a further 104, so there was certainly a demand.

Educational opportunities, too, received a boost from the German community, (see chapter 11) and the idea of allotments had been one of the strands of the Chartist movement.

The Great Exhibition

Having lived all his life in Bavaria before he married Victoria, Albert was more aware than many in England of what was happening on the Continent. His good friend Sir Henry Cole, inventor of the first Christmas card, organiser of the Penny Post and one of the four assistant keepers of the newly created Public Records Office, had just returned from the eleventh Quinquennial Exhibition held in Paris in 1849. He was impressed with it but thought it would have been better to include other countries alongside France, so there would have been an international aspect to the event.

Albert had fond memories of the Frankfurt Fairs he had attended as a child, and thought what a splendid idea it would be to organize an Exhibition in London – a Great Exhibition, which would outshine the French and bring together people and ideas from a variety of countries. It could also promote the advances in technology he was so interested in and be a showcase for British invention and enterprise. Prime Minister Peel agreed with him.

From conception to opening day took two years, a period of time in which funding had to be found, a site located, a building constructed, and governments and individuals throughout the world informed and encouraged to exhibit.

The funding was supplied by public subscription. At the Hope and Anchor in Bradford a money club was established so people could visit the exhibition, while Provident Societies and workplaces held collections to fund the great exhibition. The *Huddersfield Chronicle* of April 13th, 1850 records that Her Majesty's Commissioners were touring the district to explain the aims of this Great Exhibition and to ask for a committee to be formed to help carry out the project., while the issue of April 20th apologises for having left out of the list of subscribers Mr James Learoyd, who contributed £45-5-0d and Mr Henry Robinson £3.

A meeting at Honley, reported in April 1850 in the *Huddersfield Chronicle*, shows that alongside merchants and manufacturers the room was half-filled with working men. The young chairman, Thomas Brook Junior, in his first excursion into corporate life, urged both masters and men to exert themselves, and 'produce something for the Exhibition that would give prestige to the manufacturers of the district, not only in the estimation of England herself, but among our rivals in Belgium and France'. This was one of the occasions where a subscription list was not opened.[176]

The Queen gave £1,000 while the Rothschild family gave the same, but no donation was too small. James Randle, Parish Constable of Braintree, sent one shilling, being all he could afford, as he had four children to support.[177]

The specially constructed pavilion to house the Exhibition was a marvel in itself. Designed by the Duke of Devonshire's gardener, Paxton, builder of His Grace's cast-iron glass house, the largest glass enclosed building in the world at that point[178], the Crystal Palace covered 16 acres, with 293,655 panes of glass, more than 4500 tons of iron and 24 miles of guttering. The Astronomer Royal predicted it would collapse in the first gale, probably killing everyone in the building. The glass was made by Chance Bros of Smethwick in 39 weeks, something of a miracle in itself[179]. The site chosen was Hyde Park, a decision which angered the aristocratic members of Parliament, since they took their recreation on Rotten Row and did not want it disrupted by an influx of the working classes! Victoria Park, 213 acres of greenery opened in 1845 in Bow, they thought would be a better venue.[180]

Albert was distressed by the vituperative comments aimed at destroying people's confidence in and enthusiasm for the Exhibition, and he received a further blow when Robert Peel was thrown from his horse and died of his injuries. But the project must be completed.

Space had to be found for 14,000 exhibitors, many of them from the West Riding, wooden planking had to be laid. The opposition said this would set up vibrations which would destroy the whole building, but three hundred workmen were sent in to jump up and down on the structure to ensure that it was safe. Elm trees which had been incorporated into the building were full of sparrows, for which the Duke of Wellington provided a brutal but effective antidote – 'Sparrowhawks, Ma'am' he said to the Queen.

By mid-February 1851 Crystal Palace was near enough finished to be able to start taking exhibits. People had already ordered their season passes priced at three guineas for men and two for women, while paying at the door would cost between £1 and 2 shillings and sixpence.

The Exhibition was seized on with enthusiasm by manufacturers in the West Riding. Forty-three firms sent material to be displayed in the Woollen and Worsted Class, showcasing a bewildering variety of cloths for every kind of use. Black alpaca (first introduced into England by Titus Salt of Saltaire), blue and white mohair, dog-hair cloth, cashmere merinos, silk chine dress, linseys, woaded doeskin, Double Napier cloth. Vicuna wool from South America, super Angola mix for trousers. And so it goes on: buckskin, crape, drab kersey for trousers or coats, Scoured Sydney skin wool, grown in New South Wales and washed by J.T. Armitage Brothers. Patent woollen cords, velvet and leather cloths. Then the really fancy stuff: cotton shot with woollens and silk shot with woollens, waistcoating comprising figured quiltings. Persian velvets, Challi wool plaids for children's dresses, rabbits' down glove-clothes. Table covers, stockinette trouserings, crocheted counterpanes. Even cotton made it into the list of entries from the Huddersfied area: Jonas Brook of Meltham Mills showed throstle yarns on bobbins, mule yarns in cop and hank, sewing threads of various thicknesses and thread and crochet cotton wound onto spools.

Frederick Schwann alone, a German immigrant living in Huddersfield and trading with Germany, displayed: fancy vestings called valencias or toilinets, and quiltings; fancy pantaloons stuffs; fancy dresses; cassinets, cashmerettes, summer paletots, and merinos; shoe and boot fancy cloths; woollen beavers, pilot cloths and napped Petershams; tweeds, plaids and checks; buckskins and doeskins; fancy woollen pantaloons, and overcoat stuff; mohair, alpaca and vicuna;

Huddersfield cloth hall

friezed coatings; and shawls. A whole new vocabulary to describe the variety of materials to cater for every occasion.

Eleven of the Huddersfield exhibitors were awarded medals. The variety and astonishing complexity of the materials on show and the uses they were put to seems to have been all-encompassing, from merinos for the tops of ladies' boots to tweeds and shawls, West Riding cloth manufacturers and merchants had cornered the market.

This was due in no small measure to the introduction of the Jacquard loom in about 1830 which enabled fancy patterns such as flowers to be woven into the cloth and stimulated designers to incorporate silk and even cotton into the basic woollen weaving. The coming of the railway in the middle of the century had led to the development of trade in the West Riding and they had made the most of the new means of transport.[181]

The Exhibition made a profit and the money raised bought eighty-seven acres of land opposite the site of the Crystal Palace and the Natural History Museum, the Science Museum and the Victoria and Albert (the V and A) were built – a truly wonderful monument to Albert's vision and determination.

Sadly for Victoria and the country as a whole, Albert died in 1861 supposedly of typhoid fever but the impetus he had given to British society and trade lived on.

PART II

Women's Struggle for Independence

Chapter 10 - Education and Employment in the Second Half of the 19th Century

One of the four necessities for working class life identified by Albert was education, in particular technical education so Britain could maintain its lead in the new technological age. So what did the educational scene look like by 1850? Something of a mishmash is the answer. There were voluntary schools, charity schools and private schools, the charity schools generally being free while the others were not.

Albert's friend Lord Ashley had been keen to set up Ragged schools, which had seen only limited success since 1844 in providing elementary teaching to the urchins who roamed London's streets. It must have been difficult for many families to see the relevance of confining their children in a classroom to gain irrelevant skills when they could be out among the crowds earning or stealing a living.

In the West Riding however matters were becoming more organized as the century progressed. In his study of education in the Huddersfield area in the 19th century, Lockwood has shown that while in the early years of the century there was only one school in the whole of the Colne Valley at Slaithwaite, so elementary education was just not available to most children in the area, by 1820 Marsden Charity Town school had been established catering for 80 to 100 children. The Poor Law clerk had however been informed that poor families could not afford to send their children, even though it cost only pennies a week[182]. Almondbury Township had a day school for 60 boys while a mistress taught twenty small children and Huddersfield itself had 15 schools containing 745 children. They were not charity or voluntary school so must have been unendowed schools for middle class children.

The great strength of the area lay however in the dissenting chapels -Quaker, Methodist, Baptist, Unitarian which had been established throughout the region. The good people who attended chapel felt the urgent need to teach children to read so they could read the Bible and as the only time in the week that they were not working was Sunday, Sunday schools were opened to teach children to read, though not necessarily to write.

By 1820 Huddersfield Sunday School Union recorded that there were 10 schools in or near Huddersfield catering for 2,163 pupils and taught by 584 adults[183]. The Methodist Old Connexion Chapel alone had 540 pupils. All the Sunday schools were supported by subscriptions and collections and the number of children gaining some sort of education before the growth of a separate, more prosperous, middle class demonstrates an interest by the working classes in the education of their children.[184]

By 1833 Huddersfield had 31 public elementary schools as well as private schools, and since no public money was available for buildings until 1833 shows a remarkable dedication by working class families to improve the lives of their children. If they were very poor however, families tended to pay for boys rather than girls, and the percentage of girls attending was in consequence slightly lower than boys.

When Prince Albert wrote about 'industrial training' he may have been thinking about the Mechanics Institutes which began to spring up from the 1820s onwards. They were aimed at those men who serviced the machines which were increasingly being introduced into the mills, and attendant engineering works. The first two Mechanics Institutes were formed in Edinburgh (1821) and Glasgow (1822) and the first one in England was in Liverpool. These establishments aimed to provide a library, lecture courses, a laboratory and

Huddersfield Hall of Science

sometimes a museum.[185]

The idea of forming a Mechanics Institute was taking place in Huddersfield in 1825 with the aim of instructing mechanics and tradesmen in 'scientific principles on which their operations chiefly depend'. It was also intended to have a library freely available to the general public. The implementation of it however had to be deferred because of the financial crisis of 1826, when local banks failed. It was refounded in the 1830s as the Huddersfield Philosophical Society along with another twenty establishments in the Pennine area[186]. It met in the Hall of Science in Bath Street, built in 1839 by local disciples of Robert Owen such as Joshua Hobson and Lawrence Pitkethley and was intended 'for the education of the ordinary people'. It was here also that the Chartists held their meetings.[187]

In 1841 a group of five young men employed by Frederic Schwann formed the Young Men's Mental Improvement Society which aimed to 'reach the working man and to teach him' and was based on mutual improvement societies where working men passed on their knowledge and skills to other working men[188]. It actually taught basic literacy to semi literate boys, some as young as nine, and as such was highly successful. Schwann was treasurer of the association, and no doubt provided funding if there was a shortfall.

As we have seen, Frederic Schwann was a keen exhibitor at the Great Exhibition. He had come to Britain on the death of his brother Sigismund in a riding accident in 1828, a young man who had established himself as a merchant in Huddersfield. Frederic knew no English when he arrived so had to learn fast. He married Henrietta, daughter of the Reverend Kell of Edgbaston and they had six children. He had a very well developed social conscience, due perhaps to his Lutheran upbringing. In Huddersfield the nearest church he could find to Lutheran principles was the Unitarian, which he duly attended. He joined the Temperance Society in 1830, which at that point had a membership of 30, and during the Irish Famine of the late 1840s, used one of his warehouses as a base to distribute food to the destitute new arrivals.

Over time the Young Men's Mental Improvement Society changed its ethos somewhat. It grew and began to hold classes in the British and Foreign Society's school in Outcote Bank where, as well as reading, they taught arithmetic, grammar, geography, design and French, the relevant staff being drawn from Huddersfield College and Huddersfield Collegiate School. In addition there were lectures in the Hall of Science while social events were held at Fixby Hall and Kirklees Hall. The organization therefore was no longer a self-improvement society but something much more ambitious.

By 1842 the society had 100 members all over fifteen and taught clerks, warehousemen, shopmen, designers and weavers with an administrative committee formed from the membership[189]. By 1843 the membership had reached 200, with each member paying threepence ha'penny a week and in that year they joined the Yorkshire Union of Mechanics' Institutes. Chair of the Institute that year was J. Kell, a member of Schwann's extended family and a business partner.

The Huddersfield Female Educational Establishment

Frederic Schwann's wife Henrietta was as keen on education for girls and women as her husband was for the education of young men and in 1848 she helped organize a Female Educational Establishment, to provide evening classes for working class girls and women. This idea must have been discussed among the congregations of dissenting chapels in a wider circle than Huddersfield since in the same year Hannah Ford, a Quaker and mother of Isabella Ford, well known later in the century for her encouragement of trade unionism among the mill girls of Leeds, organized evening classes for mill girls[190]. However the Leeds organization seems to have been very slightly later, though starting in the same year, and possibly less successful. The Huddersfield Institute was up and running by March of that year.

Attendance records for the Huddersfield Female Institute in 1848 show that on Monday, March 18 there were ten staff attending, four men and six women teaching sewing and reading, with a committee member on hand to take responsibility for the evening.

On Tuesday March 19th the two-hour evening session was split between ten people teaching reading, spelling and geography, with in the second hour the number of staff whittled down to six, two women, Miss Routledge and Miss Barnes, along with four men.

On Thursday, March 21st much more detail is given about who was teaching what. For the first hour, Miss Cheetham and Miss Batley taught reading and writing, but in addition a whole phalanx of other tutors concentrated on writing: Messrs Kell, Roebuck, Nelson, Heywood, Shillitoe, along with Miss Balon. Mrs Tom Innson did dictation, and Miss Wright and Mrs Pesel dealt with anyone who turned up who did not fit in to the classes already arranged. The second hour was largely given over to arithmetic.

One peculiarity of the teaching of arithmetic was that the different things that can be done with numbers: addition, subtraction, multiplication and division were each taught separately by a different man. It must have made life for the teachers fairly difficult. How do you do long division, for instance, if your students are not confident adding up or multiplying? It must also have been difficult for pupils to learn to manipulate numbers. Perhaps they didn't! Robert Kell, Frederic Schwann's business partner and brother-in-law, taught division. Friday saw ten teachers provided for the first hour, five men and five women among them Mrs Schwann who did writing. The committee took it in turns to supervise the evening. By the end of the month there were 39 students.

The start of the following year, January 1st was marked by a tea party for students instead of study. January saw a simpler system than that of the previous year. On January 4th the first hour was spent writing while the second was spent doing arithmetic while the following day everyone did writing for the first hour and reading for the second hour.

By June 1848 the numbers had risen to 59 with staff being a mixture of volunteers and paid teachers. Five years later the annual subscription list for 1853 contained 55 contributors, most giving relatively small amounts. The Earl of Carlile of Castle Howard contributed £2, as did Mrs Schwann and Robert Kell, with sixteen people or businesses giving one guinea. The rest were half guineas and even small amount down to 2 shillings and sixpence. If the amount given demonstrates the prestige of an organization, it seems the Female Education Institution did not rank highly.

Like the Mechanics Institute, high on the list of priorities was a library. In September 1852 the Institute took out a subscription costing one guinea to the Yorkshire Village Library, which was now circulating in some forty villages throughout the county. Among its patrons were the Duke of Devonshire, the Marquis of Ripon, the manufacturer Sir Isaac Holden of Keighley, who gave £50, and Sir Titus Salt who gave a box of books – the Saltaire Box. Lord Lytton gave copies of his own works, which are not, as one might think, very dry and worthy history books, but highly dramatic works such as *The Last Days of Pompeii,* and who coined phrases such as 'The pen is mightier than the sword' and 'Twas a dark and stormy night'[191]. There were 40 boxes in circulation at that point and committees could select from shelves at the library in Leeds or from the catalogue. The library provided a box for carrying the books, but carriage had to be paid by the borrower.

The Institute must have flourished because White's Directory of 1858 shows that the Mechanics Institute 'now occupies a commodious building in Queen Street, purchased and altered in 1850 at a cost of £1600.' It had by that time acquired 1000 members and a library of 2000 books, and there was a School of Design attended by 100 pupils. The building was shared by a branch of the YMCA and the Female Educational Institute, with about 100 pupils.[192]

There was no means of assessing progress until in 1858 a sub-committee decided they needed to look at measures of uniformity of attainment. This Female Education enterprise was obviously a voyage of discovery for more than the pupils.

Eight years after the founding of the Institute, the report for 1856 spells out the aims of the organization:

> To provide for females of this town and neighbourhood increased facilities for mental improvement by means of Evening Classes, a Library, Addresses and such other methods as may appear suitable for imparting a sound moral and secular education; not inculcating doctrinal theology on the one hand, or permitting any studies hostile to religion on the other.

By this time the rules for running the Institute had been worked out in detail. They were as follows:

- Members included people who were annual subscribers, quarterly or fortnightly members, honorary members and presentees.
- Subscribers of ten shillings annually, in addition to their own privileges as members, were entitled to present one female to all the benefits of the institution for every ten shillings subscribed.
- Presentees paid only one penny a week.

The committee which ran the Institute should consist of twenty ladies and gentlemen, sixteen chosen from among the voluntary teachers or honorary members and annual subscribers of ten shillings upwards. Four were to be selected from the classes, one from each class and one from the class for adults. The President and the treasurer were to be elected annually and nobody under eighteen could be a committee member. The committee was to meet once a month and would choose a vice-president, an honorary secretary and a librarian. Five was to be a quorum.

The treasurer would be allowed to spend up to two shillings and sixpence without scrutiny from the committee and when the treasurer was holding £10 it was to be paid into the bank. If a committee member missed three meetings they could be asked to resign.

The Minute Book also records that the committee organizing the annual soiree intended to ask Mrs Sunderland to sing at the event. Girls could take two friends with them. Front seats were priced at one shilling and back seats at 6d.

The rules therefore show a body of people prepared to commit a considerable amount of their time to running what they must have felt was a significant and systematic contribution to female education. The Schwanns, the Kells, the Huths and the Pesels, all represented among the committee members and tutors, were German immigrants, and therefore likely to attend one of the various dissenting chapels in the town.

The 1858 report also demonstrates the Victorian propensity for collecting statistics. The annual meeting was held at Netherwoods' Buildings in King Street and comments that the classes had been reorganized in the Spring of 1857, and that attendance had been more satisfactory since then. The course of instruction, they felt, had been more connected and systematic, which must have resulted in more customer satisfaction.

The number of pupils now stood at 104 with an average nightly attendance of 50. Average weekly attendances were 275. There were 54 pupils under 15 years of age, 49 above 15 and under 20, and 15 over twenty. 86 of them also attended Sunday School and the remaining 32 were mainly older pupils of the Institution. Of the 118 pupils on the books 75 paid 3d a week, 40 were presentees paying 1d and eight were honorary pupils.

There were 22 classes taught by eight paid teachers and ten unpaid who taught ten classes.

No. of classes	Topic	No. of members
6	Reading	75
13	Writing	115
6	Arithmetic	90
3	Grammar	52
2	Dictation	50
1	Composition	21
3	History	56
4	Geography	72
1	Singing	34
2	Sewing	40

Women were involved in teaching five of the subject areas but not Arithmetic, Geography, Dictation, Grammar and singing.

The Minute Book, as already mentioned, suggests that they should find ways of measuring how much learning had occurred. They suggested offering Physiology, Health and Domestic Economy and thought there was too much time devoted to writing and not enough to Arithmetic. There was also a need for more class books to keep pupils stimulated.[193]

The 1859 annual report gives yet more statistics. The ages of girls attending the Institute were

Under 15	0
15 and under 20	54
Over 20	33

Of these students 111 also attended Sunday School.

The financial contributions were:

3d a week	94
Honorary	2
Presentees	61

22 classes were conducted by eight paid teachers, who taught

twelve of the classes, the other ten being taught by volunteers.

The singing class was very popular, as was the sewing. A letter from a student going on to study at Homerton Training School to qualify as a teacher was very appreciative of what she had learned at the Institute. 'I am glad I was ever a member of the Female Educational Institute', she wrote. 'What I learnt there will be useful for me through life – every dress I have taken with me I made myself at the Institute'. The Institute also provided lectures on a variety of topics. Astronomy with lantern slides was very well attended, as was the soiree in the Philosophical Hall.

Work available for women

Mrs Schwann must have been very pleased with the progress the Institute was making. But what were the opportunities for girls and women in mid-19th century Huddersfield? What would they do when they had finished paying out their threepences? Well, as we have seen, one of them went on to teacher training. But there were other business opportunities available. White's directories for 1837 and 1870 show how the town itself was changing and growing, and with it, how opportunities for women were expanding. The population of the Huddersfield Township in 1821 had been a mere 13,284 which grew to 30,880 by 1851. By 1871, with the expansion of the township boundaries following the 1868 incorporation of the town, the population was 70,253. So while we are not comparing like with like in population terms, we can see that the overall trend is one of a rapidly expanding population and an increasingly sophisticated society.[194]

In 1837 the businesses being run by women were:

Tea Dealer	Hotel, innkeeper
Baker and flour dealer	Music preceptor
Game dealer	Tailor

Milliner and dress maker Wine, spirit, porter merchant
Shopkeeper Beer house keeper
Straw hat maker Painter
Toy dealer Slay and heald maker
Cloth dealer

Seventeen different jobs, though keeping an inn, hotel or beer house must have had rather a lot of similarities. Dealing in foodstuffs and drink were four of the seventeen, while three categories covered women making clothing of some kind. Two, shuttle making and slay and heald making, were involved with items for the handloom trade - slays were the reeds which separated the threads on a loom - while two, the music preceptor and the painter were earning a living with their artistic ability.

By 1870 business opportunities had more than doubled with 39 different jobs being listed. They were:

Artist in wax Grocer and tea dealer
Butcher Inns and taverns (21)
Confectioner Newsagent (5)
Fent dealer Register office for servants (5)
French polisher Staymakers
Greengrocer Tea dealer
Hosier Umbrella maker
India rubber dealer Brewer
Music teacher Clothes broker
Pawnbroker Corn and flour merchant
Smallware dealer Flock dealer
Tailor Ginger beer maker
Toy dealer Heald, reed and slaymaker
Wine and spirit merchant Beer house keepers (10)
Baby linen dealer Milliner (87 women, 14 men)
Cabinet maker Painter

Draper
Fishmonger
Furniture broker
Lath render

Stone mason and builder
Temperance hotel keeper
Whitesmith

As well as the increase in numbers of jobs, it is immediately apparent that life has become more sophisticated. Selling foodstuffs is now much more differentiated: butcher, confectioner, fishmonger, greengrocer, grocer and tea dealer. While inns, taverns and beer houses still provide a substantial number of jobs, there is now a Temperance Hotel. Providing clothing and cloth again shows more specialization with a fent dealer, baby linen shop, hosier and staymaker. As there was one man and one woman employed in this category, it is a reminder that men at this period also wore corsets, if need be[195]. The rising middle classes are catered for by the French polisher and, very noticeably, by the five agencies for domestic servants. The poor now have a pawnbroker, which at least implies there are people with something worth pawning. The new inventions and discoveries being imported into the country is shown by the india rubber dealer.

One possible source of employment not appearing in White's Directory was that of nursing.

Hospital-Nursing

Following the ground-breaking work of Florence Nightingale in the Crimean War, and her subsequent use of statistics to show that more soldiers died of disease than were killed in battle, nursing became an honourable calling for women. In 1855 the Nightingale Fund for training nurses was set up, closely followed in 1860 by a training school. In 1865 the first women to emerge as fully trained nurses according to Miss Nightingale's stringent requirements were looking for posts and found them at the Liverpool Workhouse

Infirmary on a scheme financed by William Rathbone. There were twelve nurses and the whole hospital was overseen by a matron, Agnes Jones. The nursing was done by these twelve, assisted by probationers and able-bodied women inmates. These latter, however, needed close supervision as many of them used every opportunity to get hold of alcohol.

Separating patients with infections such as cholera and fevers from other patients was one of the many improvements to be introduced while cleanliness, good sanitation, fresh air and a decent diet were now on the agenda, with patients nursed in long Nightingale wards with beds spaced at a reasonable distance from one another.

In the Huddersfield area a dispensary had been established in 1814 ministering to out-patients. There was no place here for women doctors, as the medical profession would fight long and hard to keep women out of medical training. Only Elizabeth Garrett Anderson's grit and determination got her on to the British Medical Register in 1873, and that because of a qualification gained in Paris, not Britain. Sophia Jex-Blake was the woman who finally beat down the medical establishment but it was not until 1892 that Edinburgh University agreed to take female students, the first of the British universities to do so.

Marland lists the diseases to which people might succumb in the early 19th century: airborne bacterial infections such as TB, scarlet fever and whooping cough; waterborne bacteria causing cholera and typhoid, and typhus, a bacterium carried by body lice. Then there were the viruses: measles, smallpox and influenza, not to mention diarrhoea. In the rapidly expanding towns and cities people were often living in crowded, dirty homes with very limited access to clean water. Cows, whose milk could carry tuberculosis, were often kept in cowhouses with no running water, and no system for clearing away manure. Peter Brears quotes a rate for TB of 90% infection in the milk sold in Leeds at the end of the nineteenth century.[196]

Somewhat earlier in 1850 a report on the living conditions of people in Haworth showed that the lack of any kind of sanitation was polluting the water supply, and that the graveyard was so crowded and the soil so poorly oxygenated that even the contents of the graveyard were adding to the pollution. The average life expectancy in Haworth then was 25.8 years and 41.6% of the population died before the age of six[197]. How, one wonders, did our ancestors survive long enough to procreate?

Infectious diseases were usually treated at home[198] by a dispensary doctor or, if the patient was very poor, by the workhouse surgeon. By the 1850s there were over twenty doctors practicing in Huddersfield, though it has to be said that there were many diseases they could not treat.

Victims of accidents - and there were many - would be taken to the Infirmary to be cared for till they either recovered or died. In 1825 Huddersfield Infirmary had been propelled into existence by a horrific accident when scaffolding collapsed, killing or injuring sixteen of the men working on the erection of a new chapel in Ramsden Street. They had fallen from a height of fifty feet, and there was nowhere to take the injured. A linen draper, Samuel Clay, started the subscription ball rolling by raising £3,329 in a week! The foundation stone was laid in June 1829 and the building was completed in two years, ready for action in 1831. It was meant to cater primarily for the many accidents that happened in mills and workshops in the Huddersfield and Upper Agbrigg area.

There were no women doctors, obviously, but there must have been women nurses though we don't know how many, how much they were paid, and certainly not their names. It may be that the recruitment of women into the new voluntary hospital was run on the same lines as St Bartholomew's in the 1830s, St Thomas's in the 1850s and Guy's in the 1870s[199]. Here sisters of the different wards and the matron, in other words the women who made decisions on budgets and nursing care, were recruited separately from the women doing the actual caring. Each sister was responsible for running her own ward and took on casual labour depending on how many patients there were and what their needs were. Sisters and matrons had often been upper servants in private families. The matron was a senior administrative officer and an advertisement from Leeds General Infirmary of 1852 spells out the kind of person the hospital was looking for: somebody middle aged and free of family commitments, 'of good address', able to manage accounts, 'staid, sober and discreet', kind but firm and 'experienced in the management of a family and the duties of the sick room.'[200]

Governessing

Another suitable occupation for respectable girls and women was that of governess. This was a live-in post for girls and women to earn a living by educating the young boys and older girls of the wealthy. Older boys would be sent off to a public school but the girls were kept at home, secluded from the outside world, a custom surviving well into the 20th century. Virginia Woolf, for instance, born in 1881, was educated at home along with her sister. Any poor woman trying to impart skills they did not want to learn, then as now, struggled. The person giving Virginia and her sister singing lessons was a devout Christian. When she asked Virginia what Christmas commemorated, Virginia answered 'The crucifixion' then collapsed into such a fit of giggles she had to be sent from the room. Not so clever governesses trying to teach clever children must have had a hard time of it.

Socially, too, it was a difficult position to hold. Above the servants – even the lady's maid – so unable to socialize with them, but unable to interact with her employers, unless, of course, you were Jane Eyre and had to contend with an amorous employer with a mad wife in the attic. This was an unusual situation however and the majority of governesses must have felt very isolated.

Help was at hand to some extent, however, at least for women in London. Frederick Denison Maurice, Professor of English Literature and History at King's College, London, had a sister who was a governess. Sensitised to the difficulties of their situation and seeing a possible gap in the market, in 1848 he organized a series of evening lectures entitled 'Lectures for Ladies' with the aim of increasing the knowledge and therefore the professional standing of governesses. The lectures were so popular that they were continued and extended down the age range to include thirteen year olds. In 1853 this organisation obtained a royal charter from the Queen and became Queen's College. The Queen strongly approved of a sound Christian education for girls though opposed 'this mad wicked folly of women's rights'.[201]

Higher education

Higher education was also moving forward. Up to the mid-nineteenth century there had been only two universities in England, those at Oxford and Cambridge. They were open only to men who were members of the Church of England, so young people from dissenting families were excluded not only from these institutions but also from the professions which the universities served. Owens College in Manchester was set up in 1851 as a non-denominational college, thus opening the way to a wider clientele than the old established colleges, though not, of course, providing education for women.

Two women in the North who were interested in education for girls were Josephine Butler and Anne Jemima Clough. Josephine Butler was the wife of the headmaster of Liverpool College. She had lost her youngest child, Eva, in an accident, and was so desperately unhappy that she looked for other women who were suffering as much as she was. She found them in the oakum shed of Liverpool workhouse, women without hope, many of whom had been forced into prostitution as the only way to keep themselves from starvation. 'It was not difficult to find misery in Liverpool', she commented.

She realised that women, whatever their station in life, needed education so they could have access to work which did not involve selling their only asset, their bodies. 'Economics lie at the very root of practical morality' she wrote. She became well known for her work with prostitutes who she sought to save from their misery through Christian faith and education.

It was not surprising then that a woman with such a high profile should be approached by Anne Jemima Clough, and asked to join the newly formed North of England Council for Promoting the Higher Education of Women. Their first venture in 1867 into the field of women's adult education was a series of lectures, again called 'Lectures for Ladies'. They asked a young Cambridge don, James Stuart, to give a series of lectures on astronomy in various northern towns and cities.

They were afraid that very few people would turn up but they need not have feared. Young Mr Stuart, travelling between Manchester, Leeds, Sheffield, Rotherham and Crewe, met with crowded lecture halls wherever he went.

Such was the demand that circulating libraries had to order new consignments of books, and the editions of several scientific works sold out. James Stuart would have liked to have a question-and-answer session but this was deemed too daring so he agreed to have questions printed and promised to read and correct them. He expected about thirty but had underestimated the enthusiasm and received 300.

These lectures formed the basis of the University Extension Scheme, which soon began to admit men and was copied by Henry Sidgwick, Professor of Philosophy at Cambridge University, who hired a house to accommodate women students. This developed into Newnham College.[202]

The University of London was the first to admit women in 1868 though they were not given degrees but Certificates of Merit. At the turn of the century the university extension scheme also laid the foundation for women's access to universities in the North, with Liverpool, Leeds and Manchester forming part of the federal Victoria University.

While this was a significant step forward for the more affluent women in society, it did not touch the lives of working women in any meaningful way. For that we have to look to the workings of an organisation set up by working people and run democratically by them: the Co-op.

Chapter 11 - The Women's Co-operative Guild

The Women's Co-operative Guild was an off-shoot of the Co-operative movement. The Co-operative movement is often said to have started in Rochdale in 1844 by the Rochdale Pioneers, twenty-eight working men who came together to sell goods that offered value for money. The business was owned and run by the men, who had put their own money into the venture. They began opening for two nights, then four and after a year their membership was 74, their capital was £181 and the year's takings amounted to £710.[203]

This successful co-operative venture was however built on the foundations of several failed ones, some having begun and faded away across the Pennines in the West Riding. The original co-operators followed the tenets of Robert Owen, their aim being to build co-operative communities, and as such came together to make their cloth, but being working class they had difficulty accessing enough money to make their ventures successful. In 1827 however a co-operator from Brighton, William Bryan, suggested that if they controlled the selling of their goods, they could amass a lump sum, perhaps even a substantial one.[204]

In the following five years thirty-eight co-operatives established themselves in the West Riding, the first being at Meltham Mills in 1827, and the most important being the Huddersfield Co-operative Trading Association, founded in 1829. The Association had nineteen shillings to begin with and after twelve months had accumulated £700! They were not at this stage selling groceries and other foodstuffs, but were concerned to sell the cloth they had made.

Every year saw a Congress of Co-operators and in 1831 the Birmingham Congress decided to spread the word with a national network of lecturers, chief among whom would be Thomas Hirst (1792-1833) who wore himself out with his tours across the north of

England, expounding the virtues of co-operation. By 1835 the movement had lost the energy it had had and it gradually faded away, though the Huddersfield Association survived longer than most and contributed financially to the Chartist demonstration at Peep Green in 1839.

What made the Rochdale Pioneers so successful and what separated them from the Owenites was the payment of a dividend. The more you bought at their shop, the more you saved. The dividend was paid quarterly, six-monthly or yearly and was an easy way to amass a lump sum for working class families. They were also dealing in foodstuffs, rather than manufactured goods, and aimed to provide wholesome, unadulterated food at reasonable prices. These rules were followed by subsequent co-operators and, with clear-cut guidelines, the societies flourished.

An important part of their responsibilities as they saw it was to educate their fellow co-operators and as the movement spread, to pass on examples of good practice. To this end in 1871 they established a news sheet, the *Co-operative News*, and employed as editor a man with a similar name to the radical witness at Peterloo – Samuel Bamford. Samuel Bamford the co-operator was born in Rochdale in 1846 and had a son and a daughter. The son, William, helped his father with the editing of the *Co-operative News*, while his daughter, Annie Tomlinson, became editor of the women's section in 1904. Involvement with the Co-operative Movement seems to have run in families.

On first opening the Huddersfield Branch in Buxton Road in 1860, business was slack and committee members had to go in and out of the shop to give the impression that trade was prospering. The manager, however, had to pretend to be away when creditors called[205]. Gradually however trade increased and in 1862 they were able to buy a sugar chopper for young John Horsfall who had broken sugar till his fingers bled.[206]

When more branches were opened the minutes show how carefully expenditure was managed – micro-managed, one might say. In 1862 a looking glass was bought for the drapery department, and instructions were issued that the horse was not to be lent out on a Sunday. They also needed a rat trap. Sausages were to be taken to Lockwood by John Nutter on the bus not later than six o'clock every Friday evening (presumably any later and the shop would not be able to sell them) and if anyone complained about bad eggs they were to be given replacements. In 1861 smoking in the shop was forbidden, with a fine of 3d imposed for any breaking of this rule. They decided to close the shop for the funeral of Lord Palmerston in 1865, as other shops were closing, and that the old horse be sold.

Meanwhile there were problems with the carter. J. Johnson was instructed to rebuke the carter for being drunk and ask him to be more civil. The horse was given a nosebag, perhaps to make its life more bearable, since it was being driven by a drunken, foul-mouthed carter![207]

While the carter would not be drinking champagne, by 1868 the Co-op was selling it, so it had moved away from serving just the working class customers and lured the middle classes into its orbit. They were also selling snuff alongside tobacco in 1870, though it was beginning to go out of fashion.

They were also spending on essential items for the shops such as a piggin (a small pail with a handle at one side) for the Lockwood branch, an ounce- and half-ounce weights for Moldgreen and a brush for Paddock.[208]

The National Organisation

The Women's Co-operative Guild began with a corner of the *Co-*

operative News put aside for topics that might interest women, and came about because of Mrs Alice Acland's friendship with Samuel Bamford. Mrs Acland was married to an Oxford academic, Arthur Acland, an administrator of the Oxford Extension Lectures who in 1879 helped found Somerville College, the first non-denominational college for women in Oxford. It was some thirteen years later that the Huddersfield branch of the Guild was founded so we need to look back to the beginning of the movement to see why it was so important and to see who made it so.

Mrs Acland suggested that the Women's Corner of the *Co-operative News* should contain a series of topics that might interest women, then moved on to suggest that women might like to gather together with their knitting or sewing to listen to someone reading from the literature that circulated to members about the co-operative movement.

By 1883 a group of women attending the annual congress along with their husbands gathered together and formed an organization, promptly electing Mrs Acland as their President. They agreed to pay 6d a year, and appointed secretaries in areas where there was already some interest in their ideas. Hebden Bridge set up the first of these guilds with 60 members. There was also one in Rochdale, three in London, and one in Coventry. The last quarter of the century saw a huge increase in the number of co-operatives, and with it an equivalent increase in branches of the Women's Co-operative Guild.[209]

To begin with the guilds concentrated on what was considered women's sphere of influence: the welfare of the family, their health, and how to manage on a restricted budget. In 1889 however, the Guild elected as President Margaret Llewellyn Davies. As a suffragist who was very committed to the welfare of women in general, she realised the potential of the Guild to change attitudes towards women and the attitudes of women themselves to their position in society. When she took over as General Secretary she sent out a winter circular in which she urged women not to allow their meetings to degenerate into discussion solely about cooking and sewing. As members of the Guild they should remember that their aim was to spread co-operation and they could do that by educating themselves and others about the movement. 'Draw up a programme of meetings', she said, 'and organize a series of lectures'. And in 1892 she wrote, 'There is a good deal yet in the lives of women that is not exactly rose-coloured and changes are not likely to occur without determined action on the part of women themselves.'

The Guild, under the guidance of Miss Llewellyn Davies, developed campaigns for changes in society that still resonate today. They campaigned on financial matters, for a living wage for Co-op employees. In 1908 the Co-operative Congress drew up a scale of wages for female co-operative wages which was implemented four years later. They supported an old age pension for all and at the age of sixty-five, not seventy, as originally mooted by Lloyd George.

On the question of divorce, they supported a change in the law bringing it into line with the divorce law for men. In the nineteenth century a woman could not divorce her husband for adultery. If he were violent or unfaithful, all she could do was apply for a separation. Miss Llewellyn Davies took the view that the value system that stigmatized divorce took the subordination of women for granted. The change however was slow to be implemented and precipitated a crisis in the Guild. Roman Catholic members of the Co-operative movement were incensed at this proposed change and the grant to support the Guild was withdrawn, which for a time limited its expansion. The First World War changed attitudes considerably and in 1923 the Matrimonial Causes Act evened up the laws regulating divorce.

The Guild wanted women to be included in jury service because they thought women could provide greater understanding of the stresses that had brought women into court. This was not implemented until 1921.

On the matter of women's suffrage, the women of the Guild did not necessarily support demands for the vote. Those who did saw the vote as a means of increasing their political clout and obtaining improvements that were difficult to get accepted by the male political establishment. Those who did not support this position were put off by the violence of the suffragettes and considered that the wider political scene was the province of their menfolk, rather than themselves.

For women interested in the political process, their way into it had been at the local level via representation on school boards (since 1870), on parish vestries, which before the 1832 Poor Law managed the maintenance of the poor of the parish and even after that responsibility was taken away still looked after local services such as road mending, keeping the peace and ensuring markets were properly run. These political possibilities however were being eroded. The London Government Act of 1899 abolished parish vestries and brought in Borough Councils, from which women were excluded and the 1902 Education Act barred women from the management boards of local schools.

This made votes for women much more of an issue for the Guild women, who decided that their first priority should be to change the attitude of the men in the Co-operative Movement. In 1906 the Co-operative Congress refused to accept a motion proposing support for women's suffrage. Women members spent the following two years leafleting their local co-ops and conducting a postal vote of the husbands of Guild members. This tactic paid off and in 1908 at the Co-operative Congress there was only one vote against the resolution calling for the enfranchisement of women.

Perhaps the greatest contribution to women's welfare however was the Guild's concern with the health of women at a crucial time of their lives: during pregnancy and in the period following the birth of children. Doctors were taught little about this. Isabel Hutton, writing about her training as a doctor in the early years of the twentieth century in Edinburgh, says the teaching in gynaecology was perfunctory. 'It seemed as if gynaecology was considered a second subject', she writes[210], and 'on the 'change of life' there was but one page of notes in our lectures, on sterility only half a page with never a whisper as to the husband's possible share in an infertile marriage'.[211]

Miss Llewellyn Davies lectured on the links between poverty and infant mortality which she blamed on the poor diet of the mother at a time when she should have been well fed, and lack of knowledge about pre-and post-natal hygiene. The Guild also collected first hand accounts of members' experiences of sickness and poverty. These were published in 1915 under the title *Maternity: Letters from Working Women* and make humbling reading. What leaps from the pages of this eloquent book is the effects of multiple pregnancies, the lack of knowledge by the medical profession of women's health and the effects of heavy work such as lifting loads of wet washing. Anaemia was taken for granted as one of the things to be expected especially during pregnancy. The exhaustion experienced by mothers of small children is expressed vividly by one writer. 'Many a time I have sat in Daddy's chair, a baby of two and a half years old at my back, one sixteen months and one month on my knees and cried for very weariness and hopelessness'. (Letter 20).[212]

A husband's poor health could lead to poverty if he was paid only for the work he did. Poverty meant lack of food and no money to pay for a doctor or midwife. And the number of children who died at a young age, added to the number of miscarriages some women suffered must have been well-nigh intolerable. Of the 400 women who replied to the survey, 26 were childless and 26 did not give definite figures, which left 348. Of these 348, 37 had stillbirths, 89 had miscarriages. One poor woman had had eight miscarriages while another had had six. Of the 348 women, 86 lost children in the first year of life and of these deaths half occurred within the first month or from ante-natal or natal causes after the first month.[213]

Several of the women wrote about losing their mothers when they were very young, and felt the need for the guidance and knowledge they might have gained from them. The lady who wrote letter 20, however, had different views. 'I was married at the age of twenty-eight in utter ignorance of the things that most vitally affect a wife and mother', she writes. 'My mother...thought ignorance was innocence and the only thing I remember her saying on the subject of childbirth was "God never sends a baby without bread to feed it". Dame Experience long ago knocked the bottom out of that argument for me.'

Having started their married lives as strong and healthy young women, after multiple births many were left with varicose veins, prolapsed wombs, anaemia, incontinence and debt. Combined with grinding poverty, it says much for the human spirit that these women had not only survived but were prepared to put their energies into an organization which would work towards improving the health of the next generation. They were the first working class women to write openly about contraception, and the effect of childbirth on their health. They pulled no punches.

A delegation led by Miss Llewelyn Davies used the information the Guild had gathered from members to lobby the government about maternity provision. In 1914 a government circular was issued to local authorities offering a grant of 50% towards any expenditure incurred on health and welfare work.[214]

The book of letters was an immediate hit both in Britain and America and influenced public opinion. The Maternity and Child Welfare Act of 1918 contained several of the Guild's proposals for improvements in health care during pregnancy and in the post-natal period, and was a major achievement of the organization.

The Huddersfield Branch

In Huddersfield it was not until 1892 that the Guild was formed with twenty members, funded by a grant of £2 from the main society and following an address by Miss Llewellyn Davies[215]. By this time the Society was very firmly established in the area with a Co-op in almost every district. The local branches were mainly groceries, but there were a substantial number of butchers', there was a drapery at Milnsbridge, a branch at St Thomas' dealt with property and the laundry was established in Princess Street in the centre of town. The laundry had washing machines, soap boilers, starching troughs, ironers, goffering machines and two drying stoves.

Aware of the threat to workers' health from the steam and heat, a dining room was provided so there was some escape from the damp, as in the country as a whole the incidence of TB was high and people were very aware of the need for fresh air. The directors had produced a list of prices and regulations printed on a card attached to a postcard which could be completed by any co-operative member and posted back to the laundry, showing what needed to be collected. Needless to say, the workers sweating over the goffering irons and the washing machines were women, with a man managing the whole

The Co-op laundry
By kind permission of the Huddersfield Exposed web site

process.[216]

By 1902 women were beginning to make their presence felt in the running of the different strands of co-operative undertakings. Miss Mayo succeeded Mr Arthur Smith as editor of the local news incorporated into the co-operative magazine, *The Wheatsheaf*, and Mrs Marshall succeeded Owen Balmforth as chair of the Education committee. This committee awarded scholarships to adult students who came top of their respective exams. Two members of the Balmforth family, one a daughter and the other a niece, came top in 1902 and 1903: Miss A. Balmforth in 1901 and Miss G. Balmforth in 1903, Miss A having studied 'Co-operation' and Miss G having studied 'Industrial history'. The scholarships were worth £2-10 shillings and were tenable at the summer meetings of the University Extension Scheme held alternately in Oxford and Cambridge. Miss Amy Balmforth was later to resign her position in the drapery department because of her approaching marriage.[217]

Back in 1892 the first president of the Guild was Mrs Alfred Shaw with Mrs Merrifield as treasurer and Mrs Henry Hirst as secretary. By the following year there were 119 members. They heard lectures from Miss Murray of the Nurses' Home in Trinity Street[218] on sick nursing and in 1897 were given a grant of £10 to pay for a series of lectures by Miss Ravenhill, 'well known authority on public hygiene.' They also invited Miss Margaret McMillan from Bradford to speak on 'The Early Days of Childhood'. Miss McMillan and her sister Rachel were pioneers in the provision of nursery education in Bradford and later in Deptford. They knew that children could not learn if they were hungry, so lobbied for local authorities to provide free school meals for poor children. They also knew that children with body and head lice, with scabies and impetigo were unlikely to be able to concentrate on education, however imaginatively presented, so wanted bathrooms installed in schools and knew that young children learned best by doing, not sitting learning by rote. Margaret McMillan published several books on childhood education, so would have given the ladies of the Huddersfield Guild an insightful talk about the needs of young children.

The Guild helped at the Jubilee celebrations in 1910. The ladies of the Guild were among the organisers of what must have been a great event in the Huddersfield social calendar.

The Children's Field Day was arranged for July 9th, 1910 and for once it didn't rain. A procession headed by the Huddersfield Military Band were at the head, followed by decorated wagons showing the goods sold by the Co-op. It wound its way round central Huddersfield before heading off down the hill to Aspley and from thence to Longley Hall Park. There were 3,600 children in attendance, 164 of the younger ones being crammed into a large motor wagon, (It must have been huge!) with four contingents of older children walking the whole way.

The attractions available in the park were bands playing for concerts and dancing, the Band of Hope children giving a display of dancing round the maypole, a gymnastic display, a Punch and Judy show, and songs by the Co-operative choir. Those children who were not worn out by walking to the park could then compete in the various races: egg and spoon, potato race, obstacle race and sack race. There was also a spoon-cleaning competition organized for the girls, while the boys could compete to produce the greatest shine on a pair of boots. For the ladies there was a cake baking competition. 250 gallons of coffee were consumed and 3,600 buns! There were also commemorative mugs.

Owen Balmforth concludes his booklet about the Co-op with the following words:

> The principles for which Co-operation stands – thrift, cash payments, pure commodities, fair conditions of labour, education, mutual help and co-partnership of profit – are principles which are needed not only for today, but for all time.

Well said, Owen!

Chapter 12 - Florence Lockwood nee Murray. 1861-1937[219]

It is sometimes useful to see a society not from within but observed by an outsider, an 'off-comed un'. An outsider may see things that are particular to the area but which the natives consider to be the norm. Such a one was Daniel Defoe, though he spent only a short time in the region. Florence Murray, however, made her home permanently in the Colne Valley when she was 37 and stayed for the next twenty years, married to a local mill owner and embedded, as far as she could be as a southerner and an artist, in the local culture. Florence had the eye of an artist and the descriptive skills and curiosity of an anthropologist. Her descriptions of life in Linthwaite in the Colne Valley bring the place to life and in this unfamiliar place she would become an ardent suffragist and pacifist.

Born in Devonport in 1861 where her father was a doctor in the Navy, she was the youngest of six children. The family was familiar with the North, because after Devonport they moved to Birkenhead. A family tragedy, the suicide of her eldest brother aged twenty-three, precipitated a move away from the North back to the West Country where their mother fell into a severe depression, refusing to take the girls to social events. With teenage girls this was a major drawback, as this was the way they met suitable young men.

At the age of twenty-six, still single, Florence decided to study art. She had £18 in a savings account and her parents agreed to support her by paying her board and lodging, so she could afford a year at the Slade School of Art. Her eldest sister, Jessie, was already nursing in Huddersfield when her parents died within a short time of one another, and these events scattered the family, with her other sister, Nellie, joining Jessie, and Florence moving to London, where she was

A Huddersfield electric tram

able to make a living by selling her paintings.

She met Josiah Lockwood when she came to Huddersfield to stay with Jessie, who had opened a nursing home in Trinity Street. One cold, rainy day, with nothing better to do, Florence accompanied her sister on a visit to a patient of hers, the housekeeper for Josiah Lockwood, at the mill owner's house at Black Rock Mill in Linthwaite. The old lady had a broken leg. They took the tram to Linthwaite, 'Electric trams were still a nine day wonder,' Florence comments.

She describes the scene as they approached Black Rock Mill.

'The mill was just losing', she wrote. The workers came clattering out in their clogs, each woman having a bucket on her arm and the men a little tin box. Florence and her sister were directed to the mill by a local man. 'Yond's the chimney and th'house is in t'yard', were the directions.

As they approached the mill they could hear and feel the pulsing of the mill engine and the roar of a swollen mill stream. The mill was dimly lit for the night shift and neither Josiah nor his nineteen year old son, Sam, were there, as they had gone to London, but Florence and Jessie were assured by the old lady that Josiah would be 'fair sorry' to have missed them.

He was indeed. The following day they were invited to lunch and in the dim light of a winter's afternoon Florence watched the procession of workers passing the house on their way back to the mill for the afternoon shift. 'The women wore shawls on their heads and the men had top coats over their blue smocks, for it was cold outside, though warm in the parlour,' she wrote. The afternoon passed and eventually at half past five the whistle blew signalling the end of the shift and at that point the two women were shown round the mill, seeing the greasy wool from the sheep's back at the beginning of the process, and the finished tweed at the end.

Josiah must have fallen in love with this exotic flower from the South. The following day he sent a carriage to take them for a drive on the moor. Jessie declined the invitation, but Florence accepted. As they drove up onto the moors Josiah told her about his family, of how his parents had worked as weavers and reared a large and healthy family. He told her how his father and his five uncles, all fine lads and good weavers, were laiking (playing i.e. out of work) for six weeks at a time. 'They played in their shirts up back o't'clough yonder, they could addle no brass o' no sort, and had nobbut porridge to live on, and a muffin for their Sunday tea,' Josiah explained. Josiah had four brothers, the third of whom, Ezra, had drowned in the mill dam, though the other four were all now directors of the company.

By the end of the week Josiah had asked, 'Do you want to join us at Black Rock?' a fairly cryptic proposal of marriage. Florence treated it as a joke and headed back to London.

She couldn't get away from him so easily, however. Josiah visited her in London over the following year and at the end of the year she agreed to marry him. 'I found much to admire and love in him', she said. Perhaps this was to the people who raised their eyebrows at such an unlikely match.

When they returned from honeymoon, Josiah's sister Sarah had re-organised the household. She instructed Florence on how to run it:

> Use the back door, not the front, to keep out the dust.
> Don't have bacon and eggs on a Friday for breakfast because Friday is a fettling day and the steel fender in the kitchen needs to be cleaned.
> Polish the fender in the drawing-room yourself.
> Don't leave it to the girls, they won't do it right.

Florence realized there was a power struggle going on here and she had every intention of winning it, whatever the cost to her relationship with her new sister-in-law.

As soon as Sarah had left, she propped open the front door and began a make-over of her home. Over the following few weeks she consigned the equestrian bronzes and the beaded sofa cushions to the attic, stripped out the heavy valances, curtains and flower pots, had the sofa re-covered in chintz and the velour curtains replaced with lighter flowered ones. She gave away the brass fender and fire-irons, had some shelves put up for her books and got rid of the sideboard, the only piece of furniture Josiah was sorry to see go. 'I'm fair grieved. It cost many a pund!' was his comment. But in spite of this, he bought her a new piano.

Sarah was surprised they were not having a wedding 'At Home' day to meet the neighbours, and one can only imagine the tightening of her lips as she saw the waste of those good, heavy curtains and the cost of re-covering a perfectly good sofa with new-fangled southern light-coloured chintz which would show the dirt in no time.

Manufacturers' wives held regular 'at home' days once a month when the stuffy parlours were opened up but still smelled musty. There was cake and talk mainly about the servants. (Perhaps when Florence was not there the topic of conversation was Florence herself!) 'Cleaning down ensures a lot of conversation', Florence comments caustically. Having converted to a studio the old weaving room on the upper floor where Josiah's parents and uncles had spent so many waking hours, Florence tried to invite friends there, but the group gradually dwindled so eventually she stopped asking them. She must have felt very lonely.

She watched the work people as they passed the house on their way to the mill: Nathan, a short man in corduroys and blue smock who provided them with poultry, Sam Hayes, an old man who rarely left the clough (the local word for a valley) and had been walking to the mill since the master was a lad. Now he walked between a tall son and a small woman, his daughter. A row of women menders, arm in arm, with scissors dangling from strings at their waists. They wore black skirts and boots, not clogs, since they worked on the finished cloth in the mending room, which was light, clean and dry. The elite of the workplace.

The girl with the tam-o-shanter and gold-rimmed spectacles was the typist from the office, while the three men in bowler hats were the cashier and his two clerks. They raised their hats when they saw her watching. Edward, the teamer would set out soon with the three horses, Tom, Jim and Polly, on 'their everlasting journeys to the railway' on the far side of the valley for coal to keep the engine going.

When she went out she was greeted by the housewives. You could tell what day of the week it was by what was happening. On Mondays the clough was festooned with washing, Thursday was baking day, Friday fettling (cleaning), when they swabbed the windows and scrubbed the doorsteps, outlining the edges with white.

On Saturdays the girls would fettle and sort out their clothes for the evening when they went into Huddersfield. The lads would eat their dinner, wash and 'don up' before going to the football match. Many of the older men, Florence said dismissively, would stand in a damp field with a lot of yelping dogs for rabbit coursing or follow the Colne Valley pack of harriers.

One afternoon she sat at the top of the hill above the clough, looking down on the mill and the people going about their business. From her vantage point she could see the black smoke rising from the mill chimney, day and night. She could see Josiah and another man measuring – they must be making improvements to the mill manager's, Eli Mallinson's, already substantial house. She could see Nathan collecting eggs and wringing a cockerel's neck for Sunday dinner, and Tom the huntsman cutting up a dead horse for the hounds. The men who had been seeing to the pigs were sitting on a bench under a thorn tree, cattle were feeding in the hilly pasture just below her. There was one poor field with a few dejected stooks of corn. A woman and a small child were making their way with a tea basket for the father, working overtime at the mill. Rooks were cawing in the rookery, a train whistled on its way to Manchester, someone tuned up a concertina and the Slaithwaite church bell was ringing.

Sometimes Florence and Josiah would go up the hill to walk round Blackmoorfoot reservoir, made when Josiah was a boy. Florence, hampered by the petticoats clinging to her black merino stockings and heavy skirt, would follow a few steps behind Josiah, the wind tugging at her head and pulling her hair out from her hat, which was skewered in place by only two pins and a veil. Josiah would point out the houses he visited as a boy on his pony as he went round collecting up the pieces hand woven in nearby cottages.

Josiah's family demonstrate how the woollen industry had developed since the beginning of the century. By mid-century, Josiah's father Charles was working as a master clothier, putting out weaving to journeymen then collecting in the pieces and mending them before selling them at the Cloth Hall in Huddersfield. 'Many preferred to share their bedroom with a great heavy lumbering loom, using their own physical force to pass the shuttle, than go to work in the mill' said Josiah.

'It makes one realise that the coming of the steam engine and the power loom is not very ancient history, that the prosperous mills have not always been there and perhaps may be superseded in another age', Florence commented. How right she was!

On Sundays they went to chapel. This was the thing that least fitted her for living here, she said. You have to attend either church or chapel. The chapel was crowded and it was hot. Josiah was in his Sunday best, with hair oiled and wearing black gloves. He sweat so much he stuck to the seat. The singing was splendid but the sermon! The text was taken from Job and after forty minutes Florence had had enough. She sank into a comatose state, roused only by a whisper from her husband who said, 'Not a word, love. Remember you have to live among 'em'.

The first Monday of September was the local Feast when the mill closed for three days. The workers all went to Blackpool though in the past they would have gone to the local fair. Josiah stayed at home, he had the mill dam to sludge and machinery to move. It took thirty labourers working from six in the morning till dusk to clean out the mud from the dam.

Josiah's naivete could sometimes led to social and family embarrassment which was sometimes just amusing but often hurtful to both of them. On one occasion they were invited to a splendid house in Wath-on-Dearne for the weekend. The husband had been surprised when he visited Josiah on business to discover his intriguingly talented and, for Linthwaite, exotic wife, who played the piano, painted beautiful pictures and could discuss rather more than the state of the spring-cleaning or the difficulty of getting reliable girls to clean the fenders.

It was a real ordeal for Josiah. He was struck dumb, as Florence records, by their imposing hostess and was appalled that he had to dress for dinner. He struggled in vain with his studs until Florence came to his rescue. He forgot to change his socks, so 'large expanses of white woollen stockings showed between his patent leather shoes and his trouser legs. Fortunately he was unaware of them.

The following morning, Sunday, he was counting the hours to get home. 'An elegant maid brought us tea and proceeded to spread embroidered mats for the round baths, one in each room. Josiah, from the bed, not wishing to give trouble, exclaimed,' Nay, Nay, miss, I can wash me when I get home!' The maid ignored him.

Even more painful for both was a visit by two of Florence's nephews. The detail she includes shows just how angry Florence was with her loutish and over-indulged nephews. She would ponder these differences between what her nephews expected and possessed compared with the local people, and even more the poor people who came before her in her role as Poor Law Guardian.

The boys arrived by train. No sandwiches for them on the journey north! They ate in the dining car. They hated the tram to Linthwaite - they complained about being squashed. They didn't stand up for women. When they arrived at Black Rock they didn't want to see the mill. They didn't like the food. They sang beautifully but refused to sing much and flatly refused to sing the songs Josiah asked of them, saying they were 'rotters'. They stopped singing if Florence made a mistake in the accompaniment.

There was nothing to entertain them at Black Rock, given their attitude. Josiah struggled. The one excursion the local people went on was to the Isle of Skye inn on the Greenfield Road out of Meltham. 'We trail off to these forbidding moors, feed on rank bacon and eggs at that grim inn, and face the homeward journey (in the mill cart) by way of Wessenden Valley, and pronounce it 'fair grand!' says Florence, as her nephews' attitudes held up a mirror to her life there.

Josiah took them to watch Yorkshire playing Essex at cricket in Huddersfield, which went down rather well, but otherwise the visit was an almost unmitigated disaster. They were given a goose to take home with them. Josiah tried to give them each a sovereign as they left, but they declined it. After they were waved off at the station Josiah watched the clock and commented on where he thought they would be on their journey. He expected a letter the day after, but it was several days before it arrived.

When it did, Florence read it with dismay and anger. It was addressed to her and not to them both, they informed her that the train had been three minutes late arriving at its destination and they asked her to send all the things they had managed to leave behind. Their mother liked their new suits, they said, and ended, 'I suppose you were glad to get rid of us. Love to Uncle Josiah.' A more off-hand and discourteous letter it would have been hard to find.

They made another visit some time later with their mother and older brother Andrew and their dog. Their mother and Andrew were on their way to Scotland but the younger boys were off-loaded onto Aunt Florence. They brought huge amounts of luggage: bicycles, tennis racquets, guns, fishing rods, dress suit cases. They had needed two carriages to transport them and their luggage from the station. Andrew had brought only four dress suits so had to go shopping.

The younger boys were taken on a works outing in the mill lorry to the Isle of Skye pub again and the Bills o' Jacks pub. When Andrew returned from Scotland he looked ill, Florence supposed from late nights and too much smoking and drinking. He now insisted on smoking nothing but cork-tipped cigarettes. Florence and Josiah must have been pleased to see the back of them.

However, Florence must have felt flattered that the teamster's wife had christened her baby daughter Florence. Perhaps she was finally being granted a place in the little community of Black Rock.

The same could not be said of other mill owners' wives, among whom Florence had failed to find friendship. Progressive whist parties were all the rage. They took place in the afternoon. Everyone dressed up in satin, diamonds, and crepe-de-chine. They kept their hats on. There were chocolates on each table and a gas fire in the dining room. Someone asked Florence if she had ever been rinking. 'No, Florence replied,' I've never done roller skating. I'm interested in votes for women and politics.' 'Oh, I've no time to bother with that!' was the reply. The dreadful afternoon ground on until the mill hooters sounded at 5.30. Florence went home on the tram and was pleased to see Charlie, well known in the area because he earned a living going round the mills selling oranges, nuts and spice. (Whether this is a reference to spices such as ginger or to sweets is not clear).

He blew the organ at chapel.

On one horrendous occasion there was a fire at the mill. This was not unusual, and there was a routine to deal with such untoward happenings. Unfortunately it was the eve of Honley feast and all the men were at the feast, while Josiah was in Blackpool. Florence saw the chimney stack was on fire, and rang the fire brigade and Josiah's brothers. 'Get the buzzer agate,' ('Put the buzzer on') was the terse reply from the Lockwood men. The sound of the buzzer was so loud it was heard over in Honley. The feast ground cleared as if by magic as the men rushed back to Linthwaite. They cleared the designing room, the pattern room and the office and brought the contents to the house, stacking them up in every corner. Sister-in-law Sarah came and made coffee and handed out cake for the workers and by 3am the fire was out. The business was insured, of course, but the mess left behind was disheartening. Charred beams, broken shaftings, roofless walls and smoking piles of raw materials bore witness to the length and strength of the fire, which had started at 9.30 pm.

Politics

When Florence came to the West Riding, she was apolitical. But we have seen that by the time of the progressive whist drives with their gas fired rooms, their boxes of chocolates and everyone dressed up to the nines, she had committed herself to the women's suffrage movement. She describes how she was converted to the cause.

When she arrived at Black Rock she thought politics was not for women but if anything she was a Tory. Josiah, however, was a staunch Liberal and took her to a Liberal Party meeting at the Town Hall. She hated it. She hated the 'hoary-bearded old men and the songs they sang'.

The Colne Valley being Liberal, Liberal speakers to local political meetings were often invited to stay at Black Rock. One such was

John Ward, who was elected MP for Stoke on Trent under a Liberal/Labour ticket. He had had no education and only learned to read when he was in his teens, but in 1899 had founded the Navvies, Bricklayers' and Labourers' Union, and wore gold earrings. Josiah had met him when John Ward was supervising the building of Blackmoorfoot reservoir.

Discussing politics with him, Florence gradually changed her views but explained her aversion to politics by its links to church or chapel, which she found difficult to tolerate. She explained to John Ward that women's place in politics seemed to be to organize bazaars to raise money, and she found that distasteful.

However, one day in 1907 as she came through Linthwaite Fold she saw a crowd of people gathered round a cart on which stood a woman addressing the crowd. It was unusual to see a woman speaking so she made her way towards the cart to hear what she was saying. The woman was Mrs Pankhurst, leader of the Women's Social and Political Union (WSPU), trying to raise support in the Colne Valley for the Independent Labour candidate, Victor Grayson, in the forthcoming Parliamentary by-election. Women should be allowed to exercise a Parliamentary vote, said Mrs Pankhurst, and take part in affairs of state as men did.

Florence went home and must have told her sister-in-law Sarah what she had seen and heard. Unsurprisingly Sarah disagreed with what Mrs Pankhurst had had to say but Florence was not so dismissive. The following day they were haymaking in the field behind the mill. Florence took tea out to the workers and as she did so two young women, little more than girls really, came into the field. One of them wore a dirty, limp, print dress, she had a sunburnt, freckled face, she was perspiring and her voice was hoarse from over-use. 'They look like suffragettes', remarked one of Florence's friends.

They were indeed. Adela Pankhurst was the sweaty one in the dirty print dress. They wanted to know if Josiah would lend them a cart for their evening meeting. Then they said that they wanted to tell people that they thought the vote should be granted to women on the same terms as men. The men present laughed heartily. Josiah lent them the cart, and their meeting duly took place.

The suffragettes, including not just the Pankhursts but Annie Kenney whose two brothers were members of the Colne Valley Labour League (CVLL) were there in force to support the radical left-winger, Victor Grayson. Josiah was not too sure about the wisdom of having lent the suffragettes a cart, seeing as they were preaching against the Liberal Party, of which he was a staunch supporter.

Despite herself, Florence had been impressed with the suffragettes' sincerity. As she thought about it, she became convinced that the Pankhursts were right, but it would have been difficult to join the WSPU, given their opposition to everything Liberal and their activities among striking trade unionists[220]. They were also, on the whole, working class women drawn from the mill girls and their mothers. Florence would not have felt at home there, as she had a position to maintain as a mill owner's wife in both the family and the community.

She kept her feelings about politics quiet for a while though she discussed political matters with John Ward. After discussion with him she joined the National Union of Women's Suffrage Societies (NUWSS) and soon became one of the leading local members, organizing speakers, and making a splendid banner, now in the safekeeping of the Tolson Memorial Museum in Huddersfield. She also made one for the Scalby branch of the NUWSS. Her stepson, now married, had moved there with his wife, a Halifax girl, but that

Florence Lockwood's suffrage banner

banner does not seem to have survived.

Huddersfield had a thriving NUWSS branch drawing its support not just from the town itself but the outlying villages such as Honley, where Miss Emily Siddon, long-time chair of the Board of Guardians and a JP, even though as a woman, her responsibilities were limited to certifying lunatics, had been elected president in her absence[221]. The organization had the support of one of the Aldermen, Allen Gee JP, so the NUWSS was highly respectable and respected as an organization working within the rules of society to bring about a change in Parliamentary voting by gradual degrees. Slow but sure, was their approach. They were suffragists, not suffragettes.

Much to their surprise the Liberals lost the Colne Valley seat to Victor Grayson and the Colne Valley Labour League (CVLL). (For a full account see chapter 13.) Following this shock, the Liberals were keen to recruit new blood into the organization. Florence was invited to chair a meeting at the local Liberal club. She writes unkindly of the women assembled there that evening. 'I found a room full of women with shawls over their heads looking like a flock of penguins.' The speaker was Cicely Corbett, a product of Somerville College and the woman who had established the Liberal Women's Suffrage Group. Cicely was an experienced speaker and gave what she hoped would be a rousing speech to the assembled 'penguins', some of whom were not convinced. 'There's naught wrang wi' men,' one woman was heard to mutter.

As Florence's involvement with the NUWSS increased, Josiah's initial opposition to the aggressive tactics of the suffragettes and apprehension about her involvement with the suffrage movement changed, as a progression of articulate women stayed to enliven their evenings with their intelligent and well informed talk. Black Rock became a haven for suffrage organisers and speakers and Florence records that Josiah seemed proud of her advanced views. If she were speaking at a meeting, he would 'wave his red pocket handkerchief from the audience as a sign of distress', and she would know she had spoken long enough. He would say, 'Thou hast done well, love. Give up.'

On the suffrage front Florence had missed out on the Mud March of February 1907, the first peaceful demonstration organized by the NUWSS. Her progress in local politics however was meteoric. She became president of the Colne Valley Women Liberals and before she knew it, a Poor Law Guardian.

Many of the NUWSS members were strong pacifists, considering that while it was men who went to war, it should be women's role to work for peace. By 1913 the International Women's Suffrage Alliance (IWSA) had been organizing peace conferences for seven years and had gained comfort from the knowledge that across the world there were women struggling for the vote and for peace. Women in New Zealand had had the vote since 1893 while Finland was the first European country to follow suit in 1906, so there were signs that, world-wide, their pleas for recognition were producing results.

In 1913 the IWSA organized their seventh annual conference in Budapest. Thirty delegates from Britain were chosen, Florence being one of them. They congregated on Victoria station, a sea of red, white and green, thirty women and one man from the Men's League for Women's Suffrage – a brave man indeed! – waiting for the boat train to take them to Dover. Florence records that she did not stand out as an eccentric in this band of women. She was among the more conservative members, surrounded by representatives from the Quakers, the Fabians, the Jewish League, the Church League, the Catholic Society and others.

On the boat she shared a cabin with a woman who could get into all her clothes without help from a maid! How Florence managed is not recorded. In Dresden she shared a room with Mrs Cobden-Sanderson, daughter of Richard Cobden a founder of the Anti-Corn Law League. Mrs Cobden-Sanderson was a Socialist, a Christian Scientist, vegetarian, and founder member of the Women's Freedom League and the Women's Tax Resistance League an organization which linked paying taxes to the right to vote, formed in 1909. They travelled via Dresden to Vienna, where they spent two days, then took a steamer to Budapest. On the Austrian border they were handed over from the Austrian suffragists to the Hungarians, arriving in Budapest at 10pm.

There were 2,800 delegates congregated at the Redoute to hear speeches all given in German and French. The theme of the speeches was that women wanted the vote so they could bring influence to bear on the questions of the day: to work for purity, temperance, the care and protection of children and to work against social injustice and the causes of war. For the first time in her life Florence heard the terms pacifism and pacifist, and she met Professor Anna Ehrsam, with whom she felt an immediate rapport. She wrote,

> The greatest wonder was that we should have been there; we, a hitherto isolated and stationary sex, trained to keep our love and interest within small circles. It was wonderful that we should have travelled so far and opened our hearts to strangers working on the common ground of a need, felt by all – Women's Emancipation.

This feeling of euphoria did not last long. Professor Ehrsam's visit to Black Rock the following year was interrupted by the outbreak of war in August 1914, which sent Anna Ehrsam rushing home and precipitated a crisis in the suffrage movement.

The WSPU, the suffragettes, supported the government and suspended their work for women's suffrage. The members of the NUWSS split into two factions, those who supported the government position and felt that the movement should use its networks and structure to help the government, and those who felt that war was against everything the Women's movement stood for and who wanted to pursue the path of negotiation with the enemy. This difference of opinion led to half the executive committee resigning.

These divisions were to be found within families, too. Florence was a pacifist, though Joseph was not and this resulted in a strain in their relationship. August 4th, 1914, the day war broke out, saw her leafletting in the town centre, accompanied only by the Quakers. Pacifism was not popular in Florence's neck of the woods and she comments that 'War always breeds war'.

The immediate consequence of the outbreak of war was the decline in trade in the Colne Valley. Poor families were pushed into even more dire poverty and the Education Authority began feeding the poorest children. Then the government put in orders for khaki cloth for their soldiers, while the French ordered blue for theirs and trade picked up.

Enemy aliens were rounded up and taken away to camps before, in many cases, being deported to the colonies. A German photographer in Huddersfield disappeared, never to return. Dark blinds were fitted to mills, houses, trams because of the fear of Zeppelins overhead, and a letter from Sam in Scalby informed them that a hundred people had been killed in Scarborough by bombardments from German gunboats, and that they had been instructed by the government that in the event of invasion they should carry out a scorched earth policy: burn ricks and slaughter farm animals. Every mill had to have someone sitting by the telephone all night to receive messages of approaching raiders and warn night workers, many of them girls.

A Linthwaite War Distress Relief committee was formed, whose first task was to fit out a large house on the hill above Linthwaite to accommodate thirty Belgian refugees. There were weekly subscriptions deducted from the wages of the mill workers to help starving Belgians and a large Belgian flag flew at Royds Hall, which had become a military hospital.

Florence decided that knitting was one of the curses of the war.

On trams needles clicked. There was a Soldiers' and Sailors' Comfort Fund at the Linthwaite Liberal Club and there were knitting teas. Convalescents from Royds Hall were invited to the Drill Hall at Longwood for a 'knitting tea'. There was a band playing and cups of tea were being served. One of the soldiers told her he thought it was a nice occupation for a woman. He patted his wife's shoulder. 'This little woman here can knit without knowing it', he boasted.

'That's just why I condemn it,' Florence replied tartly. 'A machine can do better. The women ought to be thinking about how to avert war!'

With the WSPU actively supporting the war effort, militant suffragettes were released from gaol; in 1916 conscription was introduced, and younger men from Black Rock marched off to do their duty and fight for King and Country. They 'fair liked the life' when they set out, but when they returned from France - those who did return - had a visceral hatred of the Germans. A meeting held in St George's Square by the pacifists who were recommending internationalism went completely unrecorded by any of the local papers, Florence notes.

Florence listed nine of her nephews and cousins, five of whom were killed or wounded:

>Herbert Kennedy killed in 1915;
>Colonel Jack Lampton killed in 1916;
>Colonel Charlie Kennedy died 1916;
>Noel Kennedy wounded and missing;
>Captain Peter Bird wounded.

Four others seem to have escaped unscathed from the bloodbath which was the Great War. So farewell cork-tipped cigarettes and dress suits. What a waste! No wonder her pacifism was reinforced by the slaughter of her family.

At the end of the war in 1919 Florence and Josiah both caught Spanish flu, a virus that affected a quarter of the British population and resulted in 228,000 deaths in Britain alone. Josiah was now sixty-five years old while Florence was fifty-seven. Time to retire, they thought, and leave Black Rock. Josiah died in 1924 at which point Florence felt too sad to stay in the north. She returned to London and lived there until she died in 1937 and was cremated at Golders Green though her ashes were brought back to Linthwaite and buried alongside her husband[222]. Her book, published in 1932, was entitled *An ordinary life* though it patently was not.

Did Florence think she had made the right choice in marrying Josiah? Many of her friends and acquaintances must have found it difficult to understand. For such a sophisticated woman to marry such a rough diamond, must have been a puzzle. But, as she wrote, there was much to admire and love about him. He was generous, kind and loving. He adored her and encouraged her to expand her interests and he was immensely proud of her.

He also had money. This was not to be sneezed at. When Florence contemplated her future at the age of thirty-seven, when she first came across Josiah, she was earning her living in a notoriously unreliable career. She was popular enough at the time but fashions in art can change and what would have become of her in old age, if that had been the case and she had failed to save enough to see her through? Reliance on relatives? Handouts from the Distressed Gentlefolks' Aid Association? Josiah must have seemed a much better bet.

So besides financial security, how did her stint in the West Riding change her? It gave her increased political awareness and the ability to put her changed perspectives into practice. It gave her greater social awareness, and the opportunity to meet other committed and radical women who wanted to not just change the world but save it from the horrors of war.

Her graphic account of life with Josiah gives us a vivid impression of life at the end of the 19th century, and shows that mill owners such as Josiah were not much removed from the realities of the life of their workforce. When the workers went on holiday, Josiah stayed and cleaned out the mill dam. He was part of the community centred round the mill, not some remote, rich head of the company who lived off the work of the mill hands. He was seen to work hard, he was knowledgeable and shared the ups and downs of their lives. The old people of that community had known him as a boy, had seen him grow up into the man he was, and they respected him. He spoke like them, used the same language and shared their values. There would be little room here for the revolutionary ideas which brought about such momentous changes in the world. The Colne Valley and Black Rock remained a bastion of Liberal thinking for many years.

Chapter 13 - The Suffragettes

> Put me on an island where the girls are few.
> Put me amongst the most ferocious lions in the zoo.
> Put me on a treadmill – I'll never, never fret.
> But for heaven's sake don't put me with a suffragette.[223]

Florence Lockwood and her friend had met one of the Pankhurst family - Adela - and had a firm idea of what suffragettes looked like: scruffy, sweaty, uncaring of their appearance and forward - prepared to talk to people they had not been introduced to and to men at that! They had opinions. and they were not afraid to express them. Nor were they afraid to be laughed at. Tough, then, with radical views not befitting cultured and well brought up ladies and certainly not the kind of women Liberal ladies might want to befriend.

Florence Lockwood had settled for what her social position required of her: the Liberal Party, the suffragists, and peace campaigners. There was one woman, however, who, middle class though she was, and living in Edgerton, that bastion of middle class Victorian gentility in Huddersfield, went against the social trend. This was Bertha Lowenthal, daughter of the German wool merchant Joseph Lowenthal. Born in 1837, she was the third of four siblings, her older brother Arthur having died at the age of 15.

The Lowenthals were part of the German community who had settled in the West Riding because of the wool trade with Germany. By the latter half of the nineteenth century the demand for wool in the West Riding had far outstripped what the locality could provide and much of the wool used in the cloth industry was imported from Germany.

There was a nucleus of very prosperous German families, several of whom lived in the newly developed suburb of Edgerton. German neighbours of the Lowenthals at The Grange included the Fischers, the Huths, the Liebrichs, the Liebmanns, the Anders family and the Zossenheim brothers, Maximilian and Julius, shipping agents.

Some of these names are instantly recognizable from their support of the Mechanics Institute and the Female Educational Establishment[224], so we can assume that along with Frederick Schwann they were keen on promoting education among the working classes. Bertha was also librarian of the Female Educational Establishment from 1863 to 1876 and in those thirteen years must have met a considerable number of girls and women who wanted to improve their knowledge and understanding of the world around them. Not the kind, therefore, to be unaware of the injustices of society, but the kind who would have the will to change things.

We have met the Pankhursts in the Huddersfield area in the run up to the 1907 Colne Valley by-election, but that was some thirteen years after the WSPU had been formed. Mrs Emmeline Pankhurst, a formidable and impetuous woman, had been active in the suffrage movement since the age of fifteen. She had first burst on the political scene when she became one of the speakers on a series of lectures across the north of England instigated by Lydia Becker. Miss Becker was another of the German diaspora though at one generation removed. Her father had come from Thuringia and established himself in Manchester. Lydia herself was highly educated and interested in botany and astronomy. She published monographs on botanical subjects and corresponded with Charles Darwin on a variety of botanical matters.

It was at a meeting of the National Association for the Advancement of Science that Miss Becker heard Barbara Bodichon give a paper with the intriguing title of 'Reasons for the

Enfranchisement of Women'. Completely bowled over by the logic of this, on her return to Manchester she formed the Manchester Women's Suffrage Committee and became a tireless worker for the cause. She and her associates in the Women's Suffrage Committee obtained votes for women in municipal elections, on school boards, and even in the Isle of Man. She was active in the West Riding, encouraging the formation of the Batley Women's Suffrage group as early as 1876. She founded and co-wrote the Women's Suffrage Journal and in 1874 organised the lectures where Emmeline Pankhurst, nee Goulden, cut her oratorical teeth.[225]

Towards the end of the nineteenth century, trade unionism had become much more of a force to be reckoned with, with women working in the mills realising that unionism was a useful tool in the balance of power between mill owners and their employees. This was paralleled by the growth of the Labour Party. At the end of the century unions were considering introducing a political levy to support the Independent Labour party (ILP), formed in 1893. But how was a political levy to a political party going to further the interests of women, who had no vote? Not at all, as far as they could see. A petition was started in 1896 asking for the vote for women and great efforts were made to involve women workers in the northern towns. In all 257,000 signatures were collected

It was sent to Parliament, but as usual achieved very little.

The Labour Party, as opposed to the Independent Labour Party (ILP), a separate organization at that point, was not enthusiastic about the idea, either. They thought tangling with women's suffrage would damage their political agenda. There was a property qualification to the vote which ensured that only a third of men in Britain could vote. Therefore to press for votes for women would, because of the property qualification, only enfranchise better-off women. These would be unlikely to vote Labour, and would swell the numbers of Tory or Liberal voters. Not a good idea, in the view of the Labour activists of the time.

It was at this stage that Emmeline Pankhurst, previously an enthusiastic member of the Labour Party, decided it was unworthy of her support. In 1903 she left and formed the Women's Social and Political Union with the motto: 'Deeds, not Words'.

Their first political action was in 1905 when Viscount Grey and Winston Churchill were speaking in Manchester. When the set speeches were over and the meeting was thrown open to questions, Viscount Grey was asked by Christabel Pankhurst, Emmeline's daughter, and Annie Kenney whether he would support votes for women. They were ignored, so Annie jumped on a chair and unfurled her banner demanding votes for women. They were hurriedly bundled out of the hall and pushed down the steps outside, whereupon they held an impromptu meeting and were arrested for assaulting a policeman. They refused to pay the fine and were sent to prison, Annie for three days and Christabel for a week. This made the headlines in the national newspapers, and the Pankhursts realized that social disruption was an important political tool.

Annie, born in Springhead on the eastern edges of Oldham, was the fifth child in a family of twelve. She was very useful to the Pankhursts because of her working class origins, and her experiences of working in a mill as a half-timer from the age of ten. She was devoted to Christabel and remained a loyal member of the WSPU throughout its existence. She suffered imprisonment and force-feeding, and was the public face of the movement in London when the WSPU moved from Manchester. She was the link between the movement and Christabel when Christabel fled to France in 1912 to avoid prison, travelling in disguise and suffering horribly from seasickness with every crossing of the Channel.

Although always presented as a typical mill girl, Annie came from an aspirational working class family. A typical pattern in such families was for the older children to work from an early age, as did Annie, and when the family had more money from these wage earners, for the younger ones to be better educated. Two of Annie's sisters became Montessori teachers, one brother was a writer and another a successful businessman in Manchester.[226]

The following year after their confrontation with Lord Grey and Winston Churchill, there was a general election. Huddersfield was held by James Woodhouse for the Liberals, but he resigned in the November to take up a post as Rail and Canal Traffic Commissioner, so the by-election was scheduled for November 1906.

The Huddersfield Suffragettes

The WSPU set up an office in Huddersfield and Mrs Pankhurst visited to encourage voters not to vote for the Liberal candidate, Arthur Sherborne, in spite of his support for the enfranchisement of women. She failed in this respect, but gained enough support in the area to be able to draft in Annie Williams from Newcastle to support the formation of a Huddersfield branch of the WSPU. The minute book of their meetings is one of the rare survivals from this period and as such gives us an insight into the workings of the branch.

Edith Key, nee Proctor, (1872-1937) was the illegitimate daughter of a Bradford mill worker, Grace Proctor, and Joseph Fawcett, a mill owner. Raised largely by her mother's sisters, she left full time school at the age of thirteen but had been a part-timer from her tenth birthday, going to school in the morning and the mill in the afternoon one week and reversing this the following week.

By this time she was living with her aunt Martha in Huddersfield, and being musical joined the Choral Society. Here she met Frederick

Mrs Pankhurst leaving Huddersfield by train.
By kind permission of the Huddersfield Exposed web site

Key, a musician blinded at the age of six by an arrow while playing a game of Robin Hood. By 1891 when he married Edith, Fred Key was working as a piano tuner and ran his business from a music shop in West Parade (now Trinity Street). There he not only tuned pianos, but repaired them and composed music. Edith ran the business side bringing up their two sons at the premises behind the shop. Fred was a member of the ILP and was often to be found presiding over outdoor meetings of the group.

After the demise of the local branch of the WSPU, Edith still maintained contact with the Pankhursts and other figures in the movement, as her son Lancelot witnessed. Following the passing of the Prisoners' (Temporary discharge for Ill Health reasons) Act in 1913, the 'Cat and Mouse Act', which released suffragettes from prison when their health had been undermined by protracted hunger strikes, then re-arrested them after a certain time, the Key household sheltered some of those who went into hiding rather than go back to prison. The Keys were at this time living in a rambling house in Bradford Road, with a great many nooks and crannies suitable for hiding people. The Keys were risking being sent to prison themselves by their actions, but this did not deter them.[227]

Eliza Thewlis and her Daughter Dora

Back in the heyday of the Huddersfield branch, however, on March 5 1907 Mrs Eliza Thewlis chaired the meeting held at the Friendly and Trades Club in Northumberland Street. The main part of the meeting was given over to discussing what to do about the bill for the enfranchisement of women which had been put forward by Willoughby Dixon, Chair of the London Liberal Federation, and which had yet again been rejected. They were urged to take part in a protest march to Parliament to emphasise that women felt strongly about the vote, and to counteract the views of some MPs who had expressed the opinion that the majority of women were not interested in having a vote and didn't understand why yet another bill had been submitted. Ten women from Huddersfield volunteered to go to London, among them sixteen year old Dora Thewlis, Eliza's daughter.

Dora, and probably her mother and father, keen socialists, understood that she was going to represent her mother and sisters, too, and they felt she would be in the care of her fellow suffragettes so could come to no harm. Eliza accompanied her daughter to Manchester and left her in the company of other suffragettes travelling down to London, rail fare paid from the funds of the WSPU.

The protest march on March 20th started at Caxton Hall and, led by Viscountess Harberton, keen cyclist and president of the Rational Dress Society, proceeded to Parliament to lobby the politicians. At least, that was the idea. They never got as far as the Parliament buildings. Their way was barred by a line of policemen which the demonstrators tried to breach. To no avail. They were manhandled and roughed up in a way which perhaps none of them had quite expected. Seventy-five of them were arrested, including Dora, along with three other Huddersfield women, Mrs Hellawell, Mrs Pinnance, and Miss Anne Hopson. They were accused of breaching the peace and remanded to Holloway prison for a week.

The magistrate, Mr Horace Smith, was outraged to find such a young person in the court. 'Why are you not in school?' he asked in a bewildered fashion. It reflected discreditably, he thought, on the people who had helped her come[228]. Mr Pethick-Lawrence offered to stand bail for Dora and another seventeen year old from Blackpool, but the offer was refused. Dora was consigned to Holloway Prison with the rest of the suffragettes, but she was treated rather differently. She had her own clothes taken away and had to dress in prison uniform – a blue bodice and skirt, white check apron, and a kerchief, heavy shoes and a disc around her neck inscribed with a number, E.4-21.

She was kept in solitary confinement and applications to visit her were refused, until Mrs Pethick-Lawrence rang the prison governor and pleaded Dora's case. Dora hated the food, so ate very little and when a journalist from the Daily Mail interviewed her five days after her arrest, he said she was pale and thin, her spirit broken and feeling intensely lonely. 'I feel that tired,' she said. 'These clothes are so heavy.' The journalist observed that remand prisoners were not usually told to wear prison uniform as they were innocent until proved guilty, an opinion he checked with a lawyer and found to be correct. Her mother had written her a letter, in which she said,

> Dear Child,
>
> You might have told the magistrate when he said you

were too young and ought to have been in school, 'What about working at Huddersfield at a loom for ten hours at a stretch?' You know what you went to London for and what you were doing. You are a member of the Women's Social and Political Union, who are looking after you, so do your duty by the WSPU.'

Dora was finding it difficult to follow her mother's instructions. She told the journalist she had had enough of prison but was angry that the magistrate had offered to pay her fare home out of the poor box. 'My father can pay,' she said, 'and I have a little money'. The magistrate had written to her parents, rebuking them and offering to pay her fare, as Dora said, from the poor box, an added insult from a man completely unaware of the realities of life in the West Riding. Dora's parents replied in scrupulously polite language, showing they were not the poverty-stricken uneducated, careless people he obviously thought them.

The Sheffield Daily Telegraph of 28th March carries the text of their letter. They appreciated the magistrate's solicitude, they said, and hoped he extended similar to other young girls in the dock.

> We agree that seventeen-year-olds should be in school, but we respectfully remind his Honour that girls of Dora's age in her station of life are in this part of this Christian kingdom of England compelled by their thousands to spend ten hours a day in health-destroying factories, and that the conditions and regulations under which they toil for others' gain are sanctioned by law, in the making of which women have no voice.

Dora spent a week in prison and was then escorted to the station for her journey home to Huddersfield. The WSPU asked to be allowed to collect her from prison and see her off at the station, but this was refused, and a wardress accompanied her, shaking her fist at photographers and journalists as they waited to catch the two o'clock train. The WSPU had however provided sandwiches and chocolates for Dora, which may have cheered her up. She was accompanied the whole of the way to Huddersfield by the wardress and was met at the station by her mother and sisters[229]. There were, however, no other suffragettes present and Jill Liddington suggests that the local branch members may have felt alienated, feeling that Dora being so young had undermined their credibility as responsible members of society[230]. It seems very likely that the humiliation visited on Dora had a lasting effect on her. She would not forget being supervised by a prison officer on her journey home, nor the invidious treatment meted out in prison.

The meeting of July 30th asked the secretary to write to Mrs Thewlis explaining the feelings of the branch towards her and asking Mrs Thewlis to work agreeably or resign from the branch. This was carried unanimously. The letter sent from the meeting must have made Mrs Thewlis very hurt and angry. They wrote:

> Although to a woman we recognize your gifts as a speaker and your undoubted usefulness as such, we feel that your power to sway the members to certain action tends in many cases to over-ride their better judgement. In the second place the feeling is that much unpleasant contention results whenever matters arise in which you seem determined that your will shall rule. And thirdly the members feel sure that if you could only realize as they do, that the membership of the branch and its influence is being rapidly reduced, mainly on account of the above

reasons, you would, as a woman desirous of seeing the branch flourish, and its influence grow, do your utmost to make our business meetings pleasant memories in a bitter struggle for justice for women.

Having received a letter such as that, it would have been astonishing if Mrs Thewlis had continued to be a member.[231]

Dora's treatment by the magistrate was aimed at breaking her spirit and making sure she did not tangle with politics again. It seems to have succeeded in not only making her wary of English politics, but making her disillusioned with life in England. In 1912 she and her sister Evelyne emigrated to Australia. Her parents and two other sisters joined them in 1920 and Dora remained active in politics, albeit in Australia where she would already have the vote, till the end of her life[232]. Eliza died of a heart attack on her way back from Australia aboard the *Moreton Bay* as they approached the Suez Canal in July of 1930. Her husband returned to Australia in the October and lived in Geelong until he died at the age of 84.

In the wake of the events in London of March 1907, where a quarter of the women arrested came from the West Riding[233], Huddersfield WSPU held a mass meeting, suggested by Annie Williams at the May 28 meeting of the branch. It celebrated the work of the Huddersfield 'Martyrs', the ten women who had marched to Parliament alongside Dora Thewlis and were present on the stage in St George's Square.

A further outdoor meeting held in Marsden, was not a success. One of the speakers was Eliza Thewlis, so this must have been well before the branch sent its letter asking her to modify her attitude or leave. The Huddersfield women were subjected to a barrage of verbal abuse, then a rain of eggs, banana skins and assorted rubbish, followed by half bricks and stones. The women fled across a fairground to the home of Mary Scawthorne and barricaded themselves in. Mrs Scawthorne had been one of the Huddersfield women arrested along with Dora Thewlis and jailed for fourteen days in Holloway prison[234]. Fortunately, as often happens in Marsden, it began to rain, and the persecutors dispersed, it being fun to lob bricks and fish heads at women who didn't know their place, but not so good when it poured with rain.

The Colne Valley By-election

The WSPU may not have been entirely successful in the Huddersfield by-election of 1906, but there was a further by-election looming in the Colne Valley in June of the following year. James Kitson, a Liberal, had held the seat in 1906 unopposed but had been elevated to the peerage so now left a vacancy. The Colne Valley Labour League (CVLL) decided to put up a candidate, as did the Conservatives against the Liberal nominee.

The CVLL chose twenty five year old Victor Grayson, a fiery Liverpudlian with a fine turn of phrase, and plenty of experience on the ILP speaking circuit. Well known in the Huddersfield area because of this, he had no practical experience of any other kind, but it was hoped his oratory would carry the day. The local supporters were out of the stocks early. His leaflets were ready for distribution, his canvassers were prepared long before the Liberal or Conservative candidates. This was no bad thing, considering the local paper, the *Colne Valley Guardian*, was so staunchly Liberal it refused to publish anything about him. His literature said it all, however. Fenner Brockway [235] said, 'His campaign was like a religious revival… Socialism was preached as a new hope of deliverance to the poor, and the poor responded.'[236] Ironically, of course, the poor would have no vote in this election.

Grayson supported tackling the unemployment problem, old age pensions, nationalizing the land, railways and canals, free trade, progressive and unsectarian education for all, free maintenance of school children, abolishing the House of Lords, government reform, progressive income tax (i.e. wealthier people would pay more tax than the less well off), an eight hour working day for all, payment for MPs and, crucially, votes for women.

On this topic he said, 'The placing of women constitutionally in the same category as infants, idiots, and peers does not impress me as either manly or just. If returned, I am prepared to give the most immediate and enthusiastic support to a measure according women the vote ON THE SAME TERMS AS MEN.' Who could resist? Certainly not the WSPU!

Annie Kenney joined the CVLL alongside her brothers Reginald and Rowland to canvass throughout the constituency. The Labour Party decided not to support Grayson, but the ILP wheeled out speakers and canvassers. Among the more colourful characters supporting Grayson were Kathleen Bruce Glasier, a well-known and popular speaker in the area, and Daisy, Countess of Warwick, a staunch left-winger and ex-mistress of Edward VII, known as the babbling brook because of her inability to be discreet. She sent her private secretary.

The election aroused great excitement. Looms in the local mills were decorated with the colours of the candidates: red, of course, for Grayson, blue for Wheeler, the Conservative, and yellow for Bright, the Liberal. Having always been a Liberal seat, the Liberals were fairly laid back about the whole process. There was little room for doubt that they would win.

Voting day arrived, a warm and sunny June day. There were 11,771 voters registered in the sprawling Colne Valley constituency, which spread across from the Colne Valley taking in many of the moorland villages to the west. There was an astonishing 88% turnout but the locals would have to wait till the following day to know who had won.

The count took place in Slaithwaite Townhall the following day and as the morning wore on the crowds gathered. The Liberal agent was predicting a 500 majority for Bright and the Socialists sang to keep their spirits up. The voting returns were:

A. Victor Grayson	3,648
P. Bright	3,495
G.C.H. Wheeler	3,227

The CVLL could hardly believe their luck. They followed their hero to the Dartmouth Arms, some sixty yards along the way, and listened to his victory speech. He, of course, praised the CVLL workers, and finished his address with the stirring words 'We stand for equality, human equality, sexual equality… for the abolition of sex ties… It is a splendid victory, comrades.'

And so it was. A flurry of political activity followed. But in the Winter Sunday Lecture programme 1908-1909 held at Slaithwaite Townhall, only one woman, the redoubtable Kathleen Bruce Glasier, is listed among the speakers. Not much progress there, then! And in 1910 at the next general election, Grayson lost the seat and the constituency reverted to its former support for the Liberal Party.

Another Dora: Dora Marsden

We have seen how Dora Thewlis hit the headlines. There was also another Dora, Dora Marsden, (1882-1960) born in the Colne Valley some twenty-five years before Grayson's magnificent by-election victory. She was a Marsden girl who lived the first few years of her life at The Hey, in the hills above the village.

Dora was a clever girl, daughter of Fred Marsden, a woollen waste manufacturer, and his wife Hannah and the fourth of five children.

When Dora was eight years old, her father, whose business was in serious decline, left Marsden with his eldest son to emigrate to America. Hannah and his other four children were left to fend for themselves as best they could. No doubt the two older children would be able to find work as part-timers in a local mill, and Hannah could take in sewing, but it must have underlined to Dora the absolute necessity for a woman to be financially independent.

She became a pupil teacher at the age of thirteen and qualified as a teacher at eighteen. She then won a Queen's Scholarship to Owens College, Manchester in 1900 shortly before it was renamed as the University of Manchester. Christabel Pankhurst was a fellow student and Dora also came under the influence of such feminist women as Isabella Ford, Teresa Billington and Eva Gore-Booth, the Irish poet.

In 1903 Dora graduated with an upper second class degree and started work as a qualified teacher, which must have been a relief to the family, given that the job had not only a regular salary but also a pension. By 1908 Dora had become head of a teacher-training centre in Altrincham, though she stayed in touch with her friends in the WSPU.

She was one of nine suffragettes from the Manchester area who acted as a speaking corps to accompany Adela Pankhurst at a huge meeting in St George's Square in Huddersfield on October 1st, 1908. Whether because of the warm, sunny weather or the 'unsparing use of chalk' or both, it certainly brought the people out, which, given the Liberal support in the town, surprised even Dora Marsden.

There were lorries arranged in what she describes as a tuning fork layout, with Mrs Pankhurst and Miss Rona Robinson M.Sc. on the central bridge part of the fork in front of the statue of Sir Robert Peel, with Miss Lillian Williamson B.A., Mrs Morris and Mrs Lee on the right flank and Miss Drummond and Miss Capper on the left, while 'Miss Gawthorpe with Miss Clarkson, Miss Adela Pankhurst and Miss Dora Marsden B.A. were on the lorries approaching the tramlines.'

Dora was surprised at the attentive hearing given to the speakers, especially as the town was such a noted Liberal stronghold. Almost every argument went home, she said, 'especially those relating to the industrial position of women'. Presumably this is a reference to the much lower wages women were earning in the textile industry. The meeting lasted for an hour and a half when all the speakers had left the platform except for Adela Pankhurst. One man in the crowd was heard to say, 'My, but that *is* a game 'un!' and an eight year old tugged at Dora's sleeve and asked, 'Will you be open again tonight?'.

Most of the literature they had with them was sold, and there was a good collection. Resolutions were passed unanimously and 'we left feeling that another strong link had been forged in a chain of successes already long and strong.'[237]

Dora then became a paid worker for the WSPU and was arrested and imprisoned several times in 1909-1910[238]. This was the year when the suffragettes began hunger strikes. Whether Dora did this we do not know. What we do know, however, is that the same year she spent an uncomfortable and dangerous night in the cupola of the Empire Hall in Southport, in order to evade the security surrounding the visit of Winston Churchill.

She was soon disillusioned however with the WSPU. She felt they were too militant and so focused on getting the vote for women that they suppressed any discussion of feminism and analysis of what they were aiming for. She was not alone in being disappointed with the suffragette movement and Christabel Pankhurst in particular. Mrs Pankhurst and Christabel had even managed to fall out with the Pethick-Lawrences and the finances of the movement were opaque.

Suffragettes leafleting in Huddersfield
By kind permission of the Huddersfield Exposed web site

Money seemed to come in and flow out of the coffers with no accountability, as far as anyone could see.

Dora resigned in 1911 but by this time she had made the acquaintance of Harriet Shaw Weaver, who was to provide financial support for her for many years. Together they edited '*The Freewoman*', a weekly feminist review, which was extremely forthright and covered such topics as sex, marriage, motherhood and woman's sphere in the country. Rebecca West and H.G. Wells wrote for it, but newsagents in the end refused to stock it because of its outspoken content, which was deemed obscene.

The paper was then re-launched as the *New Freewoman*, and later *The Egoist*. Dora was influential in early modern British and American literature. She published *Portrait of the artist as a young man* by James Joyce in instalments but *The Egoist* collapsed in 1919.

In 1912 she was living in Southport with her mother and a friend called Grace Jardine and remained there until her mother's death in 1936, when she moved to the Lake District. She published two quasi-religious books, *The Definition of the Godhead* and *Mysteries of Christianity* in 1930 but in 1934 suffered a nervous breakdown. After a suicide attempt in 1935, she entered the Royal Crichton Hospital, Dundee, her hospital fees paid by her brother-in-law, and she remained there until her death in 1960. A sad end after such a promising beginning.

The Pankhursts

Of all the women fighting for female suffrage the Pankhurst family is probably the best known. Emmeline and her husband Richard, a lawyer, had five children: There were two boys, Francis Henry, born in 1884, who died at the age of four, and Henry Francis, the youngest of the family, born in 1889. He died when he was twenty years old, and it is the three surviving daughters, Christabel, Sylvia and Adela who were caught up in the suffragette movement, with Adela being the least well known.

We have seen that she was a hard working member of the family and participated fully in the fight for the suffrage. She does not, however, seem to have had much recognition for the part she played. This may have been something to do with family dynamics. It was a turbulent family, each member filled with a great sense of self-belief and it seems to have been Christabel, her mother's favourite, who was seen as the driving force behind the militancy of the WSPU. Christabel and Sylvia parted company because of Sylvia's dedication to socialism and her sympathy with the multiple problems of the working class women she lived among in the East End of London.

Having spent a month in Holloway in 1906 for the cause, and having worked so solidly in the West Riding, it seems odd that Adela got so little recognition from her mother. Christabel seems to have actively disliked Adela, and referred to her as 'a very black sheep'[239]. Adela was a pacifist and was critical of the militancy of the WSPU. In 1912 following a breakdown in her health, she was persuaded by Emmeline to withdraw from campaigning and took a horticulture course which led to a strenuous job which she soon abandoned, going to Switzerland as a governess. She was still however seen as subversive and as having strayed from the true path of feminism and was persuaded by her mother to go to Australia. Emmeline paid the £20 fare, and Adela sailed away from Britain, never to see her family again.

This did not mean the end of her militancy, however. She became a Communist and spoke against conscription, leading marches in Melbourne, which resulted in imprisonment from 1917 to 1918. At the end of the Great War she met and married a staunch unionist and socialist, Thomas Walsh. This was apparently a happy marriage and resulted in the birth of five children, one son and four daughters.

She was however impetuous and restless, and as she got older she became much more rigid in her attitudes. In 1929 she formed the Australian branch of a London based organization, the Women's Guild of Empire and turned against her more left wing views. In 1939 she spoke out against war, which, as can be imagined, alienated the conservative Women's Guild of Empire. As the ODNB puts it, she managed to offend 'communists, socialists, trade unionists, patriots, feminists, nationalists, imperialists, and conservatives'. Most of Australian society, in fact. She died in 1961 and is buried in Sydney beside her husband.

Chapter 14 - Greenhead High School for Girls

When Dora Thewlis came up before the magistrate in 1906 he was scandalized that a sixteen year old was in court instead of in school. Her parents were quick to point out that they agreed with the magistrate that a girl of Dora's age should be in school, not working in the mill on a ten hour shift. This spells out the ideas people had about education, and their expectations of the education system. Secondary education, from the age of eleven or twelve, was for those families who could afford for their children not to be earning a wage. Many ten year olds were half-timers.

The 1870 Education Act had allowed local authorities to raise a special rate to fund board schools offering Primary education to children from five years old until the early teens. Between 1876 and 1880 attendance at school became compulsory though it was not until 1891 that schooling became free. The middle classes could afford to educate their children beyond the age of eleven, while the working classes could not, so education was irredeemably defined by class.[240]

After the age of twelve, education was available for those who could afford it in endowed grammar schools and for a small number of bright working class children whose families prized education there were scholarships to be competed for. Hunt has pointed out that early in the nineteenth century middle-class schools had not been overly concerned with training the intellect but in turning out gentlemen and ladies, with all the skills that that involved.[241]

For girls, as readers of Jane Austen's works will know, a great deal of the curriculum consisted of deportment, music, embroidery, painting water colours, netting purses and the like, skills to attract a husband. For a discerning husband, according to Mr Darcy, a love of reading and a well furnished mind would also be required.

In 1895 the Bryce report found that the endowment and management of grammar schools had been widely reformed, that the curricula had become subject to greater scrutiny, that the middle class character of schools had been strengthened, although allowing a limited number of bright working class children access and that secondary education for girls had made significant progress.[242]

1902 saw a major upheaval in the field of education. The Education Act of that year saw school boards that had been established in 1870 abolished. Local Authorities assumed responsibility for education and administered elementary schools, which were now funded partly out of the rates and partly by central government grants.[243]

Women, who had been able to become governors of Board schools, were no longer allowed to sit on these elected boards. At government level the Education Department was renamed as the Board of Education with expanded administrative responsibilities. Government grants became available for funding new municipal secondary schools and the Board of Education assumed responsibility for their inspection. These schools were categorized as either 'recognised', i.e. for grant purposes, or 'efficient' i.e. financially autonomous but fulfilling certain criteria.[244]

The consequence of the availability of grants for secondary education meant there was an incentive to establish a municipal high school in Huddersfield, to join those already up and running in Leeds, Bradford, Wakefield, Halifax and Keighley.

The Municipal High School

In Huddersfield there had long been secondary grammar school education for boys, but very little for girls. Some girls attended the Higher Grade School in New North Road known as the Boys' College, and there were also places at Fartown and Longwood

Grammar schools. There was no secondary school purely for girls. While the 1902 Act could provide funding for a girls' school, there were so many arguments over the kind of school – technical or more intellectual – with the arguments founded on strongly held religious beliefs, that the education committee asked Sir Michael Sadler, an educationalist and descendant of Oastler's friend, a Professor of History and Administration of Education at Victoria University (later renamed the University of Manchester) to write a report on the matter[245]. He recommended a public High School for girls which should keep pace with developments in boys' education. This was opposed by the Huddersfield Trades and Labour Council who thought it was not needed! Fortunately their opinion was ignored.

On the opening morning of the new school on January 15, 1909, there were 236 pupils, giving the lie to the Huddersfield Trades and Labour Council's ill-informed opinion. A hundred and twenty-four transferring from the Boys College and girls from Huddersfied Borough were joined by scholarship girls funded by the West Riding County Council. Of that first intake 115 were paid for by the Huddersfield Board of Education, twenty by the West Riding and forty-five were self-funded.[246]

Everything about the school was new: the building, the curriculum, the teachers, the pupils. It must have been a logistical nightmare to collect everyone and everything a working grammar school needed, and ensure they were all in the right place at the right time.

The building was located on the site of what had been Greenhead Hall and the school changed its name to Greenhead High School for Girls in 1920. The last occupant of the Hall and its estate had been John Fligg Brigg, twice mayor of Huddersfield Corporation, who had died in 1899. Following Sir Michael Sadler's report, produced in 1904, enquiries about buying the Hall had begun in 1905 and in the following year the Corporation approached Sir John Ramsden with a view to buying the site. The cost of demolishing the original building and erecting a new one was estimated at £12,000, but in fact came in below budget at just short of £11,000, providing accommodation for 286 pupils. It was opened on January 15, 1909 by Lord Stanley of Alderley.[247]

The morning of that momentous day was spent rehearsing for the official opening in the afternoon, after which the girls who were within easy reach of home went and changed into white dresses, which the school magazine refers to as 'invariably associated with all school functions everywhere'. What about girls who lived at a distance from the school, such as Elsie Chapman who lived in Penistone and probably travelled to Huddersfield every morning on the train, her father being a railway employee? They would probably have been able to change in the newly built cloakrooms where they could wriggle out of their gym slips and don the requisite white dress. The weather was very cold and it was snowing, so it's to be hoped they had substantial Edwardian underwear to keep them from freezing!

In the afternoon the girls and the nine women teachers who were permanent members of staff assembled in the hall which also did duty as the gym. There were also three visiting mistresses and two visiting masters - perhaps music, art and a boost to the science side of the girls' education - but no mention is made of what they taught or whether they were present at the opening ceremony[248]. The platform party consisted of Lord Stanley, the mayor Alderman Holroyd, Mr Owen Balmforth, chairman of the Education Committee, whom we have met before in his capacity as historian of the Huddersfield Co-operative Society, and Miss Chambers, the head.

*Miss Chambers, the first head of the school.
By kind permission of the Huddersfield Exposed web site*

Now thirty-four years of age, Miss Chambers had attended Girton, in Cambridge, and completed a maths degree, though of course women could not graduate at Cambridge until 1948! She had then moved to Dublin where she could graduate, and acquired an MA in maths in 1906. Between that time and 1909 when she came to Huddersfield, she had been teaching in St Andrews. She was to remain at the school until 1918, when she moved to Chalfont St Giles to run Maltman's Green school for girls.

Miss Chambers' philosophy was that there should be no stress on individual achievement, even going so far as to exclude individual prizes at school events. Girls were to be encouraged to work for the good of the whole community. The school motto, like many other schools both in the British Isles and the Empire, was 'Honour before Honours', an admirable statement of priorities.

After sundry speeches from the members of the platform party,

The Staff in 1910

most of the girls filed out and the rest, under the direction of Miss Shadbolt, gave a drill display. Then tea was served in the common room and the dining-room and gifts of statuary and pictures were received so the bare walls of the newly plastered corridors would appear rather less stark. In the years following the opening of the school every girl surrendered one shilling and sixpence a term to the Kyrle fund, established by Octavia Hill's sister Miranda to provide art and books for the working class poor.

What Was Taught

The curriculum was a thorny problem. What did you teach girls who were expected to marry and play a crucial role in bringing up and forming the characters of the next generation? And who had the requisite skills to teach them the variety of subjects worthy of a prosperous corporation which expected value for money? And did you include religion, and if so what kind of religion in this chapel-dominated town?

Since many of the girls were expected to marry and run their household in an exemplary fashion, domestic science, a newly labelled and fashionable subject, would probably have been one of the least controversial topics. Domestic Science had been so termed by a Canadian woman memorably named Adelaide Hoodless. She had lost a child to 'summer complaint', a disease caught from infected milk, and she argued that if she and the farmer's wife who sold her the milk had had more knowledge of how to keep dairy products, 'summer complaint' would not have happened and her son would not have died.

As she was involved with the newly formed YWCA in Ontario, she set up an educational course for girls newly arrived in Canada, to teach them the skills of organizing and using cooking equipment safely, the importance of a balanced diet and hygiene in the kitchen. She called it 'domestic science' to put it on a par with the science that men were investigating, and the information in her 'Little Red Book', published in 1898, contains a great deal of information about the calorific value of food and the role of proteins, fats and carbohydrates. The suggestions for a suitable meal for four men 'at moderate muscular work' gives not only the name of the food, the quantity suitable for them and the calorific value. It also costs it to the penny, or rather the cent[249]. She was a good friend of Lady Aberdeen, wife of the Governor of Canada at the time, and came to England in 1899 to attend the International Congress of Women, so her ideas would certainly have become familiar in Britain.

A more difficult problem would be the teaching of religious knowledge. The dissenting chapels in the West Riding had been an important influence on education for both boys and girls, so to have the Church of England muscling in on what they may have felt was their territory, with ideas about worship which, in some places, under the influence of the Oxford Movement, had taken a turn towards

Roman Catholicism, was not acceptable. The 1870 Education Act had stipulated that all religious teaching in board schools should be non-denominational, and so it remained in the newly formed grammar schools.

The results of the Oxford Local Examination Board of 1912 show precisely what subjects were being taught and how well the girls fared. Twenty-four girls sat the exams. Religious knowledge was broken down into the Old Testament, the Gospels and the Acts of the Apostles. No-one was examined in the Gospels but twenty-one girls had learnt a great deal about the Old Testament with only nine people studying the Acts.

The standard of teaching in arithmetic, listed separately from mathematics, must have been high, since twenty-two girls obtained grades that were very good, good or fairly good. One just failed and one, Miss Chilton, failed miserably though she did well in algebra and geometry though again failing in trigonometry.

Everyone was entered for the English exam, though not, ironically, the grammar part of the curriculum. All twenty-four were examined in composition, but five of them failed. The sciences were not well represented. One girl took Chemistry and did well but the only other science which features is Botany which had six entrants of whom only two passed.

History and geography were also included with most girls doing well in both subjects. The rest of the results were concerned with languages – French but not German, and Latin, though not Greek. The French results were impressive. Out of the twenty-four entered, only two failed, though the results for Latin were very much less satisfactory. Fourteen took the exam but five of them had obviously not learned enough and failed badly. Perhaps the ones who passed were girls who had attended classes at the Boys' Grammar School and thus had had more time to learn.[250]

Drill featured prominently in school events and some girls were keen on sport. They played fives, tennis, netball, basketball, cricket and hockey and as the school became more established by 1913 had teams who played against other school teams such as Batley Grammar, Halifax High, Wakefield High and Keighley Grammar. Provision for games was less than satisfactory however with league features for the school hockey team having to be played away since the West Riding League refused to pass the hockey field for matches[251]. In 1918 hockey must have been suspended entirely, because the field was needed for growing potatoes. The girls got their exercise by going out to dig, rather than hitting a ball.

There was a drama group which was supported by several members of staff, including Miss Chambers, who played the part of Miss Betsy Parker in the 1910 production of *Cranford*. There was also a production of *Everyman,* an early sixteenth century morality play which uses allegorical characters to examine the question of Christian salvation. Not a jolly romp, but useful for a girls' school as all the parts can easily and convincingly be played by girls and the costumes - Greek tunics - would be easy to make. It would also be well known by the staff, since the play was popular at women's colleges. *Antigone* by Sophocles which the drama society put on in 1913 would be similarly easy to stage though the report in the school magazine for that year notes that because of the simplicity of the setting and the starkness of the plot 'the play stands or falls by the acting'. Fortunately the standard of acting was so high that for the two hours of the performance the actors and audience found themselves 'transported to another world' and the writer of the review felt the performance would be remembered for the rest of their lives.

Music also played an important part in school events. The school of course had a school song. At the beginning the song was copied from that sung at Harrow public school and written in 1872: 'Forty years on'.

> Forty years on, when afar and asunder
> Parted are those who are singing today,
> When you look back and forgetfully wonder
> What you were like in your work and your play,
> Then, it may be, there will often come o'er you,
> Glimpses of notes like the catch of a song –
> Visions of boyhood shall float them before you,
> Echoes of dreamland shall bear them along,

Presumably they changed the reference to 'boyhood' and omitted the chorus, which is staggeringly inappropriate, referring as it does to the Harrow football game. The Boys College song would have been even less appropriate. That begins:

> We're boys of the sturdy northland
> 'Midst mills and mines we live.
> And to our well loved homeland,
> The best we can we give.

It was not until several years later that a song specifically written for the school by Peggy Madden was adopted:

> We shall look back when we are here no more,
> Some memory or echo of a song,
> Will bring before us half forgotten days,
> Then all red-lettered as they sped along....
>> Breeze of the field, gleam of the sun,
>> Well remembered faces and laurels hardly won,
>> Will be with us till our working days are done,
>> Till our working days are done.

A school magazine was established though only three still exist in the Kirklees archive, for 1913, 1916 and 1918. They are packed with worthy accounts of speakers, essays on topics such as 'The Celtic Element in Literature' and accounts of events in other schools where girls have moved from Huddersfield.

The girls are obviously enjoying themselves in a quiet, well behaved sort of way, reproducing what they have been taught and being made aware at every turn of their duty to others less fortunate than themselves, be it helping at children's play centres, dressing dolls for sick children or collecting money for the Cinderella society. Even the holidays had tasks to be undertaken: dressing the said dolls, designing a heading for the form notice board featuring the school motto or drawing a map - any map - and drawing a twig.

Nowadays the curriculum and the ethos of the school appear stultifyingly worthy, but if the alternative were ten hour shifts in the local mill with the incessant clack of the shuttle as it clattered back and forth across the warp, then they were privileged indeed and knew it.

So what were they going to do when they left the shelter of the municipal high school and ventured out into the wide world? Teacher training college was one favoured destination. In 1913 twelve girls qualified for admission to training college, of whom five girls went on to Leeds Training College while one went to Ripon. Fifteen were admitted as pupil teachers.

The 1916 magazine was a much slimmed down version due to the scarcity of paper. It still contains the best of the writing the girls produced and they were still enjoying amateur dramatics but now their good works were aimed at supporting the war effort. They sent money to the British, French, Serbian and Russian Red Cross associations, they gave £3.5.6d to the YMCA hut and bought a table and a tea urn for the Belgian Recreation hut. They donated to the Royal Navy, the Polish Relief Fund, the British Ambulance Company, a Star and Garter home (for disabled ex-servicemen), and the British Blue Cross, the charity caring for injured animals, of which there were many because of the number of horses used at the Front.

As there was no Whitsun holiday that year, two afternoons were spent knitting and sewing for the troops. The Huddersfield War Bureau provided the material and the girls produced 170 bandages, 31 T bandages, 39 vermin shirts, 70 casualty bags, 184 pugarees (long scarves), 328 washing cloths and 30 shirts prepared for the badly wounded. By Christmas the girls had amassed enough knitted goods to fill several crates which were sent to one of the hospitals at the Front.

There was also a War Savings Club, one of several schemes recommended by the government. 'It is hoped the scheme will be effective,' said the account in the magazine, 'not only in aiding the Government, but also in helping the girls to lead simpler lives by denying themselves luxuries such as sweets and picture shows'.

'The Green Leprechaun', a short story, was written by Peggy Madden, who was later to compose the school song. The story itself is well told but it seems a strange sort of topic to write about, until one remembers that the Cottingley fairies made their appearance in 1917. They were photographed by two cousins living in Cottingley and were thought so realistic that Sir Arthur Conan Doyle, inventor of Sherlock Holmes, believed them to be true pictures of fairies. Sir Arthur, though, was a fervent spiritualist. *The Strand* magazine itself in 1920 published a serious article on fairies, so the little people were obviously a popular subject for study.

After leaving school the first intake found that for some not much had changed. Fifty-three girls were living at home, presumably helping their mothers in good works in the community. Some however had rather more opportunities than they might have expected in the past. Margaret Kathleen Darment, daughter of a french polisher, went on to the technical college to learn to be a dispenser, one of seven girls to follow that course. Then there were apprenticeships in millinery and dressmaking and tailoring. Some even went into the mill as menders or clerks. Some worked for the Post Office, some became shop assistants. One became a hospital nurse and one worked in cigar manufacturing. Six went to teacher training college and six became pupil teachers. A high school education would certainly have helped them gain work, since they were obviously better educated than the general run of girls, probably spoke nicely and had been trained to think of others.

In 1916 the school magazine reveals some of the work ex-students had moved on to: six were working in banks, one was a VAD (Voluntary Aid Detachment) at Royds Hall military hospital, one was farming in Devon and one was nursing in London. One was at the Labour Exchange, another in the Post Office, a third a typist in the British Dye Works (later ICI.) Three were in London, one at the Froebel Training College, one at Battersea Polytechnic, and one at Royal Holloway. One had reached the giddy heights of Somerville College in Oxford and two were at Bawtry Agricultural College. There was a surprising number of girls interested in agriculture and market gardening, though perhaps less surprising if one considers that the girls were actively engaged in growing food crops such as potatoes on the hockey field and botany was virtually the only science subject taught at the school.

They had also had a visiting speaker called Miss Hartop (was this the Miss Hartop who had spoken at the Suffragette demonstration in

Leeds organized by the WSPU on Sunday July 26 1908?) Miss Hartop had spoken to the High School girls about the importance of war work for women. Marjorie Moore had listened to what Miss Hartop had to say and taken her words to heart. She first of all spent two weeks at Garforth Training College learning some of the skills she might need on a farm. Then nothing! She waited patiently at home for a month, then received a telegram from the Labour Exchange telling her that farmers in North Yorkshire were finally putting their prejudices to one side and were now prepared to accept women as farmworkers

She was sent to Boroughbridge but not told the name of the farmer she was supposed to be working for. She joined up with about a dozen other young women, however, who were living in a cold, sparsely furnished old house and was told that farmer Peacock, who already had three girls working for him, might be prepared to take on a fourth. When she turned up at his farm, she was told by the maid that he wasn't at home but the hoes were over in the corner and the turnip field was down the road. Undaunted, she picked up a hoe and walked half a mile until she found a turnip field that needed hoeing, and spent the best part of eight hours hoeing it without, apparently, having met a single other person. She worked there for four weeks, presenting a bill of twelve shillings to the farmer every Saturday, at the end of which he must have decided she deserved more interesting work, and she was given the job of driving the harvest carts. When the corn was harvested she went tattie-scrattling – digging up potatoes on all fours, with a sack wrapped round her waist and pads on her knees to give some protection while she crawled along the rows of potatoes. When that was done, the farmer dismissed his casual labourers and Marjorie returned home.

But not for long. It must have seemed very uneventful at home, so she went to work on a dairy farm in Lincolnshire. In her position as second cowman she had to rise at four a.m. and milk the cows by the glimmer of an oil lamp. She was glad in the Spring to be able to move on to a farm in Devon where the locals were pleased when she made a mistake and enjoyed laughing at her misfortunes. They disapproved of women doing farm work, especially a town-bred one. She loved the countryside, however, and seems to have developed a skin thick enough to withstand the jibes of the locals. She concludes by saying that hitherto, farming has been done by the working classes but she firmly believes that when the war is over farming will be a common occupation for people of all classes and that many women who have come to farming out of necessity during the war will be happy to continue in the work in peacetime.

The 1918 school magazine is pared back to the bare minimum containing news of happenings in the school and a welcome to the new head, Miss Hill and a regretful farewell to Miss Chambers, whose character has so influenced the ethos of the school.

The number of students had increased from the original 286 to over 500 and something had to be done to accommodate them all. As building was forbidden, presumably because of shortage of materials in the last few months of the war, an old house further up Greenhead Road, Longdenholme, had been purchased and several forms moved there. The hockey field was still under cultivation so games were a difficulty, and matches with other schools were also well-nigh impossible because of the difficulty of travelling. However they did manage to organize a cricket match against the Pupil Teachers from the Technical college, and won by three runs.

A school choir was formed which had sixty members and in May the King and Queen (George V and Queen Mary) had visited Huddersfield, when the sixth form girls were allowed to visit the

Townhall so they could see the royal couple. The head girl, Gladys Cotton, was especially privileged to be spoken to by Queen Mary.

The war was still in its final months when the magazine was printed, and the girls were still supporting various war efforts. For the previous two years they had been sending money for their adopted prisoner of war, O. Beaumont A.B. R.N.D, imprisoned in Frankfurt but in April they heard the good news that Mr Beaumont had been released and had arrived back in England. He and his wife came to the school, so he could tell them about his experiences.

War Savings had raised £2,920.1.6d in the previous twelve months, half of it paid in the Huddersfield Tank Week and the girls were also sending small contributions to the St Dunstans Hostel for Blinded Soldiers and Sailors. The War Bureau had received from the High School girls 124 scarves, 90 pairs of socks, 15 pairs of mittens, 2 helmets, 9 casualty bags and 171 shirts. They sent Christmas parcels to a hospital on the Italian Front which was gratefully received by the matron though it didn't arrive till Easter. And still wanting to be of service to their country, Peggy Madden, Gwen Dyson, Sallie England and Chrissie Turner spent a great deal of time copying and colouring plans of farms for the Land Surveyor.

The examination results in the summer of 1917 show that twenty-four girls took the Senior Oxford Examination, in which Peggy Madden achieved distinction in English and French. Gladys Cotton, the head girl, did not obtain as high a mark as Peggy, only being awarded Class II Honours, though she did get a West Riding County Scholarship for Women while B. Kahn, no first name given, won a scholarship tenable at Ashburne Hall, University of Manchester. Three girls passed Responsions, the first of three examinations instigated by the University of Oxford to ensure they were of high enough standard to take the degree course. They were asked simple questions in Latin, Ancient Greek and Maths.

Girls who had left the school often kept in close touch with an establishment that obviously meant a great deal to them. Several of them had become secretaries or clerks of one kind and another: one at the Boys' College, others at the West Yorkshire Bank, Huddersfield Building Society, the Post Office and the Office of the Commissioner of Liabilities. War work had absorbed others: one in the WAAC (the Women's Auxiliary Army Corps, founded in December 1916), one in the WRAF only very recently established and having a very short life, being disbanded in 1920. One girl had joined the Women's Legion, which provided cooks for army camps, while another was nursing at Royds Hall military hospital. One girl had become a gardener in Scotland while two others were following courses at the Technical College, one in medicine and the other in office skills. One had become a dancing mistress at Mrs Dyson's school of dancing.

Five girls were at university: Freda Gee and Margaret Hurst at St Hugh's College, Oxford, and Enid Moore at Somerville, Helen Lefevre had won an open scholarship to Royal Holloway College, Kathleen Scholefield and the intrepid Marjorie Moore, who had expended so much energy on hoeing turnip fields and milking cows, were now at Studley Agricultural College. No doubt the muscles Marjorie had exercised to such good effect in Boroughbridge and Devon, would be put to equally good use in Warwickshire. Three girls had graduated that year, Jessie Davies from Oxford in English Language and Literature, Marion Draper from Leeds with a M.B, and Doris Mellor also from Leeds with a BA.

The school and its pupils obviously aimed high academically and achieved their goals. A substantial number of the girls reached the highest level of education in the land, while many of the others, if not achieving quite the same level as the high-flyers, were nevertheless finding employment in local businesses. There would no doubt still be a substantial number of young women whose families would not encourage them to seek work and who would be expected to marry, and some of those who did have jobs would in all likelihood have to surrender them when the men came home from the war. Nevertheless, the school had opened up higher education to a greater number of girls than ever and provided at least some of them with opportunities that had not existed before.

Chapter 15 - 1808 to 1909

A hundred and one years is a long time: four generations in human terms, so one might expect there to have been substantial changes between the year when the Marsden Female Friendly Society was formed and the year when the girls of Huddersfield were given their very own high school.

Seven miles separate the centres of the two locations, but in the course of the century Huddersfield had spread and with it the textile industry, so huge mills now occupied much of the valley floor. Trains chugged along that same valley carrying passengers and goods from Manchester and Liverpool in the west to Leeds and east coast resorts and ports.

In 1907 the *Daily Mirror* sent a photographer to record the political event of the decade in the Colne Valley: the by-election when Victor Grayson overturned the Liberal majority and gained a seat in Parliament as a Socialist and supporter of women's suffrage. One of the photographer's most charming photographs was of a lively bunch of young mill girls, posing for the camera, having just come from work in one of those huge mills. The photograph is of poor quality and cannot be reproduced but it shows grubby little faces above long skirts, shawls over their heads and greasy aprons. The material their clothes were made of, however, would be the same as in 1808: wool, cotton, or linen, their shawls knitted or made from a piece of local cloth, petticoats of cotton.

But if we could have seen those girls at the mill workers' annual feast, they would have looked different, when they were off to Blackpool for the day in their Sunday best, and, for the more daring among them, hair crimped with the curling tongs; ready for a good time, excited at the thought of that first view of Blackpool Tower that told them they were at the seaside long before they actually arrived. And of course, they travelled by train, an innovation which opened up the world not just to trade but to pleasure.

Their domestic lives would also have changed. While the rivers and streams of the area had been known for their purity and softness at the beginning of the nineteenth century, this was far from the case by 1900. In 1835 'few towns had adequate supplies of water', says Cyril Pearce, and the water in the rivers in the course of the century had become filthy, polluted by the expansion of the woollen trade and the increase in population with its attendant increased discharge of sewage into the water systems.[252]

Huddersfield was incorporated in 1868 largely because the leading lights of the town promised to provide an adequate supply of water. This they set about immediately by buying out the Waterworks Commissioners and establishing the Huddersfield Corporation Waterworks. In the following forty years they built reservoirs in the hills to the west of the town: Deer Hill, Blackmoorfoot, Wessenden Head, Blakeley and Butterley. By 1900 the Corporation had laid 240 water mains which provided 500 million gallons of water, not just to the town, but to the surrounding districts.[253]

So those girls with grubby faces in the 1907 photograph would have witnessed enormous changes in the countryside around, as the moors were re-shaped to form the reservoirs. They would have had plenty of water to scrub themselves clean when they finished their shift at the mill. They would also have had clean water to drink, which must have cut the incidence of cholera and typhoid.

Having begun to get to grips with the water problem, the Corporation turned its attention to the gas supply, which in the 1860s was provided by a multiplicity of small companies. In 1871 the Corporation started buying them out and selling the gas they made at a good profit. Gas light was used in the mills to extend the working day, and in houses to provide lighting[254]. So by 1907 many of the houses of these mill girls would have been lit by gas in the downstairs room or rooms, though they probably still went to bed by candle-light.

What they had to contend with which could not have been a problem in 1808 was the air quality. The air was thick with the fumes from mill chimneys caused by the vast quantities of coal burnt to keep the machines in working order and making a profit. It is no coincidence that the colour of the sky in Florence Lockwood's suffrage banner is a murky yellow. She was not colour-blind; she was representing it as it was on many days of the year.

The cooking arrangements would also have changed over the course of the century. The side oven, heated by the coal fire which warmed the living room, had been introduced and was common by the 1840s[255]. The creel which held the oatcakes would still be in place, though often used for drying or airing clothes, as well. Wheat bread began to be widely made after the repeal of the Corn Laws in 1846 while home grown wheat was increasingly supplemented by cheap imports from the USA, Canada, Australia and the Argentine as the century progressed.[256]

The generation of electricity by the Corporation soon followed the establishment of a corporation-controlled gas supply. The local tramway system, which had been first established in 1882 using steam trams, could now be run on electricity, though this was only within the borough.

So the lives of our mill girls in 1907 would in fact have been very different from those of their ancestors. In some ways they were cleaner, and healthier and could travel from the village or town if not by tram then by train. Children under ten were no longer being employed in the mill though half-time working for ten to fourteen year olds would persist until 1918.[257]

The reality of their lives might well change when they married. No contraceptive advice, little medical advice when pregnant, no doctor on hand at a difficult birth, and the awful statistic quoted by Margaret Macmillan of 120,000 babies a year dying in the country from a variety of causes[258]. The babies of these young girls might well form part of that statistic in the years to come.

But their horizons had been broadened. As Florence Lockwood said, women, an 'isolated and stationary sex, trained to keep our love and interest within small circles' were suddenly presented with the whole wide world to explore, if they had the means. Not only could they undertake a day trip to the seaside, they could contemplate travelling across the world. Dora Thewlis and her sister emigrated to Australia not as a family but as young women on their own. Their parents followed later. Mary Scawsthorn and her family went west to Canada.

Others stayed in Britain but climbed the slippery pole from working- to middle-class via the education system. Clever, ambitious girls could become pupil teachers and from there progress to training college or to one of the new universities which were admitting women, as Dora Marsden did, or they could train at the Technical College in technical subjects such as dispensing which had been a closed book for the majority of them in the past.

Even for girls who had had a minimum of schooling, their level of literacy would have been higher than in 1808 since they had to attend school and take a test to show they had learnt something. The curriculum would have contained chunks of Shakespeare to learn by heart which would add to the richness of the language they already had, founded on a familiarity with the Bible and the oratorios which were such a staple of chapel life and music.

And what of relationships within the family? At the beginning of the nineteenth century, women in the domestic textile industry were an integral part of the cloth-making process, and therefore their worth within the family and in the wider society outside the home was easy to recognize. In 1840 from his cell in Lancaster prison R. J Richardson was arguing that unmarried women and widows were entitled to full political and social rights. Thompson points out that 'his case was argued from the standpoint of a north country workman, who saw women as the educators in the family, and as workers in the industry of the locality.'[259] The women of the first Female Reform Societies in the 1820s also saw themselves as primarily home-makers and educators of their children alongside their work in the textile trade. This precipitated them into political action as they complained bitterly of their inability to keep up the high standards they had maintained in the past. But they were proud of their work, whether domestic or manufacturing, and were valued for it by the society they lived in.

The transfer of the trade from home to mill, more or less completed by the time of the Great Exhibition in 1851[260], had changed women's role. They had moved out of the domestic sphere and until the age of about forty many were earning regular money in the mill. This went strongly against the Victorian model of ideal womanhood, which was, as Florence Lockwood identified, to be gentle, kind, nurturing and focused on the home. Mill girls were considered unsuitable for training as servants because they were accustomed to saying what they thought and did not take kindly to the quiet, subservient attitude of the housemaid or the ladylike behaviour of the lady's maid.

They could afford to be similarly assertive in the home since they contributed to the family income. Not that they necessarily enjoyed the hard physical work of ten hours in the weaving or warping shed. They would no doubt be pleased to retire when they reached their late thirties. By this time the family would still have money coming in from the children of the family, who would in all probability tip up their wages to the mother. In middle age a woman might well be seen as a manager of the household, so still maintaining a clear, unequivocal role which earned respect.

Throughout the 19th century and beyond, it appears the economic realities of the area fostered equality of responsibility within the family, even though those responsibilities were clearly defined by gender. Perhaps the woman who muttered 'There's nowt wrong wi' men' at Florence Lockwood's meeting was expressing what many women felt.

The role of men working in the mill had also become more standardized. As more and more machinery was introduced into the textile industry, men became associated with these machines, so spinning, which had been women and children's work, with the introduction of the mule became a man's job. The time-keeper was a man, as were the design team. By the beginning of the twentieth century supervisory jobs were often taken by men, who were also in charge of sharing out the work. Since all the work was piece work, the longer it took to process a batch of yarn the less money was taken home at the end of the week. Consequently if the overlooker had favourites among the women, they could be allocated the best work, i.e. the easiest to process and therefore the most lucrative. This was also a situation which could lend itself to sexual exploitation.

People in supervisory jobs were paid more than other workers, so women were routinely paid less than men, though this could be justified by the different roles they played. It would take the rest of the twentieth century for women to establish some parity of earnings between the sexes and indeed the battle continues to the present.

The greatest step forward for women was the reliable control of their own fertility which freed them to participate in a full life outside the home if they so wished. Contraception, which had been considered an obscenity for much of the nineteenth century, was by the nineteen twenties considered by most as a blessing and considerably safer than trips to a helpful woman in Leeds who would help distressed women out of difficult situations.

Many of the changes in society that we value today came about after 1909 and it took the terrible upheavals of the First World war to bring them into being: votes for women over thirty in 1918, safe contraception in the 1920s with Marie Stopes and now finally in the twenty-first century a willingness to tackle sexual molestation. No need now for women to pass on information about who not to share the lift with. There is still a mountain to climb, though, and the gains that have been made need to be protected. Let us hope we go forward in the future, not backwards.

Notes

[1] *Huddersfield Exposed* web site.

[2] Brooke, Alan and Kipling, Lesley. *Liberty or Death. Radicals, Republicans and Luddites 1793-1823* (Huddersfield Local History Society, 2012) p.26

[3] Holmes, D.H. *The Mining and Quarrying Industries in the Huddersfield District.* (Tolson Memorial Museum,1967) p.6

[4] www.ColneValleyTreesSocietyBlogspot.co.uk

[5] Defoe, Daniel. *A Tour through the Whole Island of Britain.1724-1726.* Abridged and edited by P.N. Furbank and W.R. Owens (Yale University Press,1991) pp.256-257

[6] Holmes, D.H. pp.25-30

[7] Huddersfield Exposed: *The History of the Valleys of the Colne, the Holme and the Dearne.* (1906) Ch. V

[8] E. Irene Pearson. *Marsden through the Ages.* Published privately, 1984. p.12

[9] Crump, W.B. and Ghorbal, G. *History of the Huddersfield Woollen Industry.* (Tolson Memorial Museum, 1935) pp.89, 90

[10] Stead, Jennifer. 'The uses of Urine Part 1.' In *Names, Places and People,* (Huddersfield Local History Society publication, 2019) p.64

[11] Hudson, Pat. Cardiff Historical Papers www Cardiff.ac.uk *The Limits of Wool,* Pat Hudson 2007/7)

[12] Atkinson, Frank. *Some Aspects of the 18th Century Woollen and Worsted Trade in Halifax.* (Halifax Museums, 1956) p.vii

[13] For detailed descriptions of oatcake making see chapter 9, and for dairy products see chapter 15 of Brears, Peter. *Traditional Food in Yorkshire.* (Prospect Books, 2014)

[14] Heaton, Herbert. *The Yorkshire Woollen and Worsted Industries, from the earliest times up to the Industrial Revolution.* (Oxford, Clarendon Press 1920) p.345

[15] Stead, Jennifer. 'The uses of Urine Part 1' in *Names, Places and People.* p.70. Urine was a valuable commodity and if a family had collected more than they needed it could be sold for 1d a bucketful or three ha'pence, if one were a red head, the urine from redheaded people being thought to be more effective!

p.76. The urine was usually stored in a barrel outside the house and in the mills in large tanks.

[16] Heaton, p.274

[17] WYAS KC5/69. Kay family papers. Domestic bills and receipts.

[18] Hudson, Pat. Cardiff Historical Papers www Cardiff.ac.uk (The Limits of Wool, Pat Hudson 2007/7).

[19] Crump and Ghorbal, p.132

[20] Crump, W.B. *Huddersfield Highways down the Ages*. (Huddersfield The Tolson Memorial Museum, 1949)

[21] Family notes

[22] Thompson, E.P. p.460

[23] Marland, Hilary. *Medicine and Society in Wakefield and Huddersfield 1780-1870* (Cambridge UP 1987) p.176

[24] ibid. pp.387-388.

[25] Stead, Jennifer. Chapter 24 'Changing the Pattern: Everyday Life 1800-1900' in *Huddersfield, A Most Handsome Town* (ed. E.A. Hilary Haigh, Kirklees Cultural Services, 1992) p.637

[26] Seidal, Hazel. Laithes and Looms, Cows and Combstocks. (Marsden History Group, 2013) p.132. Seidal suggests 55% literacy in Marsden for the years 1750 to 1800, using the marriage registers to fix the rate.

[27] Brears, Peter. *Traditional Food in Yorkshire.* (Prospect Books, 2014) p.52

[28] *Laithes and Looms, Cows and Combstocks,* p.101

[29] National Archive: How much is that? Currency converter)

[30] Minelotti, Paul. 'The importance of ideology: the shift to factory production and the effects of women's employment opportunities in the English Textile Industries.' Discussion papers in Economic and Social History no. 87, Feb.2011, University of Oxford. p.6

[31] This is reminiscent of the requirement in the Church of England from 1597 onwards that the incumbent and two churchwardens with separate keys had to be present in order to open the parish chest.

[32] Parliamentary papers. Report from the Select Committee on the state of the woollen textile industry 1806.

[33] Liberty or Death, p.13

[34] ibid, pp.22-23

[35] ibid pp.22-23

[36] Framework Knitter Museum, accessed 18.10.2019.

[37] ibid, p.30

[38] *Liberty or Death*, p.26

[39] *Liberty or Death*, pp.27-36

[40] Huddersfield Exposed web site. Accessed 3.9.2018

[41] Peel, p.120

[42] *Liberty or death*, p.36

[43] Luddite bi-centenary blogspot compiled from *Leeds Mercury* account and letter from Col. Campbell to Grey (HO 42/123). Retrieved 10.3.2020

[44] *Liberty or Death*, p.47

[45] ibid.62

[46] *An historical account of the Luddites of 1811, 1812 and 1813 with Report of their Trials at York Castle*. At Huddersfield Exposed web site.

[47] Chase, Malcolm. 'York Castle and it political prisoners: the Luddites in a broader context'. Retrieved at Huddersfieldhistory.org.uk. 18. 9 2018

[48] ludditebicentenary.blogspot.com; article by Pamela Cooksey on the website The Luddite Link

[49] Chase, Malcolm. A*n historical account of the Luddites,* p.106

[50] ibid. p.128

[51] King, Steven. Poverty and Welfare in England 1700-1850: a regional perspective. Manchester University Press 2000, p.190

[52] E.P. Thompson: the Making of the English Working Class. p.462

[53] Leeds Mercury .mirfield –second look.info retrieved 10.3.20

[54] King, p.25

[55] South Crosland overseer's book. WYAS archive.

[56] Walvin, James. 'William Wilberforce, Yorkshire and the campaign to end transatlantic slavery, 1789-1820' in Hargreaves, John A. and Haigh, Hilary eds. *Slavery in Yorkshire*. (University of Huddersfield, 2012)

[57] Marland Marland, Hilary. 'Health care in Nineteenth century Huddersfield' in Haigh, Hilary ed *Huddersfield, a Most Handsome Town,* pp.46-47

[58] *Liberty or Death,* p.83

[59] ibid pp.78-88

[60] ibid p.87

[61] ibid p.69

[62] ibid p.70

[63] ibid p.72

[64] ibid p.72

[65] www.histparl.ac.uk

[66] *Liberty or Death,* p.92

[67] ibid p.92

[68] Mather, Ruth. *Return to Peterloo,* p49

[69] ibid p.50

[70] ibid p54

[71] The Guardian on line, 14 August 2019

[72] Bamford, Samuel. *Passages in the Life of a Radical.* First published 1844. (Macgibbon and Kee Ltd, 1967) pp.121-122

[73] ibid p.123

[74] ibid p.131

[75] ibid p.141

[76] ibid p.149

[77] Gutenberg Press on line: Campbell, Theophila Carlile: The battle of the Press as told in the story of the life of Richard Carlile by his daughter 1899. Ch.3

[78] Bamford. *Passages in the Life of a Radical,* p.151

[79] ibid pp.152-153

[80] Carlile, Theophila. *The Battle of the Press,* Ch.3

[81] Bamford. *Passages in the Life of a Radical,* p.154

[82] ibid pp.154-155

[83] ibid pp.161-164

[84] ibid p.167

[85] ibid p.360

[86] Bamford. *Passages in the Life of a Radical*, pp.193-194

[87] Mather, Ruth. *Return to Peterloo*, p.60

[88] Janette Martin. 'Huddersfield and the Peterloo massacre' in *Hudersfield Local History Society Journal 2020/2023, Issue 31*, pp.9-14

[89] Katina Bill, curator of Kirklees museums and galleries, describes how it was made. 'The main body of the flag is cotton and is made of one piece of fabric with the vertical patterned borders and central divide woven in as part of the cloth. The cross borders are appliqued. The four dark corner segments are velvet. The writing and illustrations are all applied in ink. We think the writing is by two different hands.' She points to the difference in the 's' in each quadrant and to the difference in spacing in the two left hand squares. ' The lettering beginning 'May never a cock…' is finer and well-spaced but the lettering in the quadrant beginning Skelmanthorp, which is misspelt, does not fit in the segment well, overhangs its borders and is generally cruder than the one below.'

The long 's'. which looks more like an 'f' was gradually dropped in the course of the 19th century, though it lingered in hand written correspondence much longer into the 1840s or even later. Charlotte Bronte's letters for instance sometimes contain the long 's'.

The Skelmanthorpe Historical Society web site (skelmanthorpehistoricalsociety.btck.co.uk) has an interesting document written in 1922 by a Skelmanthorpe man, Fred Lawton. It is a whimsical piece written as though by the flag itself, but has concrete information in it which is useful. The maker, he asserts, is a Mr Bird, a pattern maker, who fashioned the flag from cotton and nailed it to a frame 5ft by 5ft 8". It was made in the aftermath of Peterloo, its first outing being to the meeting at Almondbury bank in November 1819. This document states that the flag was buried afterwards in Skelmanthorpe and resurrected for various meetings – a meeting in Wakefield in1832, in support of the Chartists, at the end of the Crimean War and finally in 1884 at a meeting about the Third Reform Bill introduced into Parliament by Gladstone and which extended the franchise to two in three men in England.

[90] *Liberty or Death*, pp.89-95

[91] Chase, Malcolm. *1820,* pp.44-45 and Wikipedia

[92] ibid p.13

[93] Wikipedia

[94] Chase, p.13

[95] Opie. *The Lore and Language of school children*, 1959, p.218

[96] Chase, *1820,* p.173

[97] ibid p.147

[98] ibid pp.175-177

[99] Hargreaves in 'A Metropolis of Discontent'. Popular Protest in Huddersfield c.1780-c.1850' in *Huddersfield a most handsome town*, p.207

[100] Dictionary Of National Biography

[101] (Retrieved at Expanding ethical discourse in Wooler's Black Dwarf. www.ethicalspace.org/archive/2005_V2_1_feature-1-htm Malcolm Conbury

[102] Chase, p.191

[103] Theophila Carlile Campbell. *The battle of the Press as told in the story of the life of Richard Carlile by his daughter,* 1899, Ch.XV

[104] ibid Ch.V

[105] I. Loudon considers that chlorosis, which disappeared as a disease of adolescent girls at the beginning of the twentieth century, was closely related to what we now call anorexia nervosa. Chlorosis was a form of anaemia which resulted in a pallor which may or may not have had a green tinge and which was linked to a disturbance of eating habits. I. Loudon, BMJ Vol. 281. Dec. 1980 *Chlorosis, anaemia and anorexia nervosa.*

[106] *Liberty or Death,* p.116

[107] Halstead, Ch.4 'The Huddersfield Short Time Committee and its Radical associations, c.1820-1876' in *Slavery in Yorkshire.*

[108] Halstead, Ch.4, *Slavery in Yorkshire,* p.117

[109] Wikipedia – List of constituencies enfranchised and disenfranchised by the Reform Act 1832.

[110] Before 1830 publicans were licensed twice, once by the Excise to sell drink

and once from the JP to open a public house. The Beer Act abolished the need for this second licence, (Paper press p.38), hoping that by so doing the price of beer would decrease and encourage people to drink beer rather than spirits, notably gin.

[111] Hansard

[112] Stead. *Huddersfield a most handsome town*, p.635

[113] Halstead p135 *Slavery in Yorkshire*, ch 4.

[114] Theophila Carlile Cambell. *The Battle of the Press as told in the story of the life of Richard Carlile by his daughter*. 1899. Gutenberg Press on line. Retrieved 24 Oct. 2019.

[115] Thompson, D. *Outsiders*, p.89

[116] Hollis, Patricia. *The Pauper Press*. (Oxford University Press, 1970)

[117] Newspapers had begun their life at the beginning of the eighteenth century as advertising sheets. The size of the paper was limited by the Newspaper Stamp Duty to one sheet of paper folded which would give four pages of foolscap size paper. Printing them was a slow business because each letter had to be placed individually, and papers were printed during the week, with only the last page having anything resembling what we would think of as news, the rest being advertising. They were all of necessity weekly papers.

To begin with, the news parts of these papers were careful to avoid strong opinions on any matter, but towards the end of the century, the momentous events in France had fuelled a hunger for news of what was happening abroad, and papers began to publish opinions, dividing between a radical point of view and a more conservative loyalist position.

[118] Ibid p.97,98,116

[119] ibid p.116

[120] Royle, *Slavery in Yorkshire*, pp.154-159

[121] Hargreaves, ibid p.14

[122] ibid. Halstead p.119

[123] ibid. Hargreaves, p.208

[124] Place, Allan. *Pray Remember the Poor*. Holme Valley Civic Society, n.d. p.8

[125] ibid p.10

[126] ibid p.19

[127] Stead, p.89

[128] Driver, Felix. Power and Pauperism. The Workhouse System 1834-1884. (Cambridge UP, 1993) p.113

[129] Hargreaves, *Slavery in Yorkshire*, p.209

[130] Place, *Pray remember the poor*, p.92

[131] Huddersfield exposed

[132] D Thompson, *The Dignity of chartism*, p.39,40.

[133] ibid p.39

[134] Huddersfield Exposed

[135] Wikipedia. Bronterre O'Brien

[136] Chase, Malcolm, *1820, Disorder and stability in the United Kingdom*. pp.16,17

[137] *Huddersfield a most handsome town*, p.214

[138] ibid p.213

[139] Hargreaves, pp.178-199

[140] ibid p.223

[141] *Remember the poor*, pp.150-155

[142] Huddersfield exposed retrieved 11.11.19

[143] The conditions in the Birkby poorhouse of 1848 is reminiscent of descriptions of the field hospitals on the Eastern Front in Serbia during the First World War some seventy years later. There typhus raged in the winter months, killing many civilians and soldiers and though the cause of the disease, bacteria carried by lice, was not discovered until 1928, the nurses of the Scottish Women's Hospitals seem to have been aware that the disease was spread by lice. To reduce the infection rate, all patients were stripped in the bathroom, the first port of call, and their clothes were disinfected. The symptoms of typhus are a raging fever and loss of control of bowels and bladder. The nurses kept the patients clean, fed them every hour on a mixture of brandy, sugar and egg, which they could take in even when only semi-conscious. (p.175 Isabel Hutton. *Memories of a doctor in war and peace*. Heinemann 1960)

[144] By some miracle, the last volume of Swift's diary was discovered by Jennifer

Stead in an old furniture warehouse in Huddersfield. She subsequently undertook a considerable amount of detective work on the Swift family and produced *Diary of a Quack Doctor*, an edited edition of his diary. It is so personal it is surely not meant for publication, but thank goodness Jennifer Stead found it. It contributes substantially to our knowledge of everyday life in Huddersfield in the mid 1800s and casts light on the situation of women at that time.

[145] Private correspondence

[146] Stead, Jennifer ed. *The Diary of a Quack Doctor.*) Huddersfield Local History Society,2002) p.12

[147] Ibid p.49

[148] What these multiple rejections did for Kezia is not known, though modern thinking about the need for security in a child's early life would indicate that she might have problems. Whatever she felt, she grew up to marry John Lodge, at Kirkheaton church in September 1860, with James Lodge named as her father on the marriage certificate.

[149] Janis Lomas. 'Delicate Duties', Women's History Review Vol.9, number one, 2000

[150] Stead, p.56

[151] ibid pp.57,58

[152] Thompson, Dorothy, *Outsiders. Class, Gender and Nation.* (Verso1993) p.79

[153] Chase, Malcolm. *Chartism. A new history.* (Manchester University Press, 2007) p.15

[154] ibid p.12

[155] Thompson, Dorothy, 1993 p.94

[156] ibid p.18

[157] Web site: The National Archives

[158] Chase, Malcolm. 'Chartism in Huddersfield, the cultural dimension' in Hargreaves, John A. ed. *The Charter our Right (Huddersfield Local History Society,* 2018) p.66

[159] Chase, *Chartism, a new history* p.13

[160] Chase, *Chartism, a new history,* P.342

[161] Ancestry.co.uk.

[162] Chase, *Chartism, a new history*, p.27

[163] Underground histories.wordpress.com.

[164] quoted in Thompson, Dorothy *Outsiders* p.83

[165] Ibid p.99

[166] Chase. *Chartism, a new history*, pp.205-206

[167] nationalarchives.gov.uk Power, politics and protest. (cat.ref.HO45/2410A). Extract from the handbook of the People's Charter Union, 17 April 1848.

[168] Chase. *Chartism, a new history* p.100

[169] ibid p.140

[170] Chase, 'Chartism in Huddersfield' in *The Charter our right,* p.78

[171] ibid p.645

[172] Ashton, Rosemary. *Little Germany. Exile and Asylum in Victorian England.* (Oxford University Press. 1986) pp.56-58

[173] ibid pp.85-88

[174] ibid pp.94-96

[175] ibid pp.98-99

[176] Huddersfield Exposed

[177] Stewart, p.110

[178] Stewart, p.113

[179] tomchance.org/wp-content/uploads/2018/03/Glazing_the _Crystal_Palace.pdf

[180] Stewart, p.114

[181] Crump and Ghorbal, pp.128-132

[182] Lockwood, John. An investigation into the development of the provision of public elementary education and the changing levels of iteracy in the census district of Huddersfield from 1811 to 1851. Unpublished thesis, p.6.

[183] Ibid p.10

[184] ibid p.17

[185] Grace's Guide to Industrial History, gracesguide.co uk

[186] O'Connel, John. *The Making of a University,* Huddersfield University Press 2016, p.1

[187] Minter, Gordon and Enid. *Discovering Old Huddersfield.*
[188] Huddersfield Exposed web site
[189] ibid
[190] Hannam, June. *Isabella Ford.* Blackwell, 1989, p.14
[191] One popular parody of this still extant in the 21st century is:

> Twas a dark and stormy night.
>
> The rain came down in torrents.
>
> The captain said to Antonio 'Tell us a tale'.
>
> And the tale ran as follows:
>
> Twas a dark and stormy night. etc.

[192] University of Huddersfield Archive GB1103HUD2
[193] University of Huddersfield Archive.FEI/3/2/a
[194] Griffiths, Making up for lost time, p.3
[195] Unless this is some kind of piece of equipment for the textile trade, though I have been unable to find any reference to it!
[196] Peter Brears. *Food in Yorkshire.* Prospect Books, 2014
[197] British Library web site. *1850 Report on the sanitary conditions in Haworth*
[198] Marland, Hilary. (HAMHT) p.599
[199] Dingwall, Robert, Rafferty, Anne Marie, Webster, Charles. *An Introduction to the Social History of Nursing.* (London, Routledge. 1988) p.15
[200] Huddersfield Exposed web site
[201] Private letter to Sir Theodore Martin, quoted in Wilson, A.N. *Victoria, a Life.* (Atlantic Books, 2014) p.218
[202] Strachey, Ray. *The Cause.* First published 1928 G. Bell and Sons Ltd. Published 1978 Virago Press. p.16
[203] Wikipedia. Rochdale Society of Equitable Pioneers.
[204] Thornes, Robin, 'The Origins of the Co-operative Movement in Huddersfield' *HAMHT,* p.172
[205] Huddersfield Exposed web wite. Owen Balmforth, The Huddersfield Industrial Society Limited: Fifty Years of Progress, p.41
[206] ibid. p.45

[207] ibid p.52

[208] ibid. p.55

[209] Gaffin, Jean and Thoms, David. Caring and Sharing. A Centenary History of the *Co operative Womens'Guild.* (Co operative Union Ltd, 1983.) p.5

[210] Hutton, Isobel. C.B.E., M.D. *Memories of a doctor in War and Peace.* (Heinemann, 1960) p.59

[211] ibid p.60

[212] Davies, Margaret Llewellyn ed. *Maternity. Letters from Working Wives.* (Virago, 1978).

[213] ibid pp.194-195

[214] Gaffin, p.72

[215] Huddersfield exposed. Owen Balmforth The Huddersfield Industrial Society limited. Fifty years of progress, 1860-1909, pp.229-256

[216] ibid p.197

[217] ibid p.195

[218] This was Mrs. Josiah Lockwood's sister

[219] Lockwood, Mrs Josiah. *An Ordinary Life.* (Echo Press, 1932)

[220] Liddington, Jill. *Rebel Girls.* (Virago, 2006) p.157

[221] Huddersfield Exposed web site

[222] Liz Quinn. 'Linthwaite's suffragist' in Huddersfield Local History Society *Journal 2020/2021 Issue 31,* pp.29-31

[223] Bamforth of Holmfirth picture postcards.

[224] Hargreaves, John A. *The Villas of Edgerton.* (The Huddersfield Civic Society, 2017) p.48

[225] Dictionary of National Biography on line.

[226] Wikipedia

[227] Jill Lidington, *Rebel girls,* p.274

[228] Daily Mail 22 March 1907

[229] A variety of accounts are recorded in the *Daily Mail* 22 and 27 March, 1907, *Sheffield Daily Telegraph* 27, 28 March 1907 and *Leeds Mercury* 25, 26, 27 March 1907, all available on *Huddersfield Exposed* web site.

[230] Jill Liddington. *Rebel Girls,* p.130

[231] WYAS .WSPU minutes 1907-1909, Ref KC/1060

[232] Huddersfield exposed. Retrieved 30.9.19

[233] Rebel girls, p.120

[234] Huddersfield Exposed. The Scawthornes, like the Thewlis family, emigrated to the USA in 1912.

[235] Fenner Brockway, left wing activist, MP, vegetarian, journalist, Humanist. Died 1988 aged 99. Wikipedia accessed Oct 2019.)

[236] Clark, David. Colne Valley. Radicalism to Socialism (Longman, 1981) p.151

[237] Huddersfield exposed web site. Ret. Oct 5, 2019

[238] Oxford Dictionary of National Biography

[239] ibid

[240] Hunt, Felicity, ed. *Lessons for Life: The schooling of girls and Women 1850-1950.* (Oxford, Blackwell 1987) p.xvi

[241] ibid p.xvi

[242] educationengland.org.uk on 1.1.2020

[243] Hunt, p.xvii

[244] ibid p.xvii

[245] K.M. Cocker, Jubilee history of Greenhead High School p6. WYK 1788 Box 14/128-138

[246] Admissions register 1909 WYK 1788. Box7/36-42

[247] *Jubilee history.*

[248] ibid p.6

[249] Retrieved 8 Jan 2020 at Gutenberg.org

[250] Oxford Senior exams 1912-1914. WYK1788 Box 14/128-138.

[251] Jubilee history, p.14

[252] Pearce, Cyril in 'Huddersfield in 1867' in Griffiths, David, ed. *Making up for lost time,* Huddersfield Local History, p.44

[253] ibid p.45

[254] ibid pp.49-50

[255] Brears, p.87

[256] ibid p.139

[257] On line. Gillard, Derek. Education in England: a history. Retrieved July 16, 2020.

[258] Quoted in Reynolds, Melanie. *Infant Mortality and working class child care, 1850-1899.* (Palgrave Macmillan, 2016) p.160

[259] Thompson, Dorothy. Outsiders. Class, Gender and Nation. (Verso 1993) p.94

[260] Crump, W.B. and Ghorbal, G. *History of the Huddersfield Woollen Industry.* (Tolson Memorial Museum, 1935) p.116

Appendix 1

Rules and Orders of the Marsden Female Friendly Society

RULES and ORDERS
To be observed by
THE FRIENDLY

Female Society

Established on
THE SEVENTH DAY OF JUNE, 1808
AT THE HOUSE OF

MARTHA LINDLEY
INNKEEPER

IN MARSDEN
IN THE
PARISH OF ALMONDBURY AND COUNTY OF YORK

HUDDERSFIELD
PRINTED BY THOMAS SMART, BOOKSELLER,

1808

RULES and ORDERS

We, whose names are, or hereafter shall be subscribed, being duly sensible of the great Benefits arising from Friendly Societies, and feeling an earnest Desire to meet together as Sisters, and form a Society for the mutual support of each other, when it shall please Almighty God to afflict any of us with Sickness, Lameness, or any other Infirmity, whereby we are incapacitated from following our usual Employments, have mutually agreed to conform ourselves to the following articles.

I It is agreed by this society (with Intent to accomplish the good Design above expressed,) that everyone, that entereth into this Society, from and after the Seventh Day of June, 1808, shall be considered by the Committee, to be of sound Body and Mind, and under the Age of Forty Years: each Person shall pay at her Entrance One Shilling and Tenpence for Ale, every Quarter, so long as she continues a Member. Every Member to be in the Club Room by Two of the Clock, in the Afternoon or depute some other Member to pay her Contribution, or she will be deemed an absent Member.

II That this Society shall be governed by two Wardens and three Stewardesses, one warden to be chosen by the Committee, yearly and every Year, for which Service there will be allowed her Four Shillings a Year out of the Stock, so long as she shall continue in that Office; and then another shall be appointed by the Committee as aforesaid, to serve in like manner, and receive the same Allowance so long as she shall continue in that Office; and if any Member of the Society shall refuse to serve, when duly chosen by the Committee, she shall forfeit to the Stock, Two Shillings and Sixpence, and another to be chosen in like Manner as before, and the other Warden and Stewardesses must serve according as they stand in the Book of Accounts; any Person refusing to serve, shall forfeit Two Shillings and Sixpence to the Stock; and the next in Order shall serve as above, or forfeit the same; a Clerk shall be chosen by the Majority, who shall keep an Account of the Money that shall be collected and paid., for which Service he shall have allowed as the Majority of the Society shall direct.

III There shall be a box provided with five Locks and five Keys, one Key to be kept at the House where the Box is lodged, one by the Warden and one by each Stewardess; and if any Warden or Stewardess come not each Quarter Day by Half past One o'Clock, and bring her Key shall forfeit twopence and if not by Two o'Clock, shall forfeit Fourpence; and any one Key that is missing by Half past Two shall forfeit Two Shillings; and if the Clerk do not attend each Quarter Day by Two o'Clock and bring the Society Books in his Custody or depute a sufficient Person to officiate in his stead, he shall forfeit one Shilling.

IV Ordered that the Quarter Meetings are Whitsun Tuesday, the Fourth Tuesday in August, the Fourth Tuesday in November, and the Fourth Tuesday in February; also the Six Weeks Meeting to be the Tuesday six Weeks after the Quarter, at which Time the Wardens, Stewardesses and Clerk are all to attend, to inspect the Affairs of the Society at the Quarterly Meeting, for which Service there is allowed One Shilling out of the Stock towards their Expences; and any of the Officers that does not attend by Four o'Clock, shall forfeit Sixpence to the Stock.

V Every Person before she is admitted a Member shall appear personally in the Club Room, before the Committee, and give her Name, Age, and Place of Abode; and if she be thought proper to be admitted, she shall pay as directed in the first Article; and if any Person enter her Age under what it really is, the Committee shall have power to exclude her, or she shall pay extra till she hath made her Age equal with the Rule in the first Article.

VI That everyone that enters into the Society, after having passed one Year and one Quarter after her Admittance and paid her Contribution and Forfeits (if any) that are due, if she be visited with Sickness, Lameness or any other Affliction, whereby she is rendered incapable of working for one Week, she shall make Application to one of the Officers, who shall that Day, or the Day following at the farthest, visit her, and if she find her incapable of working, she shall receive, out of the Stock, Five shillings a Week, for Twenty Weeks, if she continue for long incapable; but should the Disorder continue above that time, she shall receive Two Shillings and Sixpence a Week so long as she remains in a State of Indisposition; but not any to be entitled to any Benefit till she hath been a Member one whole Year and one Quarter; and be it further observed that no Member shall have any Allowance from the Stock, for the first Four Weeks after she is delivered of a Child or Children; but if after that Period, she continues unable to follow her usual Employment, she shall have the usual Allowance, and it is also further agreed that if any unmarried Member have a Child by a Married Man or a married Member have a child by any other Man than her Husband, they shall be excluded.

VII That if it happen that the Stock should ever amount to Two Hundred Pounds, then, and from that time, the Sick Members shall receive Six Shillings a Week (any Article or Order to the contrary notwithstanding), till it come to One Hundred and Fifty Pounds; at which Time the Allowance shall be as in the VIth Article; and if then it should be reduced to One Hundred Pounds, then every Member to pay Sixpence more every Quarter, till the Stock amount to One Hundred and Fifty Pounds.

VIII That when any Sick Member who has received the weekly Allowance, be recovering and able to work a little, yet not a sufficient Week's Work, she shall be paid any Sum under Two Shillings and Sixpence, as the Wardens and Stewardesses in their Discretion shall think reasonable.

IX It is ordered that the Officers and Committee shall not admit or cause to be admitted knowingly, any Person who shall enter themselves with Intent to come burthensome and to be supported at the Expense of the Box; but if any have been entered unawares, they shall on Discovery be immediately excluded, provided it be before the Expiration of the Year and a Quarter after their Admittance; also to return her the Money she has paid into the Stock. But if any Person be not excluded within the said limited Time, she shall be looked upon as a good Member, and entitled to all its Privileges.

X That if any Member of this Society shall by her irregular Way of Living, or by any notorious evil Practice, after her Admittance, bring upon herself any Maimment (manument?) or Disorder, she shall not receive any Allowance from the Stock; and if she make Application to the Officer for Relief, she shall forfeit the Sum of Five Shillings, or be excluded, as the Committee shall determine.

XI That if the Officers, upon Notice given them, do not that Day or the Day following at farthest, visit the Sick, and provide for them according to Article the VIth, shall forfeit Two Shillings to the Stock, except the Officer to whom Application is made is sick herself and not able to pay a personal visit, in that Case she shall immediately send to one of her Sister Officers who shall not deny going, under the Forfeit of One Shilling to the Stock.

XII That if any Member of this Society shall have Occasion to leave her Place of Abode, to go into another part of the Kingdom, if she continue her Contribution to the Stock, and be visited by Sickness, upon receiving a proper Certificate, setting forth the Nature of her Disorder, attested by the Minister, Churchwarden and Surgeon, of the Parish where she resides, she shall be relieved as aforesaid; and she is hereby directed to send a Certificate, so long as she continues sick, every fourteen days.

XIII That if any Member of this Society receive the Allowance, under a Colour of being Sick, or Lame, and being suspected of such Deceit, by the Officers and Committee, and not giving a sufficient Proof of her Ailment, in Opinion of the Major Part of the Committee, then they shall cause her to be examined by some learned Physician or Surgeon, to be chosen by a Majority of the Committee; and if it appear that she hath no Ailment to hinder her from following her usual Employment, her Allowance shall cease, and she shall be excluded, if the Majority of the Committee consent thereto.

XIV That when it shall please God any Member of this Society shall depart this Life, and hath paid her Contribution according to VIth Article, the Officers shall pay out of the Stock, Four Guineas towards her Funeral Expences, to her Husband or nearest Relative, except the Deceased in her Lifetime ordered it to the contrary; and it is also agreed that if any Member's Husband happen to die, there shall be paid out of the Stock, One Guinea towards his Funeral Expences, except she have received the Allowance to the Funeral of a former Husband, and if any Member dies and leaves her Husband Widower, and he never marries again, but dies, there shall be paid the same to his Funeral Expences, as if his Wife was living, except she had received the Allowance to a former Husband.

XV That the Officers shall take out of the Stock, at the Quarterly Meeting, as much Money as shall be deemed necessary till the next Quarter, which shall be lodged with the Landlord or Landlady where the box is kept; and when Application is made by the Officers to the Landlord or Landlady, they shall deliver a Ticket to receive as is specified in the said Ticket; which Ticket shall be the Landlord or Landlady's Receipt, as specified herein.

XVI Ordered, that the Wardens, Stewardesses and the next member in the Roll after the last Stewardess, shall attend the Funeral of every deceased Member, if within the Township of Marsden, and likewise it is agreed that they shall attend Divine Service together the Sunday following , at the Place where the Corpse was interred, and there shall be provided for them Six Pairs of Gloves and Six Scarves, which shall after their Attendance, on the Sunday following, be deposited at the House where the Box is lodged; and if any Officer, or that Member that is hereby appointed, does not attend or depute some other sufficient Member in her Room, shall forfeit Two Shillings to the Stock.

XVII There shall be two Doorkeepers appointed by the Wardens every Quarter, and on the Feast-Day, whose Duty is to take an Account in Writing of the Members who come after the appointed Time; also there shall be a Committee appointed every Quarter and on the Feast-Day to consist of Eleven Members, Two to be chosen by the Wardens, One by each Stewardess and Six by the Society, whose Office shall be to refuse or admit new Members, to settle and adjudge all Disputes (if any should arise) or any other Matter or Thing belonging to the Society, (except in particular Cases) and their Decision shall be final.

XVIII That if any Member of this Society be convicted of Felony,

Perjury, or Treasonable or Seditious Words, Deeds, or Actions, against the sacred Person of our lawful and gracious Sovereign, or the Constitution, as at present established in Church or State, shall be excluded. And if any Member during the Time of Meeting, shall use any scandalous Expression or give bad Language to any Member, but if she hath any Complaint against any Member, she shall call the Committee into another Room; and the Member so complained against shall have Liberty taken to make her Defence; and she that is found guilty of abusing any Member, by a Committee aforesaid, shall be fined in any Sum not exceeding Three Shillings; not under sixpence and if she refuse to stand to the Determination of the Committee, she shall be excluded.

XIX That if any Disputes arise concerning the true Meaning of these Articles, or if any Member or Members? to wrest or give a false(?) Explanation of any Article, the Committee shall immediately retire and if they find her or them guilty, they shall deem a Penalty which she or they shall be obliged to pay, and if any of the Committee divulge any Thing that has been discovered in Debate (when charged to the contrary) she or they shall forfeit Sixpence.

XX There shall be a Dinner provided on WHITSUN TUESDAY, yearly, and the Contribution on that Day shall be Two Shillings and Sixpence, out of which Sixpence will be allowed for Ale; the Time of Meeting will be Eight o-Clock for the Officers , or they will be subject to the same Fines as on the Quarter Days, and the other Members at Half past Eight, or forfeit Twopence; and as soon as the Roll is called over, and everyone paid her contribution, they shall repair in orderly Manner, according as they stand in the Roll, to MARSDEN CHAPEL, alternately, that is one Year to the old Chapel, and the next to the new Chapel, where Divine Service will be performed, and a Sermon preached suited to the Occasion; for which Service the Minister shall receive as the Committee from Time to Time shall direct; and then return in the same Manner to Dinner; and hereby it is agreed that every one that does not attend at Divine Service, except in Case of Sickness or other Infirmity, or can give a sufficient Reason, to be approved by the Committee, shall pay a Fine of Sixpence. As soon as Dinner is over, the Clerk is to settle the Accounts of the preceding Year, to be inspected by any or all the Members if they choose and report them to the Society, after which the new Officers are to be appointed in the Manner as before directed, and the old Officers to deliver up their Keys and an Account of the Sick (if any) and retire to their usual Seats, and it is also agreed that if any Member suffer any Person to pay her Contribution that is not a Member, or be the Cause of any Person, Man or Woman, coming into the Room that is not a Member, shall pay a Fine of Sixpence; and if any Member go to the Chapel or Dinner, that has not paid her Contribution, (or caused it to be paid) shall forfeit Sixpence.

XXI That if any Member refuse to keep Silence, after demanded three Times by the Warden, she shall for every such Offence forfeit Two-pence; and if any Member tell another Member, in a scornful Manner, either in or out of the Club Room, what she has received out of the Stock, when sick or lame, and adjudged worthy of it by the Officers, she shall for every such Offence forfeit Two Shillings or be excluded, and if any Member shall propose Gaming, Wagers or Quarrels, in the Club Room, or come intoxicated by Liquor, or presume to smoke Tobacco, or sing any kind of Songs in the Club-Room during the Time of the Meeting, shall for every separate Offence forfeit Four-Pence, to be excluded; and if any Member Curse or Swear during Club Hours, shall for every profane Oath forfeit Two-pence, or be excluded.

XXII That if any Member or Members call for any Drink in the Club-Room during Meeting-Hours, the Officers excepted, they shall for every such Offence forfeit One Shilling, or be excluded; and if the Officers call for more Drink than the Club Allowance, they shall pay the Over-charge out of their own Pockets; and it is also agreed that if any Member refuse to pay her Forfeit, and doth not pay them when demanded by the Warden, or along with the next Contribution, she shall be excluded.

XXIII That if any Member neither bring nor send her Contribution, at the first Quarter Meeting, not at the Six Weeks Meeting next after, she shall forfeit Twopence; and if she doth not pay at the next Quarterly Meeting, she shall forfeit Sixpence; and if she doth not clear off all Arrears at the next Six Weeks Meeting, she shall be excluded. And it is also agreed that the major part of this Society shall have Power to continue the Box where it is, or remove it where they think most convenient, provided it be within a Quarter of a mile of the Town of Marsden; and whoever hath the Box in keeping, shall give such Security to the Officers, as the Committee for the Time being shall think proper.

XXIV Every Member of this Society shall pay Sixpence for a printed Copy of their Articles, or forfeit Sixpence; and every Member of this Society shall take her Seat according to her Admittance; the Officers first, and the next in Order according as they stand in the Roll; and if any Member be found on a wrong Seat, she shall forfeit Twopence.

XXV That if any Member of this Society stand at the Door when the Roll is called over, or listen or inspect where the business is carried on, or be any Hinderance to the Officers in the Execution of their Office, shall for every Offence forfeit Sixpence, or be excluded. And every Member missing the Roll called, and not deputing some other Member to pay her Contribution, shall forfeit Twopence.

XXVI That if any Member or Members shall entice others to the breaking up of the Society, or dividing the Stock, or if any Member privy to such unjust Proceedings, doth not inform the Officers thereof, shall be excluded. And this Society established purely for the Relief of the Sick and Afflicted, shall not be broke up while Three sound Members deny their Consent; and lastly, that every Member shall to the utmost of her Power, by Precept and Example, promote the Interest and Happiness of the Society, by their mutual Affection and Respect, and unto each other their Affection prove by Acts of Kindness and unfeigned Love and above all, earnestly and humbly praying that the Lord would make us thankful for all his Blessings we enjoy, under our present mild and happy Constitution and that he would shed his peculiar Blessings on all the

Members of this Society, preserving them in Health, comforting them in Sickness, supporting them in Death, and crowning them with Glory to all Eternity.

The before written Articles approved of by me, George Armitage Esquire, one of his Majesty's Justices of the Peace in and for the said Riding, Given under my Hand this fifth Day of October, 1808.

GEO: ARMITAGE

Leeds Sessions, 6th October, 1808.
    Allowed and confirmed by the Court;

WYBERGH

Appendix 2

-

Justice and Policing Before 1830

We have seen that when there was a riot in 1802 because of the price of oatmeal and wheat, the magistrate and the Volunteers dispersed the crowd. The magistrate was using the Volunteers to re-establish public order, a job that would today be done by the police force. There was no police force in England until Sir Robert Peel's Metropolitan Police Act of 1829 though both Scotland and Ireland had been policed before that.

In urban districts which had been incorporated such as Leeds there was a corporation of aldermen and a common council. In Leeds responsibility for the smooth running of the city was spread across the corporation, the parish vestry, the court leet, and an improvement commission which was established by act of Parliament in 1755.[259] Vestries were remarkably democratic. The electoral roll contained all rate payers, and elections to the vestry were open to women and to any religious denomination. Their role was to appoint a highway surveyor who collected the rates, choose annually elected church wardens to oversee the administration of the poor relief, take responsibility for highways and policing through a surveyor and parish constable and also inspect slaughter houses, maintain parish fire engines and suppress gin shops. There were also unpaid parish constables supplemented in some places by a night watch.

Huddersfield however was not incorporated until 1868 [259] so was policed in the same way as country districts. As Malcom Chase has pointed out, peacekeeping in country districts was controlled by the landed gentry which they did by a combination of economic power, patronage and control of the national political processes.[259]

The hierarchy for maintaining order descended directly from the Home Office, who chose a Lord Lieutenant of the county, in the case of Huddersfield, for many years it was a member of the Lascelles family. The Lord Lieutenant had two responsibilities: to maintain order and to restore it if it broke down. To maintain order he recommended suitable people to be

Justices of the Peace (also called magistrates), and was in charge of the militia which he could call out if necessary.

JPs were Crown appointments from within the ranks of the landed gentry. They tried minor offences locally and decided what misdemeanours should be tried by a higher court. They were also informal leaders in the county. Anglican men who owned freehold property worth £100 per annum, or were heirs apparent to property worth £300 were eligible. They were also responsible for maintaining main roads, bridges, gaols and asylums. They assembled at Quarter Sessions where they tried many serious crimes not punishable by death. These were heard by periodic Assize courts in each county which dealt with law breaking punishable by death. Grand juries at these courts were recruited from the ranks of the magistrates. Judges at each Assize used the occasion as a teaching session, summarizing the changes in the law for the assembled magistrates. Day to day justice relied on the magistracy for its smooth running and to ensure this the magistrates employed spies who kept them in touch with what was happening in the community.[259]

If law and order did break down, then the Lord Lieutenant could send in the militia or the yeomanry and the Riot Act could be read. The Riot Act dated back to 1717. If there were trouble from a group of more than twelve people, the group could be told to disperse and given an hour to do so. If not, they could be arrested and brought before a magistrate or put in prison until the magistrate could deal with them.

The Militia was kept purely for maintenance of order at home in Great Britain and Ireland. Officers were career soldiers drawn from the ranks of the gentry but the other ranks were made up of men conscripted by a Ballot. Lists of eligible men were drawn up for each township and the men were picked by ballot. Anyone chosen could opt out by finding and paying someone else to take their place. These men had to be at least five feet four inches tall, have no more than one child born in wedlock and be under 45 years of age. In contrast, the regular army which fought abroad were all volunteers.

In 1757 three regiments of the Militia had been established for West

Yorkshire with the Lord Lieutenant acting as Colonel. They only rarely served on their home ground so when they were policing an area, they and their families were billeted in local houses and inns. This led to a lot of ill-feeling between the soldiery and the local people, not made any better by the fact that the families of soldiers were often supported by the Poor tax. In the early years of the nineteenth century for instance, it was the Cumberland Militia who maintained, or failed to maintain, order in the Huddersfield area. The Militia was stood down when the country was at peace. At the time of the Napoleonic Wars the local militias often undertook duties such as doing garrison duty in the Garrison towns in order to release the regular army for fighting abroad, a sort of early version of the Home Guard.

There were also volunteer, self-financing forces. The first of these volunteer units in the Huddersfield area, was formed in 1794, and both William Horsfall, of Ottiwells Mill in Marsden, and Thomas Atkinson of Colne Bridge Mill, were officers. They were known as the Huddersfield Fusiliers and within two years of their founding had recruited 300 men. Overall was the magistrate Joseph Radcliffe, of Milnsbridge. When the Peace of Amiens in 1802 brought a temporary cessation to the wars with France, the Fusiliers were disbanded.

There were also volunteer cavalry units, the Yeomanry, who were made up usually of social classes more prosperous than the Infantry since they had to be able to provide a horse. These forces had a vested interest in maintaining the status quo so were used to subdue the working class uprisings of the Luddites and Radicals. An offshoot of this force was the Huddersfield Volunteer Cavalry, led by Captain Law Atkinson, which was well known for its poor discipline, probably caused by the antagonism between Captain Atkinson and the magistrate, Joseph Radcliffe.[259]

Because of the poor condition of many of the volunteer corps by 1807 with the corps being below strength and their members being something of a rabble, the government formed the Local Militia to which volunteers were encouraged to transfer. If a corps was below strength it would be supplemented by the Ballot. In Huddersfield this force was known as the

3rd West Riding Militia. They were only part time soldiers and had 24 training days a year. They were subject to strict military discipline. This force was not used against the Luddites and was disbanded when Napoleon offered his first abdication in 1814. Unrest at home was dealt with by the Huddersfield Yeomanry who were kept busy patrolling the highways and byways of the Huddersfield area in the following years.[259]

Minor crimes were punishable by a spell in the local gaol, in the case of Huddersfield that would have been the house of Correction in Wakefield or the local lock-up, the Towzer. If the JP agreed, it was possible to apply for bail, and it was common for prisoners with contacts on the outside to have food brought in for them, rather than them having to eat the poor food provided by the prison. Major crimes against property and people were punishable by death, and trials for these were held at York Castle.[259]

Radicals who were committed to prison for their writings and speeches were generally considered as political prisoners. They were kept separate from the criminals. If they appealed against their sentence they had to travel to London to present their case in person to the Home Office. Their accommodation in prison was better than the average criminal fraternity and they could even have wives to stay with them and have food brought in, providing they had someone to support them financially.

Bibliography

Ashton, Rosemary. *Little Germany. Exile and Asylum in Victorian England.* (Oxford University Press. 1986)

Atkinson, Frank. *Some Aspects of the 18th Century Woollen and Worsted Trade in Halifax.* (Halifax Museums, 1956)

Bamford, Samuel. *Passages in the Life of a Radical.* First published 1844. (Macgibbon and Kee Ltd, 1967)

Berg, Maxine, Hudson, Pat and Sonenscher, Michael. *Manufacture in town and country before the factory.* (Cambridge University Press, 1983)

Brears, Peter. *Traditional Food in Yorkshire.* (Prospect Books, 2014)

British Parliamentary Papers: *Report and Minutes of Evidence on the state of the woollen manufacture of England.* 1806

Brooke, Alan and Kipling, Lesley. *Liberty or Death. Radicals, Republicans and Luddites 1793-1823* (Huddersfield Local History Society, 2012)

Bythell, Duncan. *The Sweated Trades.* (Batsford Academic, 1978)

Chase, Malcolm. 1820. *Disorder and Stability in the United Kingdom.* (Manchester University Press, 2013)

Chartism. A new history. (Manchester University Press, 2007)

Clark, David. *Colne Valley. Radicalism to Socialism* (Longman, 1981)

Cordery, Simon. *British Friendly Societies 1750-1914* (Palgrave Macmillan, 2003)

Crump, W.B. *Huddersfield Highways down the Ages.* (Huddersfield The Tolson Memorial Museum, 1949)

Crump, W.B. and Ghorbal, G. *History of the Huddersfield Woollen Industry.* (Tolson Memorial Museum, 1935).

Davies, Margaret Llewellyn ed. *Maternity. Letters from Working Wives.* (Virago, 1978).

Defoe, Daniel. *A Tour through the Whole Island of Britain. 1724-1726.* Abridged and edited by P.N. Furbank and W.R. Owens (Yale University Press, 1991)

Dingwall, Robert, Rafferty, Anne Marie, Webster, Charles. *An Introduction to the Social History of Nursing.* (London, Routledge. 1988)

Disraeli, Benjamin. *Sybil.* (Oxford University Press, Reissued 2002)

Driver, Felix. *Power and Pauperism. The Workhouse System 1834-1884.* (Cambridge UP, 1993)

Evans, Richard J.*The Pursuit of Power. Europe 1815-1914* (Penguin 2016)

Gaffin, Jean and Thoms, David. *Caring and Sharing. A Centenary History of the Co-operative Womens' Guild.* (Co-operative Union Ltd, 1983)

Gleadle, Kathryn. *British Women in the Nineteenth Century.* (Palgrave, 2001)

Griffiths, David, ed. *Making up for lost time.* (Huddersfield Local History Society 2018)

Hargreaves, John A. ed. *The Charter our Right.* (Huddersfield Local History Society, 2018)

The Villas of Edgerton. (The Huddersfield Civic Society, 2017)

Haigh, Hilary ed. *Huddersfield, a Most Handsome Town.* (Kirklees Cultural Services, 1992)

Hannam, June. *Isabella Ford.* (Blackwell. 1989)

Hargreaves, John A. and Haigh, Hilary eds. *Slavery in Yorkshire.* (University of Huddersfield, 2012)

Heaton, Herbert. *The Yorkshire Woollen and Worsted Industries, from the earliest times up to the Industrial Revolution.* (Oxford, Clarendon Press 1920)

Hollis, Patricia. *The Pauper Press.* (Oxford University Press, 1970)

Holmes, D.H. *The Mining and Quarrying Industries in the Huddersfield District.* (Tolson Memorial Museum, 1967)

Hunt, Felicity, ed. *Lessons for Life: The schooling of girls and Women 1850-1950.* (Oxford, Blackwell, 1987)

Gender and Policy in English Education 1902-1944. (New York: Harvester Wheatsheaf, 1991)

Hutton, Isobel. C.B.E., M.D. *Memories of a doctor in War and Peace.* (Heinemann, 1960)

Ingle, George. *Yorkshire Cotton: the Yorkshire cotton industry 1780-1835.* (Carnegie Publishing, 1997)

James, J. *Continuations and additions to the history of Bradford* (1866)

King, Steven. *Poverty and Welfare in England 1700-1850: a regional perspective.* (University of Manchester Press, 2000)

Law, Edward J. *Huddersfield in the 1820s* (Huddersfield Local History Society, 2013)

Liddington, Jill. *Rebel Girls.* (Virago, 2006)

Lockwood, Ernest. *Colne Valley Folk.* (Heath Cranton Ltd, London 1936)

Lockwood, John. *An investigation into the development of the provision of public elementary education and the changing levels of literacy in the census district of Huddersfield from 1811 to 1851.* Unpublished thesis.

Lockwood, Mrs Josiah. *An Ordinary Life.* (Echo Press, 1932)

Marland, Hilary. 'Health care in Nineteenth century Huddersfield', Haigh, Hilary ed. *Huddersfield, a Most Handsome Town.*

Marsden, Christopher and Caveney, Andrew. *Huddersfield in 50 buildings* (Amberley, 2019)

Martin, Janette. 'Huddersfield and the Peterloo Massacre', *Huddersfield Local History Society Journal 20/21 Issue 31*

O'Connel, John. *The Making of a University.* (Huddersfield University Press, 2016)

Opie, Iona and Peter. *The Lore and Language of Schoolchildren.* (OUP, 1959)

Pearson, E. Irene. *Marsden through the ages.* (Self published, 1984)

Peel, Frank. *The Risings of the Luddites, Chartists and Plug Drawers.* (4th edition. Frank Cass and Co. 1968)

Pinchbeck. *Women Workers and the Industrial Revolution, 1750-1850.* (Frank Cass and Co. Ltd, 1969)

Place, Allan. *Pray Remember the Poor.* (Holme Valley Civic Society, n.d.)

Poole, Robert ed. 'Return to Peterloo', *Manchester Region History Review, vol.23*, (2012)

Pridmore, Elizabeth Jane. *Fabric of the hills: the interwoven story of textiles and the landscape of the South Pennines.* (Standing Conference of South Pennine Authorities, 1989)

Probert, Rebecca. BALH Journal *The Local Historian.* 'A Banbury Story: cohabitation and marriage among the Victorian poor in notorious Neithrop', pp.290-300

Quinn, Liz. 'Linthwaite's Suffragist' in *Huddersfield Local History Society Journal 20/21 Issue 31.*

Redmonds, George. *The making of Huddersfield.* (Wharncliffe Books, 2003)

Reynolds, Melanie. *Infant Mortality and working-class child care, 1850-1899.* (Palgrave Macmillan, 2016)

Riding, Jacqueline. *The Story of the Manchester Massacre: Peterloo.* (Apollo, 2018)

Royle, Edward. *Revolutionary Britannia? Reflections on the threat of revolution in Britain,*

1789-1848. (Manchester University Press, 2000)

Rusnock A. Andrea and Dietz, Vivien E. 'Defining women's sickness and work: Female Friendly Societies in England 1780-1830', *Journal of Women's History vol. 24, no.1.Spring 2012.*

Seidal, Hazel. *Laithes and Looms, Cows and Combstocks.* (Marsden History Group, 2013)

Simon, Brian. *The Radical Tradition in Education in Britain.* (Lawrence and Wishart, 1972)

Stead, Jennifer ed. *The Diary of a Quack Doctor.* Huddersfield Local History Society,2002)

E.A.Hilary Haigh ed. Chapter 24 'Changing the Pattern: Everyday Life 1800-1900' in *Huddersfield, A Most Handsome Town.* (Kirklees Cultural Services, 1992)

Stewart, Jules. *Albert.* (Tauris and Co. 2012)

Strachey,Ray. *The Cause.* (First published 1928 G. Bell and Sons Ltd. Published 1978 Virago Press)

Thompson, Dorothy.

> *The Dignity of Chartism.* (Verso, 2013)
>
> *Outsiders. Class, Gender and Nation.* (Verso, 1993)
>
> *The Chartists.* (Maurice Temple Smith Ltd, 1984)
>
> With James Epstein (eds) T*he Chartist Experience: Studies in Working class radicalism and culture 1830-1860.*

Thompson, E.P. *The Making of the English Working Class.* (Penguin, 1980)

Valenze, Deborah. *The First Industrial Women.* (Oxford UP, 1950)

Walvin, James. 'William Wilberforce, Yorkshire and the campaign to end transatlantic slavery, 1789-1820' in *Slavery in Yorkshire*

Weinbren, Daniel. 'Supporting self-help: charity, mutuality and reciprocity in nineteenth century Britain' in Bernard Harris and Paul Bridgen eds. *Charity and mutual aid in Europe and America since 1800.* (Routledge, 2007)

Wilson, A.N. *Victoria, a Life.* (Atlantic Books, 2014)

Whitehead, L.B. *Bygone Marsden* (Hotspur Press, 1948)

On line

British Newspaper Archive: Leeds Mercury and Hull Packet. 'Colne Bridge Tragedy'. 1818.

Gutenberg: Campbell, Theophila Carlile: The battle of the Press as told in the story of the life of Richard Carlile by his daughter 1899.

Dictionary of National Biography: Dora Marsden.

Economic History Society Conference 2004: 'The distribution of Female Friendly Societies across Britain in the early Nineteenth century.'

HistoryofParliamentonline.org. Yorkshire candidates for election 1790-1818

Huddersfield Exposed:

> Daily Mail account of arrest of suffragettes 22 March 1907
>
> Owen Balmforth: The Huddersfield Industrial Society Ltd: fifty years of Colne Valley Folk
>
> K.M. Cocker. Jubilee History of Greenhead High School for Girls 1909-1959
>
> Royal Commission on Employment of Children in Factories 1833
>
> Huddersfield Chronicle 21 January 1854. 'Netherton Female Institute'
>
> Female Educational Institute: first soiree.

Hudson, Pat. Cardiff Historical Papers (www Cardiff.ac.uk). The Limits of Wool, (2007/7)

Lomas, Janis 'Delicate duties: issues of class and respectability in government policy towards the wives and widows of British soldiers in the era of the Great War.' Women's History review vol.9 number 1, 2000.

Minelotti, Paul. 'The importance of ideology: the shift to factory production and the effects of women's employment opportunities in the English Textile Industries.' Discussion papers in Economic and Social History no. 87, Feb.2011, University of Oxford.

Luddite bi-centenary blogspot.

National Archive: How much is that? Currency converter.

UndergroundHistories.wordpress. The web site of Alan Brooke: Catalogue of the textile mills and factories of the Huddersfield area.

SpecialCollections.le.ac.uk White's Directory 1858. p.433.

Archive

WYAS: KC1060 WSPU minutes 1907-1909

Documents about the WSPU: KC 1060/6/006 letter from Huddersfield branch of WSPU to suffragettes in Holloway; KC1060/1.

Municipal High School for Girls: WYK 1788 school magazines for 1913, 1916, 1918. Box 15/139-146. Register; exam results; minutes; ephemera. WYK 1708 South Crosland Township 1700-1841 CP/SC

University of Huddersfield archive: Documents about the Female Education Establishment. HFE/1/1 Ledger 186; Rules n.d.; annual reports 1858-1882; Wages 1858-1881; library records; letters 1867-1883; bills.

HFE1/10/0/4a; HFE/1/10/5;HFE/5/1Adverts and notices; HFE/2/1/4 receipted bills1860-1861; HFE/7/1;

University of Leeds. Quaker collection. Brighouse meeting 1810-1822 Minute book. MS/DEP/1979/1/BRI/2/125

Index

Acland, Alice 194
Albert, Prince: 161-7
  anti-slavery campaign 163
  Buckingham Palace 163
  Chancellorship of University of Cambridge 163
  death 170
  Great Exhibition 165-7
  Palace of Westminster 63
  working class housing 163
  pensions for retired servants 164
  needs of working classes 163
Allen, Benjamin Haig 79
Almondbury 20, 106, 127-8, 172
Almondbury Bank 75, 91
Armitage, Betty 56
Armitage, Captain 71
Ashley, Lord 120, 172
assize courts 293
Atkinson, Thomas: mill fire 41, 46

baking, golden age of 161
Bamford, Jemima 78-88
Bamford, Samuel 12, 76, 78-88
Bamford, Samuel, co-operator 192
Balmforth, Owen 200, 202
Balmforth family 200
Barnsley 18, 61, 152
bastiles 131
Becker, Lydia 225
Bellas, Reverend 20-1, 32-8

Berlin decrees 48
Bills o' Jacks inn 212
Blackburn 76, 120
Black Dwarf 73, 102, 114
Blackmoorfoot reservoir 209, 214
Black Rock mill:
  chapel 213
  fire 213
  routine 125
  visit of Florence's family 204-6, 211-2
  workers 125
Blake, William 17
Bodichon, Barbara 225
Bolster moor 20
Bottomley, Luke and John 145-6
Blind Jack of Knaresbrough 28
Bradley mill 46, 48, 52
Bray, Hannah 45
Brighouse 91, 137, 156
broadcloth 32
Brockway, Fenner 235
Brook, William, Thomas, James, George 52-3, 55, 61-2
Brigg, John Fligg 245
Bryce report 244
Burdett, Sir Francis 72
Butler, Josephine 189
Byron, Lord 49

cap of liberty 75-83, 91-3
Cat and Mouse Act 229
carding 22, 26

Carlile, Richard: 72-75, 102-108
   attitude to women 83-85, 103
   divorce 104
   Dorchester prison 103
   support in the West Riding 102
   writing about contraception
      105-6
Carlile, Mrs 102-10
   character 104-5
   imprisonment 104
Carlile, Theophila 105-6
Caroline of Brunswick 97-102
   divorce 99-101
   marriage 97
   women's support of 99-102
Cartwright, Sir John 72, 75
Cato Street conspiracy 95-6
Chambers, Miss 247-8, 251
Chartism:
   Huddersfield women supporters
      of 154-5
   petitions 157-8
Charlotte, Princess 98-9, 102
Churchill, Winston 227-8
cloth halls 46
Clough, Anne Jemima 189
Cobbett, William: Political Register
   115
coal mines 18
Colne Valley:
   byelection 1907 235
   Colne Valley Guardian 235
   Labour League 235
   Tree Society 17
Combination acts 33, 44, 47

Congress of Co-operators
   191, 194, 195
contraception 105-6, 267
cooking 249
Co-operative organisations:
   Co-operative News 192,194
   dividends 192
   Huddersfield branch 191-2,
      199-202
   in West Riding 191
   minutes of meetings 193
Corbett, Cicely 217
Corn Laws 73, 128, 161, 263
Cotton, Gladys 258
cotton textiles 168
Crabtree, George 119
Croppers' Institution 47-48
   Huddersfield Union 47
cropping machines 44
Crystal Palace 167

Daily Miror 261
Dawson, Mrs 70
Deanhouse 132
Defoe, Daniel 17-19, 22, 27, 203
Demagogue, The 114
diseases, 19th century 185-6
domestic system 10, 22, 118, 122,
   124, 265
Dungeon Wood 54, 55
Dyson, Clement and Hannah 51,
   70
dyeing 19

Earl Grey 110

Edgerton 224-5
education:
   elementary, in Colne Valley 172
   Mechanics Institutes 172-6, 178
   Newnham College 190
   Owen's College 188
   ragged schools 172
   Sunday schools 173
   universities 188-90
Education Act
   1870 243, 250
   1902 196, 245
Ehrsam, Professor Anna 219
election:
   1818 74-5
   pre-1818 74
Elland Radical Association 154-5
Engels, Friedrich 162
exclusive dealing 112

factory reform 109, 114-9
family, women's role in 103, 133-4
Female Friendly Society 10, 30-32
Female Educational Establishment
   aims 179
   ages of girls 181
   classes 180-1
   library 178
   subjects 176-7
   subscriptions 178
Fenton, Captain John: Beer Bill 110
Fildes, Mary 76-7, 84, 90

Firth, Joseph 114
Fitzherbert, Maria 97-8
Fixby 132, 135, 137
Fixby Hall 116, 133, 175
Fleet debtors' prison 97, 133
Folly Hall 71
Ford, Isabella 176, 238
Freewoman, The 240
fulling 19, 22-4

Garrett Anderson, Elizabeth 185
Gaunt, Elizabeth 90
German immigrants 161-2, 168, 180
   In Huddersfield 164-5, 224-5
gig mills 44, 46, 49
Glasier, Kathleen Bruce 236-7
Golcar 20, 120, 122, 128, 141
governessing: see Job opportunities
Grayson, Victor 214-7, 235-7, 261
Great Exhibition 165-70
Great Northern Union 152-4
Greenhead Hall 245
Grey, Earl 110

Habeas Corpus Act, suspension of 72
Halifax 22, 24, 26, 46, 50, 91-2, 110, 119, 134
hangings:
   Batley 65
   Brook 61-2
   Crowther 63
   Dean 61
   Haigh 62

Hartley 63
Hey 63
Hill 64
Lumb 65
Mellor 57-9, 61
Ogden 62
Smith 57-9
Thorpe 57-9, 62
Walker 57-8, 61
Hampden clubs 69, 72, 110
Hanson, Abram and Elisabeth 153-4, 159
Harewood, Lord, Henry Lascelles 58, 118
Hartop, Miss 255-6
Hartshead moor 51, 134
Heaton, Herbert 26
Hey Green 24
Hill, Miss 257
Hirst, Thomas 191
Hobhouse, Henry 79
Hobson, Joshua 113-4, 118, 136, 139, 151-2, 174
Holland, Emma 45
Horsfall, Mary 122-3, 126
Horsfall, Sarah 128
Horsfall, William 46, 53-4
hospital nursing 184-7
Huddersfield,
  Co-operative Society 191-2
  dispensary 185
  Infirmary 186
  incorporation of 182
  Political Union 113
  Philosophical Society 174

Short-time Committee 118
Huddersfield and district:
  gas lighting 262
  transport 263
  water supply 262
Huddersfield Chronicle 141, 166
Huddersfield Yeomanry 71
Hunt, Henry 72, 75, 79, 82-9

legitimacy 66, 131
Independent Labour Party (ILP) 226
International Women's Suffrage Alliance 218
Isle of Skye inn 211-2

Jacquard loom 169
Jessop, Sarah 70
job opportunities for women
  governessing 187-8
  nursing 184-7
  White's Directories 1837 and 1870 178-82
Johnston, Joseph 73
Justices of the Peace 24, 33, 127, 292

Kaye, Charles 145-7
Kenney, Annie 215, 227, 236
Key, Edith 228
Knight, John 73, 79-80, 83
Kyrle fund 248

Labour Party
  attitude to votes for women 226-7
Lancashire 34, 67, 72-3, 79, 156
land plan 135
Lee, Richard 71
Learoyd, Emily 147-8
Lectures for Ladies 188
Leeds Intelligencer 130
Leeds Mercury 71, 112-4, 117, 139
Leeds Times 134
Liberal Women's Suffrage Group 217
Liverpool, Lord 74, 101
Lindley, Martha 29-30
Linthwaite 52, 124, 128, 203-4, 210-11, 213, 220-2
Llewelyn Davies, Margaret 194-7, 199
Lockwood, Josiah 204-6, 210-12, 214-7, 222
Lockwood, Josiah, Huddersfield 124-6
Lockwood, Mrs Josiah Lockwood
  family 203-205, 210-12
  politics 11, 213-23
  social life 206-10
Lodge, Keziah 145-6, 149
London Dispatch 154
Longdenholme 257
Longroyd Bridge cropping shop 51
Lovett, William 135, 150
Lowenthal, Bertha 224

Lowery, Robert 113
Loyal and Social League 73
Ludd, Ned 49, 55
Luddites 11, 43, 49-60

magistrates 34, 39, 58, 93-4, 120, 129, 292-3
Manchester Guardian 113
Manchester Observer 73, 76, 91
Manchester Women's Suffrage Committee 26
Mann, Alice and James 114-5
Marsden 9-10, 19, 23-6
Marsden Female Friendly Society
  accounting 43
  rules 39-40
  structure 42-3
  time-keeping 39
  wages 40-1
Marsden, Dora 237-40
Maternity: Letters from Working Women 197
Mechanics' Institutes 173-4, 176, 178
Methodists 68, 173
Middleton 79-81, 88-9
Midgely, Joshua 69
militia 56-7, 155, 293-4
Milns:
  Fanny 52-3, 55-6, 62
  William 52, 56
millstone grit 17-8
Minelotti 41
Mount Tambura 128
Mud March, Feb 1907 217

Municipal High School (a.k.a.
   Greenhead)
   academic achievement 258-9
   building 245-6
   careers 254-7, 259
   curriculum 248-51
   fairies 254
   opening ceremony 245-8
   war effort 253-4, 258
Murray, Florence: early life 203

Nadin, Joseph 88-9
National Union of Women's
   Suffrage Societies (NUWSS)
   215-9
Newport uprising 1839 155
Newspaper and Stamp Duties Act
   112
Nightingale, Florence 184
North family 142-5
Northern Star 136, 151, 154, 157
Nottinghamshire 49
nursing: see job opportunities

Oastler, Richard
   attitude to Poor Law 110, 117-8, 132-3
   imprisonment 137
   release from prison 137-8
   York pilgrimage 119-21
oats 17
O'Brian, Bronterre 135, 151
O'Connor, Fergus 135-6, 151-2, 157
   children named after him 152-4

Oldham 20
Oliver, William, spy 71, 113
Ottiwells Mill 46, 51-53
Owen, Robert 109, 135, 174, 191
Oxford
   Extension Lectures 190, 194
   Local Examination Board 250

Paddock 61, 75, 134
Paine, Tom 34, 72, 102-3
Pains and Penalties, Bill of 99
Pankhurst,
   Adela 11, 214-5, 224, 238-9, 241-2
   Emmeline 214-5, 225-9, 238, 241
   Christabel 227, 238-9, 241
Parliamentary report 1806
Peace movement 11, 48
Pease, Elizabeth 151
Peel, Sir Robert 163, 167, 292
Peep Green rally 134-7
Peterloo: 75-90
   casualties 90
   meetings after 90-3
Pethic-Lawrence 321
Pitkethley, Lawrence 106, 113, 118
Plug Riots 1842 155-7
Police, Metropolitan Police Act 1829 292
Political Unions
   Huddersfield area 113, 119
   poor houses 132, 138-41

Poor Law 1834
   radical attitudes to   132-4
   women's attitudes to   136-7
Poor Law Guardians   131-3
Poor Law Union, Huddersfield
   1837   132-3
poor relief pre-1834   65-6
Prince Regent   97-8
Pule Hill   28

Quakers   60-5, 173, 220
Queen Caroline, women's support
   of   98-102
Queen's College   188

Radcliffe, Joseph   39, 45, 52-3, 58,
   60, 64, 72, 294
Ramsden family   129
Rawfolds mill   51-2, 61-2
Reform Act 1832   109-10, 150
Richardson, R.J.   151, 265
Rights of Man   34
Rights of Women   151
Riot Act   45, 157, 293
Rochdale Pioneers   191-2
Royal Commission on:
   Employment of children in
      Factories 1833   121
   Poor Law   130

Saddleworth   20, 31, 80
Sadler, Sir Michael: supporter of
   Oastler   117, 119-20
Sadler, Sir Michael: educationalist
   245

Savings banks in the North   164-5
Saxony wheel   23
Saxton, John and Susannah   73,
   76, 83
Scammonden   20
Scawthorne, Mary   235
scribbling   22
Schofield, Kenworthy and Co.
   124
Scholes, Varley and Co.   124
Schwann, Frederick   168, 175-6
Schwann, Henrietta   176-7
Seditious Meetings Act   34, 94
Senior Oxford exam 1917   258
Sharples, Eliza   105, 107
Shaw, Sylvanus   21
Sheffield Daily Telegraph   232
short time committees   118, 120
Siddon, Emily   216
Six Acts   93
Shillitoe, Thomas   60-1, 63-4
Sidgwick, Henry   190
Skelmanthorpe   93-4, 135
Skircoat   91
Slade School of Art   203
Slaithwaite   32, 124, 172, 208, 237
slave trade, campaign against   67-8, 115-7
slubbing   23, 118
Spenceans   74
Spies   73, 95, 293
spinning   19, 21-3
   jenny   23
Stanley, Lord, of Alderley   246
Starkey's mill   41

Stead, Jennifer 12,142
suffragists 11,217-9,
suffragettes 214-5, 219, 224-9,
    238-40
Swift, John 129, 142-4
    Anne 143, 145-7
    Tom 143-4, 147-8

teasels 22,24
temperance movement 111, 158,
    175, 184
Ten Hour Act 120, 133
tentering 19, 24
textile trade 44-5, 265
Thewlis,
    Dora 230-233, 235
    Eliza 230, 233-4
Thornhill family 116
Tinker, Christopher 136
Tolson Memorial Museum 93,
    215
Towzer, The 295
Trafagar, battle of 48
turnpikes 10, 27-29

Union Clubs:
    female political 81
    Huddersfield 73, 113
    Middleton Radical 73
University Extension scheme 190

vestries, parish 196, 292
Voice of the West Riding 113-4,
    118, 136

Ward, John 214-5
warp 23, 25
Walker, Benjamin 55-8
Walker, Mary Ann 61
Weaver, Harriet Shaw 240
weaving 19, 23
weeting, a.k.a lant 23, 26
weft 19, 23
Weinbren, Daniel 38
Wesley, John 19
Wessenden 24, 211, 262
West Riding 22, 34, 44, 50, 65,
    67-8, 73, 95, 110, 113, 133,
    224, 245
Whiteley, Ben 69-71
White's Directory 178-184
Wilberforce, William 115
Women's Co-operative Guild:
    campaigns 195-199
    Huddersfield branch 192, 199-
    201
    Jubilee celebrations 1910 201-2
women's education:
    Josephine Butler 189
    Ann Jemima Clough 189
    Lectures for Ladies 188-9

Women's Co-operative Guild
    beginnings 191
    interests 192-8
    maternity 197-9
Women's Social and Political
    Union (WSPU) 219-2,
    228-9, 233-6, 241-2, 256
Wood, Joseph 60-64

Woolf, Virginia   187
woollen industry: processes   21-7
World War One:
   conscription   221, 242
   Florence Lockwood's family   221
   support for war effort   219-20, 258
   women's war work   258
worsted   22-26, 168
wuzzing   23

yeomanry   71, 85-6, 90, 293-5
York   59-62

Young Men's Mental Improvement Society   175

Acknowledgements

I have had such a lot of help from friends and professionals that it is difficult to know where to begin. It always surprises me how much time and attention archivists are prepared to give me. So I would like to thank the archivists at the University of Huddersfield and at the West Yorkshire Archive Service, in particular Rosie and Katrina, who have been so responsive to my requests for help. I am also indebted to Katina Bill of the Tolson Memorial Museum for her help and permission to use photographs taken in the museum. The Huddersfield Exposed web site has proved invaluable and I am grateful to Dave Probert for permission to use photographs from it.

I must also thank John Cater for the loan of the rules of the Marsden Female Friendly Society and to John Lockwood for giving me access to his unpublished work on schools in the Colne Valley.

In ideal circumstances I would not have chosen to research a part of the country 200 miles from where I live, in the middle of a pandemic. So I am extremely grateful for the serious commitment of Joan Smith and Barbara Lockwood, who explored the local reference libraries and archives for me. I am grateful, too, for Jennifer Stead 's insights into local customs.

Friends and relatives nearer to hand in Oxfordshire have also been helpful. My grateful thanks go to Professor Pam Clemit and to Ann Matthews for help and advice, Lucy for her rigorous and analytical reading of the text, and Stuart for providing a willing ear to listen to, question and discuss my ramblings. And lastly Ed. Thank you, Ed, for the drawings and coping with all the boring bits of self-publishing.

About the Author

Mavis Curtis was born and brought up in Huddersfield, where her family earned their living in the textile industry. She was educated at Greenhead High School, from where she proceeded to the University of Bristol where she gained a BA. This was followed very much later by a spell at the University of Sheffield where her work on children's oral tradition earned her a PhD.

She has written extensively on a variety of topics, concentrating in recent years on women's history, notably a centenary history of the Women's Institute and an account of the lives of suffragists after women were given the vote.

She is married to an old boy of Huddersfield (Boys) College and for family reasons now lives in Oxfordshire. Her heart, however, remains in Yorkshire.

Printed in Great Britain
by Amazon